Soccer in Munster:
A Social History, 1877–1937

SOCCER IN MUNSTER:
A SOCIAL HISTORY
1877–1937

David Toms

CORK **cup** UNIVERSITY PRESS

First published in 2015 by
Cork University Press
Youngline Industrial Estate
Pouladuff Road, Togher
Cork, Ireland

British Library Cataloguing in Publication Data
A CIP catalogue record for this book is available from the British Library.

ISBN 978-1-78205-126-8

Typeset by Tower Books, Ballincollig, County Cork
Printed in Malta by Gutenberg Press

www.corkuniversitypress.com

CONTENTS

ACKNOWLEDGEMENTS

In 2006, as a student in St Paul's Community College doing the Leaving Certificate with the encouragement of my teacher John Whittle, I took a notion to research the founding of the Waterford and District Football League for my research project in History. From then, I had the bug for history. So naturally it was to sport I returned when I began my PhD in 2009. That first burst of enthusiasm, finding my way around the Local Studies room in Waterford's Lady Lane Library, unravelling the mystery of microfilm, stayed with me through BA and PhD. Since then, the people who have helped to make what is before you a possibility are deserving of greater thanks than this short acknowledgement can manage. A work of this size and of this duration is not written without considerable help and support from many different people. Thanks are offered to a huge number of people I have encountered over the past number of years while undertaking this research. First and foremost, my PhD supervisor, Dr Andy Bielenberg, helped to make the thesis on which this book is based a water-tight and rigorous piece of scholarship; for his keen eye for detail and insistence on only the very best from me, I thank him – both then and now. Other members of staff in UCC I must thank for their support and encouragement are Donal Ó Drisceoil, Gabriel Doherty and John Borgonovo. The School of History at UCC has been a wonderful environment in which to complete this work. I was grateful as a student to be twice a recipient of their Tutorial Scholarship and, since then, to have had the opportunity to try out my ideas in lectures – I have learned as much by teaching as my students have learned from me. The community of postgraduates, exemplified in our Postgraduates Association, has made the work seem less like work on many occasions. The community of scholars who form Sports History Ireland, the British Society of Sports History, and those with whom I collaborate on The Dustbin of History, have all been great guides, peers, and friends.

To the staff of the many libraries and archives I have utilised in writing this book – Brian McGee and everyone at the Cork City and County Archives; Donal Moore, formerly Waterford City Archivist; the staff of Cork City Library, especially those in the Local Studies room; the staff of the National Library; the staff at The Source in Thurles, County Tipperary; Mary Lombard and the staff of Special Collections in UCC's Boole Library; Mark Reynolds at Croke Park; special thanks too are due to Catríona Mulcahy, the UCC Archivist for her considerable help in finding me many rich and varied sources; to Brendan Cowan, Ger Halley and David Byrne of Cahir Park FC for their enthusiasm and help; to people like Plunkett Carter, Michael Neary, John Hearne, Andy Taylor, and Paul Elliott I offer my warmest thanks for sharing with me their photographs, knowledge and enthusiasm; the Archivist of Rockwell College for his kind hospitality and enthusiasm; to both the IFA and the FAI for access to their archives and to Sarah Poutch and the rest of the team at UCD as well as the lovely staff of the Public Record Office of Northern Ireland; without the time and interest shown by all of these people, this project would never have come to fruition.

The staff of Cork University Press, in particular Maria O'Donovan, for her early support and encouragement and to Mike Collins too, I offer my deepest thanks for making this happen.

Thanks are also due to many people for variously reading, critiquing and encouraging my work and challenging my understanding of my topic – this applies particularly to Daryl Leeworthy, Niall Murphy, Mark Ryan, Peter Hession, Alex Jackson and William Whitmore. Other friends, Shane Forde, Kieran Murphy, Jimmy Cummins, Jennifer Rugolo, Sinead O'Brien, Colm O'Regan, Gareth Ryle and Eoin Myers, all provided much-needed and welcome distraction in various guises during the process.

Emma Houlihan has provided a level of support far beyond what any partner with her own scholarly, artistic and work concerns should be expected to offer, but did so nonetheless, helping to share the more burdensome moments of this work and enduring endless talk of soccer since the project's inception with grace and the good sense to ignore me frequently. For all the great trips to magical Prague where parts of this book were written, I thank you.

My last acknowledgement is to my family: to my siblings for their continued support and encouragement but especially to my parents, Maria and John, who far more than anyone else are responsible for my being able to undertake and complete this work. My mother gave me my sense of history and my father a love of sport. Without their continued support this would likely not be before you. My good fortune in having parents such as these is endless and I am deeply grateful for their long sacrifice. I dedicate this book to them.

ABBREVIATIONS

CCCA	Cork City and County Archives
CYMS	Catholic Young Men's Society
FAI/FAIFS	Football Association of Ireland/Football Association of the Irish Free State
FSW	Football Sports Weekly
GAA	Gaelic Athletic Association
ICICYMA	Incorporated Church of Ireland Christian Young Men's Association
IFA	Irish Football Association
IRA	Irish Republican Army
IRFU	Irish Rugby Football Union
LDFA	Limerick District Football Association
MFA	Munster Football Association
NAI	National Archives of Ireland
NLI	National Library of Ireland
PYMA	Protestant Young Men's Association
QCC/UCC	Queen's College Cork/University College Cork
QUB	Queen's University Belfast
RIC	Royal Irish Constabulary
UCCA	University College Cork Archives
UCDA	University College Dublin Archives
WCA	Waterford City Archives
YMCA	Young Men's Christian Association

TABLES AND FIGURES

TABLES AND FIGURES

1

INTRODUCTION

It was December 1877. On the road to Mallow, a group of boys from Lismore College made their way. The purpose of their trip was one that in time became common to the school-aged boys of Ireland. School pride was at stake. They were to meet boys from Mallow College to play a game of football, under association rules. This new way of playing football, using your feet but not your hands, was then only fourteen years old. In October 1863, a group of men met for the first of many such meetings, in the Freemasons Tavern, London to establish rules for a shared code of football that could be played more widely without confusion for the participants.[1] The rules that emerged from those meetings in London laid the basis for the game of soccer as we now know it. With those rules established, the game began spreading itself slowly in England, following the publication of the rules of association football in December 1863. The new Football Association's challenge cup began in 1871, its first winner, Wanderers, beating Royal Engineers 1–0, in the first of three FA Cup wins that decade. The game played in Mallow, although almost certainly not the first game of soccer played between two teams in Munster, was undoubtedly one of the earliest recorded by the press and is as good a starting point as any for our story.

The particular rules of football laid down by the Football Association in 1863 spread, though their spread was uneven and many teams continued to play under different football rules for some time to come. In Ireland, football codification at that time was restricted largely to the game of rugby football. Ireland's oldest rugby club was formed in Trinity College, Dublin in 1854, yet it would take until the middle of the 1870s before an Irish Rugby

Football Union (IRFU) would be formed. It was only a short few years beforehand, in 1871, that England's Rugby Football Union was formed. Not far from Mallow, in Queen's College Cork (QCC) the rugby club was established in 1874, though the game had been played for at least two years before that in QCC. A year after the boys of Mallow and Lismore Colleges played their game of soccer, a much more famous game took place: two Scottish sides, Caledonians and Queen's Park, played an exhibition match in Belfast that was such a success it led eventually to the growth of the game in Belfast and the eventual establishment of the Irish Football Association in 1880. This book is more about the boys of Lismore and Mallow playing in 1877 than what happened in Belfast in 1878. All of those young men were engaging in what is referred to as the Victorian sporting revolution. But it is that broader revolution at the local scale that forms our interest. Out of that revolution, in Ireland, would emerge the GAA in 1884. However, as this book will show, at the same time that many rowed in behind the newly formed GAA, there persisted, developed and grew an alternative sporting culture – a sporting culture centred around sports of British origin. This book is about one element of that other sporting culture: soccer. While soccer, for its initial impetus, relied on the influence of the British in Ireland, its continuation and expansion after Irish independence was granted with the signing of the Anglo-Irish Treaty in 1921, suggests that this alternative culture had a broad, popular support behind it. It also tells us that the introduction of sports like rugby and soccer was not simply a case of passive reception, but was part of a complex interaction between shared Irish and British culture at that time. As Jeff Dann has noted of people like the students in Trinity or QCC who set up rugby clubs:

> . . . the attitude of various Irish nationalists of the period towards British sports has been well-documented, both in histories of the GAA itself and in works examining aspects of the nationalist movement in general. What is far less well-documented, however, is the attitude towards British sports among those Irishmen who actually participated in them, particularly the aforementioned 'Castle Catholics' for whom participation in British sports was an opportunity to demonstrate their adherence to British culture and values and their possession, despite their Catholicism, of the attribute of manliness.[2]

This book seeks to understand the place of soccer in the life of people in Munster. While for some, playing soccer may well have been about demonstrating an adherence to British culture, this book will argue that playing soccer was about a great deal more. This book argues the case that soccer's spread and growth in Munster, from its sparse beginnings at the end of the 1870s to its strongest point in the 1920s and 1930s, reflected the reality that Ireland, though an island physically, was not one socially or culturally, a reality which included the playing of sports of British origin.

The history of sport in this country is slowly coming to light. This book aims to add to that growing body of knowledge about Ireland's sporting history. Discussion of sport in Irish historiography is no longer restricted to the old shibboleth that the GAA was important for its role as a breeding ground for both physical force and cultural nationalism. Yet, most other sports, soccer included, remain confined to sports historiography, and have not yet been brought into more general literature on Irish popular culture or social histories in general. This is a pity because, as Hassan and O'Kane noted a number of years ago, 'Ireland has a more varied sporting culture than many other nations due to the mix of traditional Gaelic Irish sports, colonial sports and sports introduced by economic immigrants.' As a result, they stress that 'importantly, each of the sports and their associated activities are closely bound to a range of ideas about what it means to be Irish'. With such importance thus placed on sport – 'at the same time it aids this process of identity formation, sport also retains the potential to divide people, opinions and communities in a manner seemingly unmatched by most other aspects of civil society,'[3] – it has much to tell us about the history of Ireland, and so, as this book aims to show, does soccer.

The favouring of the game by a mass audience, without the buttress of institutional support such as schools but instead in places of work, was mirrored in Ireland. The works team was a large part of the sport even in its early days in the Irish League and later Free State League, with clubs like Jacob's, Fordsons and St James' Gate providing three prime examples. As we shall see, soccer's fortunes fluctuated greatly in Munster in its early days, its players tied up as they were with wider political and social changes.

This book will focus in the main on Cork, Waterford, Tipperary and Limerick, places where soccer had its most substantial presence in

Munster, though it will also consider the game's development or lack thereof in Kerry and Clare. In the main this is a book about urban places – the cities and towns of Munster rather than their rural hinterlands. This is a result largely of soccer's greater foothold in the urban environment in Munster, rather than any overt decision to ignore the rural. But what and where was Munster? Like any large landmass, the province of Munster was and is as notable for a lack of homogenous features as anything else. A substantial land mass with wide rivers and deep harbours, deep valleys, mountains and good soil, containing as it does both the biggest county in Ireland in Cork, along with the biggest inland county in the country in the shape of Tipperary, Munster might best be characterised as a province in which all of the variety of Ireland can be found. With three cities in Cork, Limerick and Waterford, and many large and strategically important towns, the province was one in which sport was sure to flourish. Yet to look at the census from this period, Munster also saw a steady decline in its population over the course of the sixty years that this book covers:

TABLE 1.1
Population of Munster, 1881–1936

Year	1881	1891	1901	1911	1926	1936
Population	1,331,115	1,172,402	1,076,188	1,035,495	969,902	942,272

SOURCE: 1936 Census of Population

The decline in population indicated in the above table was the result of emigration, linked to a faltering economy in the 1890s, and later to the changed political circumstances that prevailed in the period between the taking of the 1911 census and the first census following independence, taken in 1926. In that formative fifteen-year period, as well as the usual economic imperatives for emigration, the changed political landscape saw parts of Munster become centres of guerrilla warfare as well as an important site of recruitment in the early years of the First World War, especially in Kerry, Cork and Waterford.

This book looks, in the main, at a sport that had its strongest concentration in the larger towns and cities of Munster. These urban areas did not have the straightforward story of decline that the province as a whole experienced as outlined in Table 1.1 above.

4

TABLE 1.2
Populations of Cork, Limerick and Waterford cities, 1911–1936

Year	1911	1926	1936
Cork	76,673	78,490	80,765
Limerick	38,518	39,448	41,061
Waterford	27,464	26,647	37,968

SOURCE: Census of Population, 1911–1936

As can be seen from the above table, each of these cities experienced demographic change over the course of the period when soccer emerged in the province. Significantly, in the period when the game would grow most in terms of participation and spectators, each of the three cities also experienced an increase in their populations. This increased population, driven in part by greater opportunities in these cities thanks to industrialisation under Fianna Fáil's protectionist policies, was perfectly placed to enjoy the emerging leisure industry of the interwar period, which included a new interest in Munster in the Free State League, when each of these three cities would at different times have a club playing at the national level for the first time. So while from the first table there is a discernable decline in the numbers living in Munster as a whole, the three cities of the province, the main focus of this book, all saw an overall rise in their populations. In Tipperary, some of the main footballing strongholds too saw demographic change. The county as a whole saw a decline in its population from the 1880s to 1930s, as the following table illustrates:

TABLE 1.3
Population of Tipperary, 1881–1936

Year	Population
1881	100,857
1891	86,381
1901	78,833
1911	73,849
1926	68,111
1936	65,438

SOURCE: Census of Population, 1911–1936

This is a staggering decline of close to 40,000 people over the course of nearly sixty years. Some of the mainstays of the game, as we will see, were the major towns of Tipperary's south riding, and in these places too, demographic change (and population decline) can be exhibited easily:

TABLE 1.4
Populations of Carrick-on-Suir, Clonmel and Cahir,
1911–1936

Town	1911	1926	1936
Carrick-On-Suir	5,235	4,657	4,840
Clonmel	10,209	9,056	9,391
Cahir	1,930	1,709	1,638

SOURCE: Census of Population, 1911–1936

So what do these figures tell us about Munster in the late nineteenth and early twentieth century? More importantly, what might we say about them in relation to the development of soccer? Obviously, since Munster as a whole, and Tipperary in particular, saw a decline over the period this book covers, we might say that population change doesn't have much of an effect on whether or not soccer emerged in different parts of the country – however, it is worth noting that the game did find its feet most readily in the bigger urban centres of the province, even if it had small but dedicated participants in places like Tipperary's south riding, in parts of Kerry, and later in Ennis. Given this concentration of the game, in areas that saw their populations rise during independence, much of this book will focus largely on the game as it developed following Ireland's political independence from Britain. These bigger urban areas were perfect for soccer to attain a critical mass of participants, across a variety of social classes, and to maintain that critical mass even when Ireland underwent demographic change in the wake of a world war and armed conflict at home.

This book will set soccer's development in the broader context of the developing leisure industries of the post-war period that were a hallmark of urban living in the early twentieth century (Chapter Three). In so doing, it will show that soccer was both a grass-roots game and a developed commercial business. The antagonism between these two aspects of the game in Munster will be important to our understanding of its development, as well as the place of the game in people's lives. As a quintessentially modern game, that the highest participation and spectating rates for soccer in the period covered occur after Irish independence confirms its modernity as one entertainment on offer among many in the new world of commercialised leisure. This book argues that soccer as a game, though a British import, was taken up by many people in Munster and made into a recreation that gave them joy and pleasure; soccer in Munster – its clubs, structures, its place in people's lives – was something built by many dedicated enthusiasts for the game, in the period from the late 1870s to the end of the 1930s, in the face of opposition from a variety of quarters who felt it did not belong. But, as this book argues, the many people for whom the game was an important recreation (playing or watching) were as much a part of the story of Ireland in those years as anyone else could claim. This book seeks to show that, more than just belonging in the great menagerie of sports played in Ireland, soccer had a central part in the lives of many people, particularly those dedicated to its development in Munster.

Although this book covers a period of sixty years that saw land agitation, the rise of the Irish Volunteers, the recruitment of thousands of Munster men to fight in the trenches in Europe, open warfare across its countryside during the War of Independence and again during the Civil War, it will not focus on those events in any great detail, except to acknowledge their role in shaping the changes of Munster's social and, as a result, sporting world. First and foremost this is a social history of soccer in the region, so the non-sporting aspects of the period will be dealt with insofar as they impacted those who played and were involved in the game.

As this is largely a history of ordinary, working-class people, the wider issues that affected them in their daily lives – things like housing, work, leisure, unemployment and access to playing spaces – will concern us just as much as their involvement in bigger national political fights. The broader context in which soccer's development is placed is the changing nature of leisure as its commercialisation changed people's relationship with their own leisure time.

Thus, general themes common to sports history will be examined in terms of their development in Munster: a nascent retail trade in sporting goods; the sporting press; sport as advertiser for drink and tobacco; the enclosing of grounds and building of stands; the role of the radio and the newsreel; the development of betting and commercially driven sports; and sport played in the local community as a means of socialising and fundraising for local causes. These are included in this history of soccer in order to place soccer's development as a commercial activity, antagonistic to the game's grass roots, in a broader context, that of the changing nature of people's leisure options – a change which benefited the game's move towards commercialisation. The less than straightforward relationship between the commercial and the voluntary aspects of sport, and soccer especially, will shine through.

Throughout the book, the examples of Cork and Waterford are particularly instructive. In Waterford, the example of one post-independence soccer club, St Joseph's, encapsulates so much of what this book is about. When St Joseph's Boys Club was formed in 1924 by then Bishop of Waterford Bernard Hackett, it is unlikely that he or anyone else would have thought that the most contested element of the club, the soccer side the boys set up for themselves, would be its most enduring legacy.

St Joseph's FC was probably one of the most significant cradles of young footballing talent in Waterford city until the emergence of Villa FC in 1953. In 2004, St Joseph's long history was recognised by the Football Association of Ireland (FAI). When it was set up late in 1923, this club had a wide remit to provide somewhere for young boys in Waterford city to be involved in their community out of school hours. In keeping with much of the ethos of the time, this was provided by a mixture of physical and intellectual endeavour. Aside from the soccer club that they would form of their own accord, there was to be billiards, quoits, chess, cards, skittles, boxing, gymnastics and a variety of other amusements including reading, concerts, learning fretwork, raffia and even woodwork.[4] It was very much of a piece with many sports-based clubs at that time, with links to their community manifested not just through representation on the sports field, but just as importantly in other elements of community life. The club catered for a huge number, with the figure at the end of 1926 being some 355 boys. The membership would fluctuate though remain high, with the numbers at the end of 1930 a strong 309, though by then the soccer club was St Joseph's main outlet and purpose.[5]

INTRODUCTION

This is the story of soccer in Munster, the story of clubs like St Joseph's and many more just the same. This story will bring us from seaside towns to riverside factories, have us dragged up in front of the courts, admonished and celebrated in the press; we will see great victories and crushing defeats. We will see how, in a province awash with sporting activity, soccer went from the humble beginnings of scratch schoolboy games like that in December 1877 to having three Free State League teams in 1937.

2

GARRISON GAME? SOCCER IN MUNSTER, 1877–1918

I can definitely state that the Munster Football Association intend to make an application for a grant to carry on the work, and try and put the branch in full working order. When the same is brought on I hope our Leinster representatives will be present, and give this deserving project their valuable support.
Sunday Independent, 21 October 1906

Compared to England, Wales and Scotland, the history of soccer in Ireland is not as well served.[1] With the exception of Neal Garnham's groundbreaking if limited work, no comprehensive academic history of the game has been written; the inclusion of the game in Hunt's work on Westmeath and, more recently, Curran's in Donegal aids greatly our understanding of the game's development at the grass-roots level, though knowledge about it generally is limited in a way that is not true of Gaelic games and, increasingly, rugby.[2] Like in Hunt's work, soccer and rugby are conflated into a single chapter in Donal O'Sullivan's work on sport in Cork, which, as the extensive research on rugby by Liam O'Callaghan in Munster has since shown, is insufficient to even begin to scratch the surface of either game's history in Cork. O'Sullivan's work on soccer in the same chapter is beset with dating errors and is unreliable as a result.[3] Local histories for the game in Munster are available, notably Plunkett Carter's *Century of Cork Soccer Memories* and Bertie O'Mahony's 75-year history of the Munster Football Association (MFA).[4] Likewise, Peter Byrne's book *Green is the Colour* provides a good overall picture of the sport, though it focuses heavily on the international squad and its earliest chapters are heavily indebted to Garnham's work.[5] Although not specifically a history of soccer in Ireland per se, Mike Cronin's work on soccer, the GAA and nationalism helps a great deal, along with Garnham's work and the contributions of Hunt and Curran, to set the terms of the debate about Irish soccer, namely to what extent was the game reliant on military involvement for its diffusion.[6]

Conor Curran's work suggests that boat crews in the Lough Swilly area had some role to play in the promotion of the game, but notes that it is difficult ultimately to assess the extent of their impact. A Donegal FA was established in 1894, running successfully for a number of years before floundering. Curran suggests that the influence of local patrons, the development of the game in Derry, as well as ship crews around Lough Swilly, all contributed to the game's development north of the Blue Stack Mountains, while to the south of these in Ballyshannon it was the military that had an influence, in the guise of the 2nd Dorset Regiment. This shows that within one county, two different processes for the diffusion of the game were possible.[7] The development of soccer in Munster is best understood by viewing it as part of the game's wider development in Ireland and Britain. By placing it in the broader context of both, we will be able to understand its development far better than if we understood it just within the context of Ireland alone. Almost every county in Munster touches the Irish coastline, and where it does not, a river described by Edmund Spenser as the 'silvery Suir' flows all the way from Templemore, County Tipperary to the sea at Waterford, plentiful with salmon and brown trout. Each of the three cities that form the main focus of this book were major port cities. Thus they were no strangers to outside influence and cultural exchange from those who came from beyond the mouths of their ports. This is why these cities, Cork and Waterford in particular, were important places for the provisions trade related to Atlantic sailing, and why Cork, with its enormous natural harbour especially, became a focal point for the British Navy. Understanding the development of soccer in Cork, Limerick, Waterford and even Tipperary requires an understanding of these aspects of each place's longer and broader history: to understand them not as on the edge looking in but on the edge and looking out, ready to take influences from across the Irish sea and the Atlantic. As Margaret Mastriani has written of the docks in Limerick, they 'offer an intriguing story that encompasses the worlds of international trade, with timber ships from Canada and Scandinavia and coal boats from England and Poland frequenting the docks'.[8] While the goods at Cork and Waterford may well have differed, nonetheless the key point remains that in cities where ports were so vital, as well as goods coming on and off the boat – different people, ideas, culture and even sport also came on and off. One of those sports, according to Mastriani's article, was soccer. She quotes one docker as saying that 'his colleagues would "often come out of the pub after five or six pints, play ninety minutes of soccer and then get up in the morning to unload coal boats"'.[9]

In that spirit then, and casting our net a little wider, the history of soccer in south Wales can be instructive to the Irish, and Munster, experience. As Martin Johnes notes, soccer was never 'popularly associated with notions of Welshness in the way that rugby had [been]'. He argues that although soccer had no claims to having as pivotal a role in south Wales as rugby, it did nevertheless have a history in the region.[10] In Scotland, Richard Holt notes that 'unlike the Irish, the Scots did not try to build up their indigenous sports at the expense of the modern team-games from England'. Rather, he argues 'industrial Scotland did not wear the kilt. Like South Wales it had its own identity to forge, its own kind of Scottishness to create that was far removed from the "Benn and Glen" variety so beloved of the romantic expatriate'.[11] Matt McDowell's recent work on Scottish football also indicates that the games development in Ayrshire and Lanarkshire is no product of the traditional diffusion model.[12] Holt's work recognises for both Wales and Scotland that 'sports were shared with the English and used as a means of asserting claims for the recognition of special ethnic and national qualities', saying that 'sport acted as a vitally important channel for this sense of collective resentment . . . cultural identity was a two-way process'.[13] His work focuses on what he calls the two quite separate elements of 'Celtic nationalism', the second being the appropriation of adopted sporting culture like rugby in Wales, or soccer in Scotland. The first element, for Holt though, is the outright rejection of British sport by Irish cultural nationalists. Although he later notes the appeal of British sports, and soccer in particular, to those in Derry, Dublin and Belfast, as well as to some for whom radical nationalism was off-putting, he does not give full consideration to the two-way process of cultural formation where, in Ireland, many people took soccer and made it their own.[14]

As with much of the rest of Britain, the history of soccer in Ireland is intimately linked with Ireland's urban working class, either as participants or spectators – soccer was more commercially developed than other field sports in Ireland from its earliest days. It is no accident that in its infancy, despite the interest of schoolboys like those from Mallow and Lismore colleges, soccer in Ireland was at its strongest in the country's most developed industrial areas, Belfast and Dublin, initially. The bulk of senior soccer in Ireland at the time came from both of these cities. In Munster, the emergence of soccer was closely allied to a combination of the British military presence, a middle-class base, sometimes in schools, and following independence, a broadly working- and lower-middle-class base in urbanised areas that played the game. That so much of the game's organisation happened after 1921 is important to note. Yet this simplistic view of soccer as the working man's game is too neat a narrative to fully explain its development in Ireland as a whole or Munster in particular. As this book will show throughout, it took a wider range of people than just working-class males to give the game its start, even if they would make it largely their preserve in time.

Just as such simplified histories serve to reduce so complex a social activity, so too the popular perception of soccer's origins in Ireland as the 'garrison game' should be challenged, since the evidence, not just in Donegal but in Munster too, points to a more varied set of reasons for the game's introduction than simply being the result of British privates playing the game, though their role was crucial too. Whatever the initial impetus the military interest in the game provided, Neal Garnham concludes that while the British armed forces were not 'intimately involved in the game's introduction to Ireland, military teams had apparently acted as an important means of spreading the game into the country's rural hinterland'.[15] But in what ways is this apparent? Certainly, as we will see before 1921, many of the teams playing football in Cork were distinctly military in their makeup. Was this true across the province of Munster? Why does the game persist, or even increase in popularity? What happened when the garrison was no longer part of the garrison game? As Hunt, Curran and Garnham note, the role of the military varies from place to place.[16] Hunt argues, in Athlone at least, that 'the school, the army and the GAA crossover were also important ingredients' ultimately; the key influence on soccer's development was the 'small core of middle-class businessmen' that transferred their allegiance from Gaelic football to soccer.[17] Similarly, in Donegal, Curran's work shows that there is more than the simple diffusion of soccer through the military in that part of Ireland.[18]

Neal Garnham's ground-breaking work on the history of the game cites a Boxing Day game in 1896 in Carrick-on-Suir as the first formal game of soccer played in Munster,[19] yet given the game that was played by schoolboys in Mallow in 1877 noted earlier, this was clearly far from the first. That game in Mallow and the game in 1878 between Queen's Park and Caledonians, usually cited as the first game of soccer in Ireland, suggests that a more complex interaction, one of broader cultural reception, between Ireland and Britain is the cause rather than just the British military presence in Ireland. Tony Mason and Elizabeth Riedi's work on sport in the British military has shown that soccer was a significant part of the sports programme in the British Army, with the Army Football Association being founded in 1888, the same year as the Football League. Soccer was the sport most popular with and familiar to privates in the army, with officers preferring rugby and cricket. Not surprisingly then, among privates stationed in Ireland, soccer was probably the most popular sport. Not only that but it was the sport civilians were most used to seeing soldiers play, particularly if they lived in those towns and cities where many barracks were situated.[20]

The perception of soccer as predominantly working class in England arose largely because only twenty-five years after the formalising of the game's rules in 1863, the game began to reflect that predominance, with professionalism being legalised in 1885 – a change cemented by the foundation of the Football League in 1888, and this association as the people's game only became entrenched as the First World War approached.[21] This transformation of soccer is significant for its historical development in Ireland. In no time at all, professional football in Ireland was played largely by the skilled and unskilled working class around 1900, in higher proportions than in England, in fact.[22]

While the Irish Football Association was founded in 1880 in Belfast on the back of increased interest in the game following exhibition games like that held in 1878, and this development was followed ten years later by the formation of the Irish Football League in 1890 and the Leinster Football Association (LFA) in 1892, the game's emergence in Munster between the middle of the 1870s and the middle of the 1890s is much more difficult to pin down. Cork, with its large and varied urban population and well-connected garrison towns, was the first place where soccer really began to take hold in Munster. So it was that sometime between the late 1870s and the end of the century, sufficient interest in the game had developed in Cork to establish a Munster Football Association.

Some games from this early period in Cork help to give a flavour of who was playing soccer in these formative years. Novelty matches like those played by noted Shakespearean actor Francis Benson in 1893 notwithstanding, two fixtures played at Fermoy in December 1896 give us some indication of who was playing in the years immediately prior to the founding of the Munster Football Association in 1901. One of these two fixtures was a return fixture, a victory for Holohan's XI against A Company, South Lancashire Regiment, by five goals to one. The other was between the Fermoy College's second XI and another side of local men, R. O'Flanagan's XI, which ended in a one-all draw.[23] This game was played sometime in the middle of December, just before the St Stephen's Day fixture in Carrick-on-Suir, County Tipperary that Garnham's work indicates as the first formal game in Munster. Certainly, the handful of reports from December 1896 suggest that the game was gaining a greater foothold than it had before. The fact that one of the games mentioned above was a return fixture suggests the game had been going probably from the beginning of that winter at least in the region. By the turn of the twentieth century, there were a great many clubs playing soccer in Cork, with the bulk of teams coming from the various barracks of the city. Yet the early story of soccer in Cork was not solely a story of soldiers at play. Among the earliest civilian teams were Cork Olympic, Crosshaven United, Shamrocks United, North Mall Swifts, R. O'Flanagan's XI, Boys' Brigade (Christ Church) and Fermoy College – a fine mixture of educational, residential and associational clubs. There were a good deal more teams playing the game, plenty of them civilian teams, although these seem to be mostly scratch teams playing one-off matches. The Boys' Brigade was a youth movement who seem to have latched on to soccer as providing moral rectitude elsewhere in Ireland with Belfast and Dublin branches of the organisation also fielding teams during this period.[24] These scattered reports offer us a tantalising glimpse of a broader soccer-playing culture which was beginning to find its feet in Cork as the nineteenth century came to a close. By 1901, as well as the various teams made up from military regiments, civilian teams included Cork Celtic, Church of Ireland, Cork City, Alexandra, St Patrick's FC and St Mary's FC. Two of these civilian clubs, Celtic and City, were able to field a second as well as a first XI. In 1901, Sir Alf Dobbin, one of the proprietors of Dobbin, Ogilvie & Co. Ltd., oversaw the formation of the MFA and a soccer league in Cork in 1901. This was an important step in maintaining competition for those playing the game, and facilitated the spread of the game in the city.

As already noted, little in the way of regular reports appear in the local press regarding soccer until a *Cork Examiner* report on a match between Cork Celtic and Army Services Corps in 1901. The game took place on the Camp Field, which was one of the most frequent sites used for soccer in this period. The Army Services Corps won the game by two goals to one. The game was seen by only 'a few spectators'.[25] In that first year, thirteen teams played in the league. Cork Celtic, Cork City, Awbeg Rovers, Passage and Millfield were the non-military teams in the league. Of the civilian teams, Celtic were the strongest, topping the league table for a considerable length of time. Close to the end of the season, the team had slipped to fourth, but with a goal difference that was ten to the good, it seems they played an exciting and attacking style of football that would have helped to make the game more popular with civilians.

The game continued apace in the early twentieth century. By 1904, soccer's popularity was growing with a good number of works teams springing up. Two examples of such works teams were the Ordnance Survey team and the Waterville Commercial Cable Company's team from Kerry.[26] The importance of works teams can readily be seen at the senior level in Irish soccer at that time with clubs such as Distillery, Linfield and St James' Gate being among the biggest in the period. Each of the three teams was linked to the drinks industry and linen mills. As we shall see below, Cork was to have its own significant works team in the shape of Fordsons FC following the end of the First World War. In the Waterville Commercial Cable Company there were a sufficient number of English and Scottish employees in 1904 to have an internal game between both nationalities, and it is likely that it was these workers who encouraged the game.[27] The Waterville Cable Company team's entry into the early league is perhaps best explained by this 'international' match held by the company. This strength of English and Scottish workers suggests that these men were most likely the ones who encouraged the playing of soccer in the company, similar to those noted by Curran in his work on Donegal.

Although soccer was strong in this early period, the game in Munster was not likely to maintain itself without some financial backing from the parent organisation based in Belfast, the Irish Football Association (IFA). The Munster Football Association, however, was the most immediate body to oversee the emerging game in Cork and the rest of the province. From the records of other bodies still extant, it is evident that the Munster Football Association were no slouches when it came to attempting to improve the standing of soccer in Cork. Thus, only weeks after forming, they sent a letter to their counterparts of the Leinster Football Association seeking an interprovincial contest, to be played in January of 1902.[28] These interprovincial matches became a staple of the relationship between both bodies in this era, though perhaps reflecting the seniority of the Leinster body, and the ambition of the Munster Football Association, it was more often than not the MFA who wrote to the Leinster body requesting a tie be arranged. Whatever use it may have been to either body as a means of promotion for soccer is questionable, however. For one thing, the Munster selection were usually heavily beaten by the opposition, like when they were massacred 8–0 in 1903, all for a gate of £4.18.9. The following year, 1904, Leinster beat them 6–1, this time playing in Dublin and the difference in the gate is startling. The total gate for that game was £16.9.0, four times the previous year and a strong indication of the gap – despite their best efforts – between the game's popularity in Dublin and in Cork.[29] For one person who wrote into the *Cork Examiner* using the moniker of 'Half-Back' this drubbing was proof that over-reliance on the military players for the Munster selection was a mistake and that more civilians ought to have been made use of in the game. Such a letter was an early sign of the differing cultures of the game then emerging in the city between the military and civilian teams.[30] The Leinster Football Association's own committee members were sceptical enough of the enterprise too. Their Finance Committee noted the expense of the 1903 interprovincial, with the hotel in Cork for that game alone costing their body £15.15.2. Their income from the game, half of the gate, was £12.9.0, while the entirety of their expenses for the match amounted to £27.11.11, leaving them out of pocket by some way.[31] The clubs and committees, not just in Leinster but also in Munster, watched money tightly too; and while the inter-provincial match would continue despite its costliness, not all clubs nor the Munster Football Association were able to keep things afloat without help from the national body for the game.

The Munster FA and the Irish Football Association

The first mention of the Munster Football Association in the records of the national body for the sport, the Irish Football Association, was at the meeting of their senior committee on 8 October 1901. The minutes from that evening's meeting note that a letter was read stating that an association had been founded in Munster and desired to be affiliated to the national body. The letter included a list of the clubs that made up this new body, all of them based in Cork. It also included the affiliation fees from the clubs. A Mr Sheehan of the IFA's Finance Committee proposed a motion that the newly founded MFA be given a grant equal to the amount sent in affiliation fees. This gesture of Sheehan's was however given short shrift by those present. When put to a vote, his motion was defeated, seven votes for with twelve against. This first interaction between the MFA and the IFA would typify their relationship in the coming decade and more.[32]

The IFA committee minute books suggest a distant relationship between both bodies. Most mentions of the Munster body in the minutes of the IFA's senior council related to grant applications which, like that first one, were rarely, but occasionally, forthcoming. In September 1904, for instance, the senior council of the IFA voted eleven for and two against to give the MFA a grant of £10.[33] Thus in May 1906 that the annual report passed at that year's IFA AGM noted that soccer was steadily progressing in Munster. So it was that in 1906 the fledgling Munster Football Association requested finan-cial aid from the IFA. In his round-up of the week, *Sunday Independent* correspondent W.G. Knight had this to say:

> [I]t was with regret that Cork Celtic found it impossible to travel up to meet Reginald in Dublin in the Irish Cup. I can definitely state that the Munster Football Association intend to make an application for a grant to carry on the work, and try and put the branch in full working order. When the same is brought on I

hope our Leinster representatives will be present, and give this deserving project their valuable support.[34]

Another grant application in the 1906/07 season was not so easily won, however. Given that previous attempts by Munster to secure grants were undone by failing to get a seconder for motions on the topic even before losing on a vote, hope that Leinster delegates would rally to Munster's cause was a touch optimistic. It was decided at a meeting in March 1907 that since the MFA 'could not state clearly as to the manner in which they desired to spend a grant of £30 passed by IFA', they would have to be satisfied with half that amount instead.[35] Another grant was awarded in June of 1908, this time to the tune of £20.[36] This was granted at a time of exceptional development in Munster soccer and driven in part by the greater role the MFA delegates began playing in the national association. At the AGM of the IFA in 1908, it was noted in the figures supplied in the annual report that Munster had by then twenty-nine affiliated clubs. The annual report itself included this passage:

> The gratifying feature of that increase [of overall affiliation figures] is that Munster has doubled its membership, and from information available, it is believed that it is only the beginning of the progress of the game in the Southern Province, which has given so many notable names to almost every other branch of sport.[37]

Indeed this proved an accurate observation as the annual report of the IFA in 1910 intimates that the number of affiliated clubs in Munster had risen to forty-three.

Yet, despite this progress, grants from the parent body still proved hard to come by. An application for a further grant in January 1911 was deferred until the March meeting of the IFA's council when a discussion took place resulting ultimately in Munster FA delegate Lieutenant Parker withdrawing the application.[38] Twelve months later the topic was raised again; however it was decided that the matter be left until the season's end to see how the financial arrangements of another grant would be worked out.[39] Perhaps predictably, no more was made of the matter that season. In April 1913, yet another application was made for a grant by the MFA; however, this time it was made directly to the IFA Finance Committee, who deferred making a decision until the next meeting of the senior council. At the April meeting of the Senior Council, which took place a few days later, we learn that the MFA requested the grant in order to improve their ground.[40]

In what must surely have been a frustrating move for the Munster delegates, any decision on the matter was deferred by the senior council until after the elections at the upcoming AGM. In practice this meant the matter wasn't raised again until September 1913. In another move, which undoubtedly made the MFA delegates feel as though the IFA cared little for the game south of Dublin, the matter was bounced back once more to the Finance Committee.[41] Incredibly, the motion to grant the MFA £25 was not passed by the Finance Committee at its October 1913 meeting, the motion having no seconder.[42] Nonetheless a sum of £35 was eventually granted to the MFA at a Finance Committee meeting in December 1913, the MFA having agreed terms with the IFA in one of the last references to the Munster body in the records of the IFA before the outbreak of the First World War.[43] The very last mention of the MFA in the records prior to the outbreak of the war was the recording of the receipt of the affiliation fees of twelve clubs from Munster on 10 February 1914. This decidedly tardy receipt of affiliation fees was it seems typical, not just of Munster clubs but clubs from all regions. Nonetheless, it points to the reason for the chequered record of the IFA in boosting the game in Munster.

The drip of affiliation fees – five shillings here, two pounds there – from Munster clubs to the IFA's Finance Committee, as recorded in their minute books, was only one part of a wider issue. The general perception, reinforced by Neal Garnham's work portraying the IFA as a national body, which in those years was more interested in its immediate surrounds of Belfast and Ulster than being truly national in scope, was not helped by the MFA's own occasionally less than stellar performance in engaging with the national body. For instance, the MFA, mirroring its dealings with the Leinster FA in the same era, sought an interprovincial match in a letter in May 1905 with Ulster. But a meeting in January of 1906 notes that there was still no word forthcoming about setting a date, the IFA having to send a reminder. A date was eventually set for St Patrick's Day 1906 for a match in Cork. Ulster won the game 3–1. Earlier that same season, when Cork Celtic met Shelbourne in the fourth round of the Irish Cup, the MFA were a pound shy in paying the referee's expenses, the referee having come from Newry. Indeed the MFA delegate, Lieutenant Brewer, wrote to the IFA complaining of the cost but was replied to and told that the choice was a resolution of the council and was made to pay the extra pound outstanding to the Newry referee.

The track record of the MFA delegates in the first decade of the twentieth century in attending the IFA's monthly Senior Council meetings was also somewhat lacking. Henry Wilson, the MFA delegate in the early years, attended only two of the meetings in the 1903/04 season, for instance. From 1905 onwards, the delegates improved their attendance records considerably. The not inconsequential distance required by Munster delegates to travel to Belfast was undoubtedly a mitigating circumstance for much of this poor track record, but it is also worth noting that the makeup of the MFA's own council was something of an own goal in this respect. At different times Lieutenants Brewster and Parker were representatives of the MFA at these monthly IFA meetings, though presumably army matters would have taken precedence on occasion. Here again we can see the divergence between the evident growing popularity of soccer in Munster among a civilian population being poorly served by the increasingly unrepresentative council.

The strongest influence exerted by the MFA on the national body in this period was when Henry Wilson's attendance improved and he was elected onto the Protest and Appeals subcommittee as well as the Senior Council at the end of 1905. Wilson was elected with some 162 votes. The trust placed in Wilson by those voters was repaid as he attended eleven of the twelve IFA Senior Council meetings that season. This was a marked improvement on his previous efforts of attending only two and five of the meetings in earlier years. His replacement in the 1905/06 season as the MFA representative, James McAnerny, a Belfast Celtic official, attended ten of the twelve meetings.

In his increased capacity, Henry Wilson had a major effect on the IFA in this period. Chiefly, this was through a motion of his that was carried whereby the Senior Council of the IFA include not just members from senior clubs but also junior ones too. Also, a reimagining of the council along a new divisional basis saw soccer divided into five districts with corresponding numbers of delegates who could be present at the IFA Senior Council meetings. These districts were Belfast and Antrim, Armagh, Monaghan, Fermanagh and

Cavan; Derry and Donegal; Leinster; and Munster. Belfast and Antrim had five delegates, the next three districts had two delegates each while Munster had just one, but also the position held by Wilson. This gave them, in theory at least, a stronger voice at the meetings of the Senior Council held in Belfast and Dublin.[44] However, as we've already seen, the difficulties the MFA had in securing grants – not helped by their own poor communications – suggests that for all of Wilson's work, and later work by McAnerny and Rev. Ruttle, another MFA delegate, the IFA's interest in the game in Munster was perfunctory at best much of the time.

While the *Cork Sportsman* was primarily an organ of the Cork GAA, it also provided extensive coverage of other football codes, including soccer. In spite of the financial aid required by the Munster FA, the game was sufficiently organised at the end of the first decade of the twentieth century in the Cork area to ensure this regular level of coverage in the newspapers, in particular in the *Cork Sportsman*. Competition was organised using a league format. The league was split into four divisions: the First Division Munster League, the Second Division Munster League, Third Division Munster League and the Munster Combination League.

The majority of the teams in the top two leagues were drawn from the British armed forces, with the Royal Welsh Fusiliers, Sherwood Foresters, South Lancashire Regiment, Army Services Corps, Army Ordnance Corps, Army Medical Corps, 38th Company Royal Engineers, 50th Battery Royal Field Artillery (RFA), and 31st Brigade RFA among the teams. A Navy side came from the *HMS Skipjack*, while Haulbowline was a civilian side. The other teams were Cork City, Cork Celtic and the Church of Ireland. In fact, the First Division was rarely if ever reported on, even in other newspapers of the time, with both the *Cork Examiner* and the *Cork Free Press* showing a tendency to report the Second Division particularly. This was due to the large number of civilian teams in the Second Division compared to the First. The Third Division was markedly different in its makeup, with Presentation College, Parnell Rovers, Alexandra, and Bandon.

The students of what was then QCC also established a soccer club in the first decade of the twentieth century, although the club was very short-lived. The records of the university contain some letters from the soccer club in its first two seasons. The club was formed in

1905, by several of the medical students. As it was with the rugby club, the president of the soccer club was a member of staff. This time it was Professor Bergin. The secretary of the club in that first year was Michael J. Horgan, who would later serve as a lieutenant in the Royal Army Medical Corps in the First World War. A similar letter showing elected officers for the 1906/07 season also exists. Unfortunately, the student magazine *QCC* only carries a small number of reports for the club in this period. This suggests that the enthusiasm for soccer was short-lived in the college at that time. This decline is especially unfortunate since, in only a few short years, the Collingwood Cup, the premier intervarsity soccer competition in Ireland, would be played for the first time in 1914, won by University College Dublin at Dalymount Park, Queen's University Belfast 2–1.[45] It is also worth noting that this team flowered briefly just before Gaelic games took hold in Queen's College Cork, which would shortly be renamed University College Cork following the Irish Universities Act of 1908, after which the makeup of UCC would change greatly, and following a push from students and some staff, the first intervarsity GAA games would be established: the Sigerson Cup for Gaelic football in 1911 and the Fitzgibbon Cup for hurling in 1912.

Other teams, about whom we know nothing but their names from the end of the first decade of the twentieth century, include St Finbarre's, St Mary's (Shandon), Berwick, Hibernians, Douglas, Rose Field, River Lee FC, Park View, Celtic Strollers, Bellevue United and Barrackton United. We can assume that the St Mary's (Shandon) of 1910 is the same as the St Mary's of 1901, in geographic location at least. Barrackton have remained the most well-known of these clubs, if, like the rest, quite ephemeral. Although considered popularly to be the oldest club in the city, this is evidently untrue. Importantly though, these teams are all based not on a specific institution, but on their localities. However the game came to be played by these clubs, the appetite for playing was evident, given the number of civilian clubs in absolute terms that existed. Barrackton United was formed by the people who lived around the Victoria Barracks and was probably among the earliest civilian teams to play against the Army sides in the city. Though we may have little more than their names left to us now, their abundance is a good indication that the game had set down popular roots

in Cork by 1910, just nine years after the attempt to formally structure the game in the city and province began.

As well as the various divisions of the Munster League, there
was also a Military League played between those who were
stationed in the barracks of the city. There was further competition
with the Munster Cup and the Chirnside Shield. The Chirnside
Shield was a charity shield played by teams from both Cork and
Limerick. Soccer was in a strong position by 1910 in Cork. There
were significant signs of the game's increasing popularity. One of
the key moments indicating and adding to this was the visit in
1909 of Manchester City to play a Munster selection in Cork, a
game which drew a huge crowd and much comment. The exhibition game took place at Turner's Cross, and was seen by a huge
crowd; meanwhile the Manchester City team were given the royal
treatment and were even brought to Blarney Castle, where they
all, management included, kissed the stone![46] When the 1909
season came to a close, 'Centre-Half' could write for the *Cork
Sportsman* that 'considerable progress has been made in the
spreading of the game and the outlying districts are beginning to
take more than a casual interest in the dribbling code'.[47] Efforts
were made to help the civilian clubs in Cork develop. In particular
the decision was made to divide the sum total of the gate receipts
collected at Burkley Cup matches among all the civilian clubs as a
means of helping them to stabilise financially. This decision,
however, revealed something of the tension between the civilian
clubs that took part in the game's official structure via the MFA
and the many military-based clubs that populated it. The final of
the 1910 Burkley Cup between Black Watch and the Sherwood
Foresters from Fermoy saw quite a poor civilian turnout, yet
overall the *Cork Sportsman* reported at the end of that season, cup-
tie gate receipts had increased by 150 per cent, suggesting that
civilian interest in the game was stronger than ever except where
the military teams were concerned.[48]

Still, Cork soccer in this period suffered a problem that was all too
familiar in developing sport anywhere in Ireland – a lack of good
playing pitches which clubs could call their own was an immediate
and pressing issue. The *Cork Sportsman* provides us with an insight
into the problem faced by the emerging soccer fraternity:

. . . the spread of the game will be even more accelerated now that the local clubs are realising that it would be to their benefit to secure more playing grounds. Steps in this direction have been taken by the Church of Ireland FC, who are fortunate in possessing a good level playing pitch at Blackrock. Cork City also opened a new ground at Victoria Cross last season, and will again be playing there when the improvements now being made are completed. Again two Third Division clubs – Glenthorne and Freebooters – have shown commendable enterprise in obtaining a field at Mayfield.[49]

Few clubs were as lucky as Haulbowline AFC, who in 1909 made arrangements with the Cove Football Club, a Gaelic football club, after previously having a tense relationship with them.[50] This indicates that previously bad relations could be thawed between two opposing clubs from opposing codes even in an atmosphere that saw the introduction of the ban on foreign games in 1905. The game continued its rapid spread approaching the 1910/11 season. While in the previous season there had been a total of nineteen teams, now there were twenty-seven across three divisions playing in the MFA's leagues. The First Division of the Munster League was still the reserve of just five teams, all of which were Army sides. This segregation of the best military sides from the civilian teams points at not just a sporting separation, but perhaps a social one too. For instance, in the Third Division there was the greatest diversity of clubs: there was Belle Vue (Queenstown) as well as a Belle Vue United, though they were almost certainly the same team; Clifton, Glenthorne and Freebooters were all northside clubs; Celtic Minors and Cork City Minors; Presentation, Barrackton Minors and Haulbowline Minors. Cork Celtic also acquired grounds of their own, opening them on St Stephen's Day in a game against Barrackton United in the Second Division. According to the *Cork Sportsman*, the one drawback of the ground was that it was not enclosed, and therefore the club could not charge an entrance fee. The fact that these civilian clubs seemed largely to be based around locales suggests they were playing the game anyway, and were familiar enough with the rules to allow them to take part in the league. Notices appear in this period too of civilian teams playing challenge matches, like those involving Friar's Walk and Victoria Rovers.[51] Indeed there were perhaps a good deal more playing the game, affiliated and unaffiliated, not taking part in the league but perhaps only in the local cup competitions. The annual report of the IFA, passed at their AGM in May 1910, indicated that there were a total of forty-three affiliated clubs by then – a good number more than those taking part in the local leagues.[52]

Another sign of the health of the game, even in the relatively young Munster Football League, was the existence of rivalries. On Cork's northside it was Glenthorne and Freebooters that were big local rivals. Their winter fixtures against each other in the 1910/11 season took place in Mayfield in front of a 'goodly number of spectators'. Like any league, the Munster League had one team that was above the ordinary level of support or derision – that team was the Royal Welsh Fusiliers. Their victory after Christmas against St James' Gate was received very well, and their return to Cork was highly anticipated:

> The time is rapidly drawing near when the Royal Welsh Fusilier team will again be seen in Cork. Arrangements are being made to have the postponed Chirnside Charity Shiel [sic] played at Victoria Cross on a Wednesday in February 1911, and the meeting of the Black Watch and Royal Welsh Fusiliers should result in a substantial sum being obtained for division amongst local charities.[53]

They also appear to have had the good fortune of being organised rather astutely, their engagement with St James' Gate at Dalymount being attended by many of their followers, thanks to the organisation of trams by the Honorary Secretary Quarter-Master E.A. Parker.[54]

Fixtures were heavy around the Christmas period at the end of the year. In all, between Christmas Eve and St Stephen's Day 1910, eleven soccer matches were played in Cork, as part of the Munster League Divisions Two and Three.[55] These games were played the length and breadth of Cork, with matches taking place in Douglas, Victoria Cross, Mayfield, Carrignafoy and Queenstown. A significant blow to soccer in Cork came with the decline of the *Cork Sportsman*. For its three-year run it had provided the game with an outlet for fixture lists, match reports and club notes and notices unlike anything in the other local newspapers up to that point. Luckily for those with an interest in the game, the mantle appears to have been taken over, following the decline of the *Cork Sportsman*, by the *Cork Constitution*, the main unionist newspaper in Cork at that time.

One of the most active teams in 1912 was Castle United, who had a great run in the 1911/12 season playing thirteen games, losing just one and drawing twice. The team took some considerable scalps, beating both Fr Hurley's and Rockwell reserves 8–0, Cathedral Rovers 7–0, likewise St Vincent's and a side calling themselves Everton 6–0.[56] Castle United and their opponents point towards a significant number of civilians playing the game who weren't involved officially through the MFA, which was dominated still by military teams, despite the increased interest of many locals in the game. The improved quality of the Cork players was notable, however, exemplified by Jimmy Sheehan of Barrackton United, who was called up to represent Ireland as a junior international against Scotland. When he began his journey for that game, the *Cork Sportsman* wrote that he would 'carry with him the best wishes of all local Soccerites for success in his first International'.[57]

Figure 2.1: *Barrackton FC, c.1910*
Seated, front row, second in from the right is Jimmy Sheehan
in international cap and jersey.
Reproduced with kind permission of Plunkett Carter.

There were two problems in particular that prevented soccer in Cork at this time from developing further among civilians than it might have. The first of these was the fact that most of the soccer was played on Saturday afternoons, usually between 3 and 4 pm. In the round-up of the 1908/09 season, 'Centre Forward' had noted that 'A great obstacle to the games in Cork being attended is the lack of a general half-holiday, and I venture to predict that when that drawback is eliminated the attendance at local Soccer matches will far exceed that of past seasons.' It was noted in the soccer column of 'Centre-Half' that because the half-holiday didn't prevail every-where it meant that many of the civilian teams in Cork could not put out full sides on Saturday afternoon as many were 'perhaps, out of town or detained at business'. The same issue was noted again in 1909 and 1910 when it was acknowledged that 'with the near approach to Xmas [sic] the local civilian clubs find it difficult to field representative elevens. Many of their prominent players being engaged up to a late hour on Saturdays.'[58] Given that the city had witnessed a major lockout in 1909 of workers who had attempted to organise themselves into unions, those with work were no doubt keen to hold on to it. As a result, fewer civilian sides were part of the game's official structure in the city and province. The issue of Sunday play was one the MFA were conscious of from early on. J.R.M. Lennon wrote on behalf of the MFA to the IFA only weeks after affiliating to the national body to ask if clubs connected to the IFA were at liberty to play matches on a Sunday. The secretary of the IFA wrote back, endorsed by the Senior Council, that 'while there was no specific rule to prevent matches being played on Sunday, the Association had invariably prohibited same'.[59] The implication was clear, that the MFA was expected to follow suit. However, a few years later a motion was passed unanimously at an IFA Senior Council meeting 'that the playing of football on Sunday is not illegal or antagonistic to the rules'.[60] This confused state of affairs resulted ultimately in the continued tradition of not having matches on a Sunday, thus debarring some from the sport. Nonetheless the general increase in the numbers of affiliated clubs in the same period suggests that the best efforts were made by those in civilian clubs to work around the issue. For those not affiliated, there were no such rules to obey.

Clearly, given the apparent ease Castle United had in finding opponents, many people were actively playing the game outside of these official structures. As Peter Byrne has noted, 'Statistically, the number of clubs in Munster didn't even begin to compare with the figures in Leinster or Ulster, but it has to be recorded that many unaffiliated teams are said to have existed in Cork and District at the time.'[61] The same period also saw Gaelic games develop on sure footing in the city of Cork, with organisations like the Cork City Football League and the Saturday Hurling League all aimed to cater especially for the games' development in the city and its immediate surroundings. Of course, the Saturday Hurling League was no stranger to the same issues that affected soccer, with a game between Sunday's Well and Dwyer's taking place a half an hour later than scheduled as a result of the players from Dwyer's being unable to get away from work thanks to the busy holiday season.[62] Games kicking off later than advertised was something heavily criticised in the GAA notes of the *Cork Sportsman*, prompting then chairman of the City Football League, later County board chairman and future TD, J.J. Walsh to write in to the paper to say that, in most instances, the games rarely ever took place much more than fifteen minutes later than the advertised time.

Not coincidentally, and perhaps mindful of the inroads being made by soccer in the city thanks to attractions like the Manchester City visit, 'Carbery', the pre-eminent journalist of Gaelic games, showed in this same period considerable concern for what he saw as the parlous state of hurling in the city, though he was sure the game would rise phoenix-like.[63] This was a period of important change for many team sports in Cork, with greater organisation of Gaelic games in Cork city at this time; rugby too was consolidating its position with similar league structures. Intriguingly, these changes in local rugby began to take shape as soccer emerged as a real force in Cork, and urban Gaelic games began to stake a place too.

Up until 1910, there were many ad hoc teams playing rugby in Cork that were unaffiliated to the Munster branch of the IRFU. But from 1910 on, there were ten clubs playing regularly in the league structure that included, for the first time, home and away ties. These clubs were Cork Constitution, Presentation Brothers, Christian Brothers, University College, North Monastery, Queenstown, Cork County, Dolphin, Wanderers and Juverna. Incidentally, there was a Juverna Gaelic football team, which may well have shared members. Three of these teams fielded as many as three XVs, with Wanderers having enough for a second XV only. This consolidation into a small number of clubs in rugby is significant as it points to the development of a more organised game, in which ad hoc amateurism was replaced by a more organised, competitively based amateur game, with the competitive cup, and to a lesser degree the league, structures that had been adopted and reformed. The organisation of leagues like those in the GAA, and the changed shape of rugby in the city were undoubtedly noticed by those who ran soccer; however, this was not always manifest in actions of the organisers, despite the desire to open the game to more civilians whose interest in the game was so evident.

With so many of the players and organisers connected to the military, winter-time furlough played a significant role in the shape of the season and was the root cause of the cluttered pre-Christmas calendar of fixtures. So, in some years football could halt for close on two months, taking much of the steam out of the leagues and competitions, particularly for the civilian sides. Despite these draw-backs, Cork established itself as the main centre of Munster's soccer world in the late nineteenth century and early twentieth century. The dominance of the military in soccer's administration in Munster hampered the growth of the game, despite the fact that the appetite was certainly there among civilians, many of whom simply played the game outside the structures available on their own terms. Still, the game was not restricted just to Cork. In the same period the game emerged elsewhere in Munster, laying the foundation for the game's future development and, in some cases, rising and falling quickly, leaving only the faintest of footprints in the sporting landscape.

'Accosted in all directions by large posters which occupied points of vantage': soccer in Waterford, 1898–1914

If the game got its real start in Cork in this period, then soccer in Waterford prior to the First World War was sporadic and without structure. We've already seen the Lismore side that played the game against Mallow College in 1877, but the report of that game was unusual. In all probability games between young boys were being played right throughout the period, but football among juveniles, if it did take place, went unreported. Between the game in 1877 and the next found reference to the game in Waterford, there is a twenty-year gap. One of the early teams to play the game was Gracedieu Emmett's, of whom our only existing documentary evidence is this photograph, from 1898, below:

Figure 2.2: *Gracedieu Emmett's Football Club*
Reproduced with kind permission of Paul Elliot.

Early games of soccer reported in the city at the turn of the century include one that was played on New Year's Day 1898. It was played at Coolfin, between a city team taking the name of Urbs Intacta and a team from Portlaw. The game was won 1–0 by Portlaw. Of the Portlaw team, six players have been identified. It included three stonemasons, a labourer, a carpenter and a beamer in the local cotton factory. A young man in his teens who was a grocer's clerk refereed the game.[64]

The next game to be played and reported on in the city was in March 1898 when the Urbs Intacta team took on a team of students from Newtown School.[65] No other game is reported in the *Waterford News* until 1899, when two teams, Manor Association and Barrack Street Ramblers, played against each other at Kill St Lawrence.[66] From 1900 to 1910, only a handful of organised soccer matches were reported in the *Waterford News*. These include games in 1902, 1905, 1908 and 1909. The teams that played were Waterpark Celtic AFC (attached to Waterpark College), De La Salle, and Tipperary side Cahir Park, in a game that predates their founding in 1910.[67] Waterpark Celtic were a club noticed in particular by those in Cork

31

soccer circles, especially when they entered the Munster Cup and were drawn against Sherwood Foresters in the Fermoy section, with the game being drawn at home in Waterford. According to the reports of the *Cork Sportsman*, a huge crowd turned out for the display and they noted of the Waterford team that they played 'a plucky never-say-die game' but lacked playing experience, being beaten soundly 9–2. Nonetheless, the visit of the Foresters team apparently encouraged two other clubs to start playing the game, 'Centre-Half' writing that 'by the way, Association football is advancing by leaps and bounds in the Waterford district. The visit of the Foresters last month has resulted in two civilian clubs being formed in that city, and it is confidently expected that next season will see a County Waterford League.'[68] Certainly to judge from what the newspaper had to say about Waterpark Celtic's abilities to promote a future game against 31st RFA, such enthusiasm was promising:

> Waterpark Celtic AFC have apparently nothing to learn from older organisations as regards making arrangements for matches. Although notice of the fixture could not have reached them until Thursday morning, yet the inhabitants of the city on Friday were accosted in all directions by large posters which occupied all points of vantage.[69]

The newspaper also claimed that 'gates of nearly 1,000 have been taken in Waterford City, and if the rate of progress is kept up, Cork will soon be outdistanced'.[70] The Cork newspaper perhaps ran away with itself when it said there were hopes of a league emerging. If there were any serious signs of this developing, the reticence of the *Cork Sportsman* on the game's development in Waterford suggests that such initial bursts of enthusiasm were just that, but in 1909 they could have been forgiven for such high hopes. After all, when the IFA became a limited company that year, one of the members of the new company was Waterpark Celtic. They, along with Cork-based club Alexandra, were the only two Munster clubs to be listed by the new company as members, both as senior and junior clubs.[71]

Like in Cork, there was in Waterford some competition for soccer from the GAA. The Waterford GAA, which had come on leaps and bounds in the first decade of the twentieth century, seemed to be working hard at sowing discord among its own ranks, driven in part by financial greed. At a Munster Council meeting of the GAA in 1909, Dan Fraher, the Dungarvan shopkeeper who was to give the

GAA its earliest start in the county, along with another man, objected to the election of two officers to the Waterford County Board. Fraher contended that his objection to these men derived from the fact that as directors of the Waterford Sportsfield Company they sought to make the Sportsfield open to any sport for use once they paid rent. Fraher and several others felt that this was against the spirit of the GAA and that they should not be giving a leg up to other sports, including soccer. Indeed at the Munster GAA Council's meeting, one of the accused men, Gallaher, was said to be unable to speak because he was breathless from having recently finished a game of soccer with some soldiers!

What was described as 'unparliamentary language' was exchanged and then withdrawn, before Gallaher admitted that he had indeed played soccer in his youth, but that he was not then in his senses. Gallaher and the other man Cooke, who stood accused of effectively being shoneens[72] by Fraher, put the argument that their decision to make the Sportsfield available to all at a rent was driven by pragmatism and that it meant money coming in from many sources that could help grow Gaelic games in Waterford. In their eyes, Fraher's offer of £1,000 if they would make the Sportsfield exclusively available to Gaelic games was insufficient. In their mind, Gaelic-only usage would not be a sustainable business model. What seemed to be really at the heart of the issue was a worry that the new city-based ground would take business away from Fraher's own field for big contests. In any event, the objection to Gallaher and Cooke's election was upheld, following a vote of the Munster Council: Fraher, who could leverage twenty-five years' plus of service to the GAA and also use soccer as a means of stigmatising Gallaher, proved effective, though both men appealed the decision to Central Council.

Away from the deliberations of the Munster Council of the GAA, another team, who would take the moniker of Celts and Celtic, had begun playing around 1910 in the seaside town of Tramore in County Waterford. When a Christian Brother by the name of McGurk joined the national school in Tramore from the Falls Road in Belfast, he brought with him tales of the mighty Belfast Celtic, and encouraged the boys to play soccer. The club went by the name of Tramore Celtic. When Brother McGurk departed, nevertheless, many of the boys whom he had introduced to the game carried on as the self-styled Tramore Celts in 1917.[73]

As 1910 approached, soccer was certainly stronger than it had been at any point previously in the province, though caution is required when reading such hyperbolic assertions as those made by the *Cork Sportsman*. Such caution notwithstanding, while small in terms of numbers, this pre-war interest in the game did provide a base which developed after the First World War and Irish independence into a more organised approach to the game in Waterford city and county. Still, nothing about the game in the period before 1914 would indicate the huge level of participation and involvement after 1922. Its relative lack of promotion in Waterford schools is proof of this. Clubs like the Catholic Young Men's Society (CYMS), St Joseph's, as well as places of work and individual streets would form the base of the game in the city post-independence, as it had done in Cork. The strong school element before 1914, especially from Waterpark, stands in contrast to its absence in Waterford soccer from 1924 onward.

Tipperary: Cahir Park and the spread of soccer

Despite Tipperary's apparent pre-eminence in the playing of soccer in Munster, as Garnham's work has it, the game faced considerable competition in the county, not just from the GAA, but also from a strong rugby network. The apparent lack of significant organisation at a grass-roots level for soccer was compounded by a much smaller population than either Cork or Waterford, and further by the fact that Tipperary's geography meant that the pockets of soccer enthusiasm were isolated and much of the competition came variously from Cork, Limerick and Waterford. Yet, despite these drawbacks, the evidence suggests that the game was played by a sufficient contingent of people for it to be considered a reasonable threat to the GAA in the county. Clonmel emerged in the pre-war era as an important site of soccer in Tipperary. As was noted in the *Cork Sportsman*, 'competitive matches have for the first time been played in Cahir, Fethard, and Clonmel'.[74] Of these three Tipperary towns, it was to be Cahir that would make the biggest mark in the pre-war era. In part this can be put down to sporting prowess, but, in addition, unlike teams in other places Cahir had significant local backing in the shape of local landowner, Col. Richard Butler Charteris.

The county's premier side throughout the first quarter of the twentieth century, Cahir Park was founded in 1910, although evidence suggests that a side going by the name Cahir Park was playing a year earlier, in 1909. From the beginning they had, as well as adults and adolescents playing for them, a team of young boys. Early victories for the club came in the 1912/13 season when they won the Second Division of the North Munster League along with the new Hogg and Tyler Cups.[75] Other clubs, such as Tipperary Wanderers and Tipperary United, also made a minor impact but Cahir Park were the most significant p. 2.1resence, provincially and nationally, to emerge in this period. One of the rare non-Cork based members of the Munster Senior League, all footballing signs suggest that Cahir Park ought to have followed Fordsons and Waterford Celtic to the Free State League, though this never came to pass. This is all the more unusual since Cahir, much like Fordsons before them, and Waterford after them, attained a high level of success, winning the FAI Cup in 1929/30. Yet where this led to a promotion to the top of the senior league for both Fordsons and Waterford Celtic, no such promotion appears to have been offered to Cahir. A centenary history of the club was able to identify many of the people in the photos circa 1910–30 and provide addresses for them.[76] This allows us to say something about the occupational makeup of the club's members.

Based on the earliest team photographs that survive from Cahir Park there appears to be a fair mixture of occupations in the teams. They can all be classed as being members of working and lower middle class. Three of the men worked in the Post Office, two as postmen and the third as a clerk. There was a butcher, a blacksmith, a stationer, a barman and a shop assistant too. There were also two labourers in the team, one a general labourer, the other an agricultural labourer. No occupation could be found for three of the men pictured. Overall, the photographs from the period suggest that people from most walks of life in the Cahir area were involved in playing with the club. The strongest elements though came from those with a small business such as a grocery shop, bakers, butchers or victuallers or from the Post Office, boot-making, tailoring and other trades. In total, across nine team photos, it is possible to identify the occupation for sixty-three of the people in those photographs, who were involved in the club. There are a significant number of skilled workers in textiles and also a large number of general and agricultural labourers.

TABLE 2.1
Occupations of Cahir Park FC players,
1910–30

Occupation/Head of Household	Number	% of Identified
Postman/PO clerk	4	6.4
General labourer	10	15.9
Agricultural labourer	4	6.4
Butcher	3	5.0
Victualler	4	6.4
Shop owner/Shop Asst./Grocer	7	11.1
Cattle dealer	3	5.0
Farmer	1	1.6
Publican/Farmer	2	3.2
Army	1	1.6
RIC	1	1.6
Religious	1	1.6
Draper	1	1.6
Tailor/Dressmaker	3	5.0
Boot maker	3	5.0
Watchmaker	1	1.6
Railway worker	2	3.2
Coach/Jarvey driver	2	3.2
Gas worker	1	1.6
Teacher	2	3.2
Miller/Mill carrier	2	3.2
Servant	1	1.6
Baker	2	3.2
Corn mill director	1	1.6
Pulleyman	1	1.6

SOURCE: Buckley, *Cameos of a Century*; *1911 Census Household Enumerator Returns*

Note the strength of both general labourers and shop assistants across the team photograph but also the sheer diversity of occupations of those involved in either playing or helping out with the club over that twenty-year period. It adds further weight to the argument that clubs playing soccer at that time were reliant strongly upon a middle and upper middle class base to provide grounds and equipment but that the game itself was played by people from diverse backgrounds, with a stronger emphasis on the working class and the lower middle class.

The president of the club in much of the pre-war era was the local Church of Ireland rector, Rev. Hogg. Significantly though, the majority of these men are Catholics. It is also worth noting of course that both general and agricultural labourers make up 22.3 per cent of players combined – just over one-fifth of all players. The club's main patron in this early period was Lt Col. Richard Butler Charteris, who owned the grounds on which the club would play. These military connections would see the club listed by South Tipperary No. 3 Brigade of the IRA as one of the enemy institutions in the area in 1921.[77] The grounds used by Cahir Park were usually used for playing cricket, but were loaned out to the football club by Charteris, making the club a rarity in Munster soccer to have had their own pitch from such an early stage in their history.[78]

Limerick emerges: 1908–14

As has been noted by historian Richard McElligott, many parts of rural Ireland, Kerry and Clare included, lacked the 'large urban centres and industrial workplaces from which many soccer clubs originated'. Indeed, McElligott's work on the history of the GAA in Kerry notes that throughout the 1890s, when the GAA was on its knees in that county, there were still only six games of soccer recorded, although rugby, golf, tennis and hockey were also played at that time.[79] While soccer appears to have made its mark in Limerick a little later than it had in either Cork or Waterford, the game nevertheless put down roots in the period before the First World War, not alone among the city's military personnel but also among its civilians, a key development for the game's continuation following the upheavals of the period 1914–23. Despite the later start than Cork or Waterford, from around 1908–14 the game was in a healthy state in the city, which by then had become very much a rugby-playing centre.

One of the key early clubs was the simply named Limerick AFC. This club would be the driving force for the game up until 1912, playing in the main against army sides, until further civilian teams began to be established in the city. Indeed, by 1912 there was a nascent Limerick Soccer League being mentioned in the pages of the *Limerick Leader*, a league which consisted of a number of civilian teams. One of the more unusual developments in Limerick soccer circles at this time was its impact on the game in the United States. Limerick-born Patrick J. Peel was, by 1918, the president of the United States Football Association.[80]

Limerick AFC, with few other options, played local military sides for the most part in the years before the First World War. Most of the activity centred around the winter of 1908 and early 1909. This period might be seen as the one when soccer truly emerged in Limerick city. The *Cork Sportsman* got wind of the developments in Limerick and saw this as a significant chance for the game to spread in the province. A report in November 1908 ran: 'Intimations of a strong civilian club in Limerick have been received, and the developments of the game in the City of the Broken Treaty will be watched with great interest by Cork Soccerites.'[81] They wasted no time in arranging a fixture between the new Limerick club and a Cork selection, yet another example of the role the sporting press played, not alone as reporter but organiser of sport in those early days. This was a significant fixture and Limerick held a colours match to select a representative side to bring to Cork in December 1908.[82] The game was considered to be a success by all involved. The report in the *Cork Sportsman* stated that 'the remarkable progress Association football is making in the province of Munster was clearly demonstrated on Saturday last at Turner's Cross grounds where the newly formed Limerick AFC put up a magnificent game against a powerful and representative eleven selected from the civilian clubs in the Cork district'.[83] From that point on the *Cork Sportsman* and the daily newspaper, the *Cork Constitution*, kept an eye on the development of Limerick soccer. Beyond their engagements with Cork, opposition for Limerick AFC locally included a team from the Royal Engineers as well as the Royal Munster Fusiliers and the Great Southern and Western Railway.[84] Mid-way through the 1909/10 season, Limerick AFC's praises were being sung by the *Cork Sportsman* where it was written, 'last, but not least, mention should be made of Limerick AFC's untiring energy in endeavouring to make soccer a success in Limerick. Though without a win to their credit, the Blues are hopeful of improving and their first victory will be welcomed by all sportsmen.'[85]

All of this activity served to see the game develop in Limerick and soon afterwards, in 1912, yet more civilian soccer teams began to emerge in the city. There was even, by this time, a Limerick Cup; one of the semi-finals was reported in the *Limerick Leader*, between Celtic and Weston, a game won by Celtic 2–0, which would see them play Dalcassians in the final. The Limerick Celtic club had also been noted in early 1911 by the *Cork Sportsman*.[86] The reporting on soccer in the newspaper in Limerick was quite sporadic in the period, meaning that a clear picture of the structure and scope of the game is difficult to ascertain. However, when reports did appear, typically they involved clubs like Celtic, Weston and Dalcassians among others. Indeed, such was the progress of the game that in October 1912 there is even mention of the Limerick Soccer League for the first time.[87] Other clubs playing at the time included Limerick United and a team from the St Michael's Temperance Society. This soccer club was just one of many sporting endeavours which would emerge from the club. The St Michael's Temperance Society soccer club's president as elected at their 1912 AGM was Richard Devane, a local curate.[88] Such positive early developments in the game did not last and the game was to go, if not completely unplayed in the intervening decade, then certainly unreported. Still, it is impressive that some half-a-dozen teams formed themselves in that brief period in Limerick city to play soccer and to establish for themselves a league. It reflected the general health of the game in the province as 1914 approached.

By 1914 nationally, soccer was at a peak – the Irish team won its first Home Nations championship, beating England 3–0 along the way, just before the outbreak of war. During the previous year's Home Championship, the gates from the first two games, coming in at over £2,000, were such that the *Cork Constitution* soccer notes were hopeful that the game in Munster would surely see a windfall from this to encourage the game more, though given the difficulties the MFA had in these years in securing any substantial grants from the IFA, this was never anything more than wishful thinking.[89] In any case, other, bigger problems would offset any benefit that such a windfall would have given the game in Munster in 1914. The considerable progress of soccer throughout Ireland from Belfast to Cork, spreading itself into Limerick and Waterford, Clonmel and Cahir, and the increased civilian participation in the game, suffered hugely as a result of the war. The war was also to have huge repercussions for the future of soccer in Ireland as it precipitated the split between the IFA and Dublin-based soccer that would lead to the foundation of the FAI in 1921.

When war broke out, the IFA, unlike the FA in England or the SFA in Scotland, did not decide immediately to put a halt to its regular competition structures, citing football matches as ideal recruiting grounds – eventually, they yielded and when they did, Dublin sides Bohemians and Shelbourne went to play in the Leinster Senior League, a practical split between north and south. When things began to normalise somewhat following the war, and the IFA made attempts to promote the game again, most of their interest and influence seemed restricted to the North. This situation was compounded by their decision to make Shelbourne replay an Irish Cup match against Glenavon in Belfast a second time, causing outrage in Dublin among the Leinster FA, and by June 1921 the Leinster FA had disaffiliated from the IFA, changing the shape of Irish soccer permanently.[90]

The number of clubs affiliated to the Leinster FA itself was decimated by the war. To give some indication of the upheaval caused by the onset of war for Cork, between the outbreak of war in August of 1914 and November of the same year alone, over 2,500 Cork men enlisted in the British armed forces.[91] In Waterford, similar numbers, around 1,569 men, flocked to the colours by August of 1915, and as has been argued by at least one historian, this was largely for economic reasons.[92]

Soccer all but came to a halt in Munster. A few games were played in Bandon between locals and men stationed there from the Royal Field Artillery in 1915 and 1917.[93] In Waterford, a munitions factory opened at a site in Bilbery, producing cartridges. Photographic evidence indicates that the different workers employed there played soccer against each other. Like any other club from the period, Cahir Park was not untouched by the advent of the First World War with several of its young players dying on duty. Given the makeup of the Cahir team, that so many young men should enlist is unsurprising. Among those who died were J.J. Walsh, D. Lonergan, E. Cubitt, B. Nolan and J. Carew, whose names are commemorated on the Hogg Cup, a trophy presented to Cahir Park AFC in 1912 by Rev. William Hogg, who had been so involved in the club. One of the few reported games of soccer in Waterford in this period was a friendly exhibition between a selected Waterford side and local jockeys in aid of the local distress fund in January 1918.[94]

As detailed above, soccer in Munster before the First World War, while not restricted to Cork alone, was strongest in that city. Generally, the game was strong in urbanised areas or in large towns, all of them with a military presence. Yet the role played by the British armed forces in helping to spread soccer was not as straightforward as it might appear. For one thing, as we saw, winter furlough had its role to play in the creation of friction between those who played soccer in Cork, military and civilian. Beyond this, we also saw that plenty of other bodies and organisations had their role to play in organising groups of boys and men to play soccer: many schools, particularly in Cork and Waterford, had students playing the game; other non-educational associations helped in the formation of teams: workplaces like the cable company in Waterville in Kerry, and the Boys' Brigade in Cork are prime examples of how broader associational culture had its role to play in bringing people together to form a team. And there were plenty of other teams who were organised around their streets and among the people they knew, and these teams were as vital as anyone else in making soccer before the First World War what it was in Munster. While we might know less about teams such as Castle United and their opponents than we would like, what can be in no doubt was Cork's centrality to the game; as the biggest city in the province it emerged as the place where a body to care for and develop the game was founded in 1901. This body succeeded largely in its mission, growing the game from those eleven clubs listed in the letter to the IFA in October 1901 to over forty affiliated and more unaffiliated clubs a decade later. This was done by the MFA and those who made up its membership, despite their own occasional poor organisation in dealing with the national body and that same national body's occasional evident disinterest. This central role of Cork city would continue when soccer reorganised and resumed in Munster in the aftermath of the political and social upheavals of the period 1914–23 which would change the demographic of those playing soccer in Ireland considerably.

3

Sporting Revolution to
Commercial Leisure,
1877–1937

*I see no reason why the working classes, say, should not be allowed to
indulge in their relaxation. It may be foolish from a certain point of
view, but if they want it they are entitled to it.*

Michael Byrne, Editor of *Sport*, before Oireachtas
Committee into Betting Act, 1926

To understand why, how and where soccer emerged in Munster, we
must ask ourselves how that sport was organised from the middle of
the nineteenth century and what had changed it into something we
would recognise today. What were the circumstances that allowed
soccer to develop in the way that it had first in Belfast and Dublin,
and then throughout Munster from the 1880s onwards? The answers
are manifold and complex and the ensuing chapter seeks to examine
and explore what shape the sporting culture of Munster took in the
period when soccer blossomed from a handful of organised matches
between schoolboys or soldiers into one of the central sporting pastimes of many of the people in the province.

The social and political world of Munster, in which soccer was
pioneered, was one marked in the late nineteenth century and early
twentieth century by an emerging nationalist movement. It was one
that fought first for land, tenant rights and home rule; it was given
cultural expression in both the GAA and the Gaelic League's language revival. An increasingly confident Catholic middle class
emerged, anxious to assume a greater role in the running of the
country. An increasingly radicalised working class emerged that
struck in Cork in 1909, prefiguring the almighty struggle for union
recognition in Dublin in 1913. If that was Ireland and Munster up to
1913, then Munster in the period 1914–37 would be marked by a
continuation and deepening of those tensions that saw people

experience and take part in further labour disputes, society's militari-
sation, the onset of world war, the struggle for independence and a
bitterly divisive civil war, before learning to adjust to life in the
emerging state.[1] Amid all of this, from the end of the First World
War, despite a general downturn in production, the leisure industry
grew and transformed as new technology altered how people enjoyed
their spare time. If the story of Ireland and Munster 1877–1914 was
one lived through and understood largely in newspaper print, then
after the First World War, the period 1918–37 was one recorded not
alone through the press but increasingly onscreen in the newsreels
and then over the airwaves as radio broadcast established itself as part
of Irish life. In addition, though on a much smaller scale to that
experienced by neighbouring Britain, it was a world where the commercialisation of leisure and the rise of spectator sports came into
their own. On the fields of play, the codification of rules was beginning to change how people enjoyed playing and watching many
sports from the 1860s onward. As sport became spectator as well as
participant oriented, it was still just one among many entertainments
on offer to the public, particularly those who made up the emerging
Irish middle class. This is an important point in understanding the
way in which soccer came to be both a grass-roots game and a commercial venture in its own right during the Free State era.

At the end of the nineteenth century, across Munster, newspapers'
'Amusements' sections were full of the theatrical productions on offer.
These included the visit of the Imperial Italian Opera Company to
Cork in 1877, where *La Traviata*, *The Marriage of Figaro* and
Waterford-born William Vincent Wallace's *Maritana* were part of the
programme; Mr & Mrs Bradman's productions of *Hamlet*, *Macbeth*,
Romeo and Juliet and *The Merchant of Venice* and an exhibition of
Edison's 'Speaking and Singing Machine', all of which were staged in
Waterford's Theatre Royal; the visit of comedian Charles Cooke to
Clonmel with his troupe in 1880; and the roller skating rinks, racquet
matches, cricket, regattas, sports days and burgeoning football codes
that were all jostling for a place in people's increased leisure time.[2]

The same era saw the growth of a circuit that was part of the
British touring route that included, in Munster, Waterford's Theatre
Royal, Cork's Atheneum and also the Palace Theatre of Varieties.[3]
The skating rinks of Queenstown and Waterford were not just places
of sport but also of socialising, entertainment and courtship, if some

news reports are anything to go by. As well as playing host to Smythe, the American postman whose major feat was to walk 190 miles in 50 hours, the rink in Waterford was also a place where the activities between the sexes appears to have scandalised some. A letter-writer to the *Munster Express*, using the pseudonym of 'A disgusted spectator', complained about the disreputable behaviour carried on in the rinks vicinity, though respondents mocked this outrage for its prudishness.[4] The well-known sportsman was emerging in Munster too, as the report of an athletic contest between Dan Fraher of Dungarvan and James Dwyer of Carrickbeg, Tipperary indicates. According to the report of the long jump contest, offers of up to 100/1 were being offered against Dwyer and the report says that 'a few fivers were picked up', indicating that substantial sums were bet on the outcome. Only shortly before that was Maurice Davin, from the same area, competing as a representative of Ireland in an athletics meeting against England being held at Stamford Bridge in London. We are told that Davin 'owes half his luck to his strictly temperate habits'.[5]

If Ireland's emergent middle and upper middle class had 'legitimate' theatres like the Atheneum or Theatre Royal, then working-class people had music hall and vaudeville, described by Kevin and Emer Rockett as 'a form of entertainment that emerged from an altogether more basic source: the pub or public house'.[6] It was in such spaces as these that the sportsman was already subverted into a figure of comedy, like the show at the Paragon Circus on Mary Street in Cork that included a sketch called 'The Cockey [sic] Sportsman'.[7] Perhaps the most famous comical rendering of a sportsman in the early twentieth century in Cork was in the ballad 'The Bold Thady Quill', described by John A. Murphy as being in the mock-heroic tradition. Detailing the exploits of Quill, the song in Murphy's words 'celebrates Thady as inveterate porter-drinker, all-round sportsman, hurler supreme, therapeutic lover, land league activist, and Parnellite orator and parliamentarian'.[8] The development of these spaces, argue Kevin and Emer Rockett, were part of the process that led to the development of cinema, but were also part of creating entertainment venues that could be controlled, unlike the unruly fairs and pattern festivals of the eighteenth century and earlier, a process similar to that which drove the modernisation of sport.[9]

The sports day persisted, if in a more civilised fashion, and was still, in the south-east, tied to the demands of agriculture, like the one held in Graigue in late September 1877, where 'the attendance [was] despite the hurry consequent upon the saving of the harvest quite equal to former meetings' and was not always a temperate affair. This meeting was very much in the vein of large fair days of the earlier part of the century, notably a lack of music and boredom for non-competitors, encouraging those who attended to engage in fighting.[10]

Football was emerging in this same period, one of the earliest reports being that of a game held at Marlfield, County Wexford between tenants of Mr Bagwell and tenants of Gurteen in Kilsheelan, County Tipperary led by Mr de la Poer in 1869.[11] This was contested as sixteen aside so a semblance of the rugby rules can be assumed to have been part of the game. A school fete and sports day in 1871 similarly saw football as part of the programme.[12] In Nenagh itself, games of football were being played by the 50th Queen's Own Regiment in 1875, though we do not know the rules by which they played.[13] Football, of one kind or another, was already popular with young boys in the area, with many being brought before the Petty Sessions in order to be fined either for playing football on the street or trespassing in farmers' fields to play games with a football.[14] Of course it is difficult to say exactly what kind of football was being engaged in but forms of football of a broadly modern mode were played as in the rest of the United Kingdom. While occasions such as these were primarily social, and ad hoc in nature, it wasn't long before such groupings formed themselves into clubs, dedicated to a specific footballing code, whether that was rugby, Gaelic football or soccer. It was this shift, from the semi-organised, crack teams of the 1870s to a more sustained club structure, that saw the sports club become, not just a body to play matches, but an important facet of social life, a key player in what we might call the social economy.

The social economy, broadly speaking, is that which exists between the purely public and the purely private sectors. This is a useful term to think of for sports clubs, which can become, and in the late nineteenth and early twentieth centuries did become, a mixture of public and private bodies. Some clubs or sports grounds were registered as joint stock companies, others were run on a voluntary basis, some for commercial interests, others not. Sports clubs were sometimes limited companies but run on a voluntary basis. These changes were marked by the commercialisation of Irish sporting culture – the building of stands, introduction of turnstiles, establishment of tournaments and leagues. Despite the introduction of these common features to most field sports, in Ireland the gap between commercial sport and its amateur volunteer equivalent was not always distinct.

These changes impact on the shape of wider society. In his work on Westmeath, Tom Hunt notes that 'the impact of sport on the business of the county is an aspect that is worthy of further examination'. Continuing, Hunt stresses that 'as the surviving quantitative data is imprecise and fragmentary, it is impossible to determine the exact amount of capital invested in sport, the number of people employed and their earnings'; nonetheless this chapter will explore, by means of the retail sector for sporting goods, the development of grounds, the sporting press and the emergence of new leisure forms like the cinema, radio, records, and betting, the significance of sport to the fiscal and social economy of Munster from 1877–1937 from a qualitative rather than purely quantitative point of view.[15]

The Business of Sport: a retail market emerges

Looking at the listings for joint stock companies in Ireland from the end of the nineteenth century into the first decade of the twentieth, we see a large number of companies established ostensibly to capitalise on the boom in sporting activity. Although the offshoots of the increased codification and commercialisation of sport are legion, the focus on the areas already identified will be of particular use. Wray Vamplew has concluded that the emergence of a mass sports industry was one of the 'economic success stories' of late Victorian and Edwardian Britain.[16] This goes not just for England, or Scotland or Wales, but for Ireland too. Hunt's words echo Neil Tranter, who says of the sporting industry that any precise attempt to assess sport's impact on the economy would be impossible, due to the scattered nature of the evidence.[17] This does not prevent Tranter from making the assertion that 'the Victorian and Edwardian sporting "revolution" was a profitable experience for many of the companies which supplied the equipment and services it required'.[18] Certainly, the considerable sporting activity in Munster means that this conclusion holds up in a wide variety of businesses in the region.

Perhaps the most well-known of all this commercial activity was the boom in bicycle manufacture in the 1890s. Prompting a stock market bubble, the eventual crash would see millions of pounds lost.[19] Many sports-related companies were listed as joint stock companies towards the end of the nineteenth century and into the first decade of the twentieth, companies like the Munster Cycle Agency Co. Ltd., and Cork Athletic Ground Co. Ltd. with a £1,000 capitalisation,[20] to take just two examples.

When players lined out on the pitches across Munster, from where did they get their jerseys, their boots, their ball? Who cast the trophy paid for by a local benefactor? In large part, from local retailers and craftsmen, some with their own brand products, many who simply sold products crafted elsewhere. This is perhaps one of the most fascinating, and still much under-researched, elements of the sporting 'revolution' of the later nineteenth century. What follows is by no means a fully comprehensive assessment of the development of sports retail in the region, though perhaps it will go some way to alleviating the lack of research lamented by both Hunt and Tranter. This chapter will give an indication of the level of commercialisation that was experienced in Munster in the sporting retail trade. It will show the relative sophistication of marketing sporting goods; its positive association with other commercial interests, particularly alcohol and tobacco. Further, it will demonstrate the ability [or undoubted ability] of Irish businessmen to exploit the emerging demand for sporting commodities.

In an era when major manufacturers of sporting goods were few and far between, the production and sale of equipment fell to local manufacturers and retailers, such as Robert Day, a Cork-based saddler whose business expanded to include their own brand of footballs. Across Munster tradesmen expanded the remit of their businesses to capitalise on the sporting boom of the late Victorian and early Edwardian periods. Taking trade directories as our main source, along with newspaper advertisements, to tentatively assess the impact sport had on small local economies in this part of Ireland, we will see those who provided trophies, boots, jerseys, posters, programmes, tickets and a range of other equipment and services. The opportunity for commercial exploitation by local retailers resulting from the boom in interest to both play and watch sport is one thing that makes the modern sporting era unique.

According to one source, the amount spent on sport and travel goods in Ireland by 1907 was some £552,000, while by 1926, according to Kiernan, the total spent on entertainment and sport was roughly £1.5 million.[21] Billiards was a very popular sport prior to the

First World War and as well as those billiard rooms advertised by hotels in the directories, there were billiards tables in places like the Catholic Young Men's Society and the YMCA and the ICICYMA. In fact, such was the popularity of billiards that it provided employment for a great many teenage boys during this period. According to census returns in 1901, there were 197 people employed in the country as billiard markers, and 52 of those 197 were between 13 and 18 (26.4 per cent), while 104 of them ranged in age between 13 and 21 (52.8 per cent), making up as it does the bulk of those working at the job. From the 1911 census there were a total of 179 people employed this way. As had been the case a decade earlier, the bulk of those employed this way were between the ages of 14 and 21. According to the census returns online, there were 49 billiard markers working aged 14–18, making up 27.3 per cent, while 77 of the 179 were aged 14–21, or 43 per cent.[22] Given its widespread appeal, it should come as no surprise that at least one enterprising tradesman should start to build billiards tables. The manufacturer of the tables was located on Tuckey Street, Cork and was a cabinetmaker by trade. This is just one of many examples of a business with a principal trade that diversified to include sport in order to capitalise on its increasing popularity. It is a salient example too, since the majority of sporting goods' provision was not by specialist retailers but by general retailers, drapers and so on who saw a way to further their businesses.

The number of examples is striking: William Egan, optician, also traded in trophies for a variety of competitions. Eustace & Co., a timber yard near the Lady's Well Brewery on Leitrim Street, began to advertise themselves as hurley makers in the mid-1920s. The same company also benefited from the maintenance of the Mardyke, being paid numerous times for a variety of jobs over the years, including one job that was worth £54.4.9 to Eustace & Co.[23] Along with these two examples, there was also Haughton's ironmongery that sold bicycles, Cooke's tinsmith that also traded bicycles, Mulcahy's saddler that traded in general sporting requisites and another saddler business, that of Robert Day, which became one of the main sporting goods shops in Cork in the early twentieth century. The Day business was a very big and busy company in the nineteenth century and was better placed than most it seems to diversify its business when the boom in sporting goods presented itself as an opportunity in the last quarter of the nineteenth century.

Making sure that the wider public was aware of their activity was vital to the success of a sports club. Advertisements in the newspapers by clubs, especially when touring sides were coming to play, or a cup final or semi-final was coming up, were common. In the account books of Cork Constitution RFC, we see many of these kinds of expenses. As early as the 1907/08 season we see mention of these things in the minute books of the club. Entries from the 4 March committee meeting indicate that 19s 6d is owed to Shandon Printing, and a similar entry from 8 April that another 2s 6d is to be paid to the same company.[24] Guy's, by 1908, also advertised themselves for outdoor photography for 'Football, Hurling, Cricket, Tennis &c.' in the *Cork Sportsman*.[25] B. Haughton & Co., or the Cork Timber & Co. Ltd., advertised themselves as having a 'Large and Attractive Selection' of 'Prizes for Sports'.[26] In Limerick Nestor Brothers of O'Connell Street were advertising their shop in 1914 as the 'Sportsman's Warehouse'.[27]

This kind of advertising shows that among sports goods' suppliers, the competition was strong. Some businesses aimed themselves specifically at certain markets, emphasising the fact that the product was Irish-made, as Robert Day would do later in ads for his Gaelic footballs in the *Southern Star* and elsewhere in 1926. Others exploited this same device in another way, with John F. Murphy advertising in the *Football Sports Weekly* that in his shop there was 'No Ban! We cater for All Sports'.[28] As well as those providing sporting equipment for playing, there were those who saw sports enthusiasts as a potential target market, such as Murphy's stout, brewed in Lady's Well, who ran an advertisement in this era which read 'ON AND OFF THE SPORTS FIELD, Half Time, Full Time, Every Time, Ask For Murphy's Stout, And See That You Get It!' Such targeting is unsurprising: throughout the British Isles, the pub was an important centre of local community and later sporting life. Tony Collins and Wray Vamplew's work attests strongly to this. Central to sporting developments in Britain in the first half of the nineteenth century, it would shift 'from being a conduit through which almost all popular sport was organized . . . becoming one of a number of recreational options available to the population at large . . .'[29] Part of this change is reflected in the advertising by pubs like The Arch, in newspapers like the *Cork Sportsman*. Of course, this ran counter to the spirit of the pioneer movement, with whom the GAA had especially strong links. As Diarmaid Ferriter notes, 'temperance advocates and sponsors of domestic sport . . . sought to dispel the seemingly interchangeability of drink and Irish identity'.[30]

Beyond displays in shop windows in small towns like Nenagh or big department shops in Waterford and Cork, recent scholarly work makes much of the development of what is called associational culture, and two of the biggest manifestations of this in Ireland were bands and sporting clubs. John McGrath, writing about a parish in Limerick, states that 'the 1880s saw a critical social development . . . with the establishment of sport and musical clubs, associations that acted as a cohesive agent for these social groups and gave parishioners something definite to identify with'.[31]

With the advances in the literature on sport history in Ireland in the past number of years, it is evident that viewing sport from a social and cultural perspective will provide a significant advancement not just for how sport history is understood but also Irish social history. It would be easy, however, to celebrate only the role of the GAA in Irish community and social life to the detriment of other sports. Plenty of other sports, we are about to see, also contributed significantly to local life, in city, town and village across Munster. The identification McGrath writes about can be seen elsewhere, in parts of Cork city's north side and in the 'up the roads' areas of Waterford city too, where bands were formed like the Thomas Francis Meagher Band and, earlier, Waterford's Barrack Street Band, founded in 1870. The bandstands in places like Youghal, Lismore, Dungarvan, in the People's Park in Waterford and elsewhere highlight the central place of the brass band in Victorian entertainment and days out. One of the earliest such bands in the country was founded in 1837 in Cork as a temperance band, the No. 1 Barrack Street Band.[32] Despite these more genteel associations with promenading by the sea, and temperance, band culture was also a major feature of sporting events and could be among the most intemperate of engagements.

The factionalism described in scholarly work by Lane on bands in the late 1870s[33] was also a feature of the band culture of Waterford, where the T.F. Meagher Band and Erin's Hope band clashed on the stage and in the street, a fight breaking out in Carrick-on-Suir in 1928 at a competition.[34]

The band was a major feature of regattas in Waterford. Almost unfailingly, reports of the annual Boat Club regatta included mention of the band to play and a fireworks display in the evenings. Throughout the 1890s, when both cycling and rowing vied for pride of place as the most popular spectator sports in Waterford, a huge number of bands, firework displays and bazaars were a part of the efforts of the Boat Club. In 1890, when Oxford competed at the annual regatta, both the Manchester Regiment Band and the Waterford Amateur Band provided the entertainment.[35] In other years, the Seaforth Highlanders Band,[36] The Band of the Buffs[37] and the Dublin RIC Band provided entertainment.[38] The Legion Band and Barrack Street Band provided the entertainment across the day in 1927, on the grandstand erected for the occasion.[39]

In north Tipperary, Nenagh Cricket Club had its own brass band as far back as 1880.[40] The town's own brass band was playing at the Aquatic Club sports day in the same year.[41] In 1910, a hurling tournament had been arranged in Carrigatoher in order to raise funds for a Ballywilliam and Carrigatoher band.[42] In the minute books of Cork Constitution RFC in one entry from 30 April 1909, we see that after a big game played at the Mardyke, a band for the day's entertainment were paid £2 10s.[43] Bands were also a major part of sporting occasions in the first quarter of the twentieth century. This was true for almost all sporting occasions, with some sports being especially disposed to entertaining spectators in this fashion.

Tom Hunt makes the point that 'GAA tournaments provide an ideal occasion for musical combinations to display their talents and provided an additional layer of entertainment at the venues. Some of these provided a comprehensive entertainment experience.'[44] Not just that, but as he notes elsewhere, the presence of a band 'contributed a sense of formality to the occasion and established status for the event'.[45] From the evidence above, it is fair to say that this applies not to the culture of a particular sport, but sporting culture as a whole at the time across Munster. Sport, through additional entertainment, like the bands, created a symbiotic relationship between one type of associational culture and another. It is plainly evident that the band culture of this period was intimately entwined with sporting culture, no matter what sport was on offer. The near ubiquity of bands at most social and sporting occasions is a strong indicator of the community aspect of sport in this period – a chance to display a level of civic, and highly localised, community pride through sport and music combined.[46] Not alone that, but it also suggests a considerable crossover in the personnel and connections between bands and local clubs.

Raffles were another important element of club life; the sum of £20 raised by Dunmanway's GAA club was of vital importance to its coffers.[47] Likewise, when youngsters in Nenagh wanted to establish a juvenile football club, they used a raffle to raise funds.[48] In Carrick-on-Suir, County Tipperary in July 1895, there was a tournament in aid of the new church in the nearby town of Piltown, including a full football and hurling schedule, a three-mile bicycle race and a horse-jumping contest. The hurling teams that competed were Clonmel Emmett's against the Waterford Commercials (Clonmel won by three points), Ballyduff versus Mullinahone and a game between Bennetsbridge and Mooncoin that was postponed. The football schedule for the following Sunday saw De La Salle take on Lisronagh; Kilmacow against Grangemockler; Tramore against Kilcash and Kilmacthomas against Dunhill.[49] As ever there was a band, and various roulette tables and fortune-tellers, 'fairy forms, or let us say, fair ladies . . . while your fortune or the latest astronomical discoveries were enlarged upon for a few coppers'.[50]

When the Bohemians Cricket Club took the cricket championship in Cork in 1908 in a game against the Army Service Corps, played in the Camp Field near the Victoria Barracks, they waited until their annual end of season dinner on 17 October 1908 to celebrate. The dinner was held in the Metropole Hotel, and was by this account something of a memorable night:

> The following contributed to an excellent musical programme: – Messrs. A. Young, C.A. Boyle, J.M. Cullinane, P. Riordan, P. O'Flynn, V. O'Connell, F. Leech, F. Cussen etc. Mr P. Belas acted in his usual capable manner as accompanist. 'The Song of the Beaux' – otherwise the topical duet – was one of the features of the evening, and was sung with much sprightliness by Messrs. Welsby and Carleton, who were also the authors of the amusing verses. When the last encore – and there were many – had been responded to, the duettists were presented with a floral tribute (uncooked) in reward for their efforts.[51]

Clearly these young men set out that night to enjoy their resounding victory in the league. Proof ultimately that the reasons why young men took up sports in this period had chief among them the fun and camaraderie that came with playing on a team, and the exultation of winning as part of that team.

As well as invading the hotels and pubs of towns, cities and villages for post-match, end or start of season meetings and socials, whether they were to be found hanging around in the new book-maker's premises, in the stands, or along the touchlines, sport and those who involved themselves in it left a deep and lasting impression on the social landscape and the built environment of Munster. Leif Jerram has offered a major criticism on the lack of emphasis on place in history, writing that 'if we want to find the point of encounter, and witness the rendezvous between big and small, we have to start thinking about *where* the twentieth century happened. We have to look at its streetlife.'[52]

Sports Grounds

Sport is a social activity that occurs in a well-defined place. Understanding that place is important. John Bale's work identified ten views of the sports landscape, including viewing them as artefacts, history and place. His work, along with that of Simon Inglis, on the football grounds of Britain, shows the deep historical layers of the sports ground – as a place of history and memory in its own right as well as being part of the historical process of modernisation and having an impact on the surrounding space and sense of place in the wake of its construction.[53] Two recent works have, more than any-thing else yet in the literature on Irish sports history, highlighted the importance of the sporting space and the significance of stadia in the Irish sporting landscape and as markers of its historical heritage. Both Mike Cronin and Roisín Higgins' *Places We Play* and John A. Murphy's *Where Finbarr Played* have indicated a way of assessing the history of sport in Ireland that stresses the importance of the physical in determining the impact of the late nineteenth-century sporting explosion. Much of the physical landscape of sport, that is to be scru-tinised in this section, has left few physical traces but there still remains a considerable amount of historical archaeology in various sports grounds across the counties examined here. Of course, as well as stadia, there are indoor halls, fields, rivers, swimming pools, tracks, beaches and so on that also provide for sporting recreation.[54]

For Welsh historian Daryl Leeworthy 'the everyday sporting land-scape does not surrender its history easily', but, he writes, 'behind each playground lies a story of struggle, jubilation, and sometimes sadness'.

He continues on to say, 'the making of the historic sporting environment is therefore a story not just of the hallowed turf upon which Wales defeated England many years ago but also, and more importantly, the people who made it'.[55] For Cronin and Higgins, writing of the sports ground in Ireland, 'what all sporting sites have in common, whether for players or spectators, is that they are part of the fabric of Irish history and society'. Their work shows 'sporting sites are not necessarily important for their architectural styles or the magnificence of the building, but rather are important venues for mass social activity'.[56] Jerram has noted about the building of the great football grounds of Europe, 'this spatial dimension of building transformed football from a participatory sport into an entertainment business'.[57]

Again Leeworthy writes that 'the story of ordinary spaces, in ordinary communities, deserves to be told in order to complement the many histories of those [more famous] fields of play'.[58] We must acknowledge then the reshaping of the public space in Munster by sport. Some of the sites which developed during the period include the Waterford City Racecourse, Powerstown Park, Tramore Racecourse, the Mardyke, Victoria Cross, Camp Field (Cork), the Bully Acre, the Waterford Sportsfield, Cork Park Racecourse, Deerpark (Carrick-on-Suir), Poleberry, Ozier Park and Cork County Cricket Ground. There were handball courts, greyhound stadiums, gymnasiums, golf courses and much more besides. Their place on the landscape and their impact on the shape of public space is significant, a physical manifestation of a popular sporting culture. None of them surrender their history easily. To look at many of these spaces in Munster you would hardly sense the breadth of use to which they have been put by so many different sports over the years. Given the urban environment, which is the main focus of this book, that such spaces existed at all was vitally important, particularly those playing pitches used by Munster's working-class inhabitants, for whom cramped living conditions were common in many cases.

These various playing pitches and grounds were an important economic asset to their communities. After all, to have a major sporting ground in an area brought benefits, not just to the organisation hosting games at a ground, but also to the local economy. For instance, publicans nearby were likely to pick up passing trade, and we know that at the Mardyke a particular trader was given special permission to have a stall at the grounds to sell to spectators; it is even noted that those who were unauthorised were a problem, suggesting that they were numerous.[59]

In Cork, when the local Catholic Young Men's Society wished to provide a gymnasium for its members' use they put the job out to tender and one builder was to profit handsomely for the building of the gym. The CYMS also had its billiard rooms, which were in constant need of furnishing and upkeep.[60] But more than their economic value, the civic value of these places was immense. As well as the libraries, courthouses and cathedrals – each important symbols of the civic identities of Cork, Limerick and Waterford – the sports grounds and the soccer grounds in particular, while in most cases perhaps not much to look at architecturally, were edifices of considerable local civic pride and identity, sites of shared public joy and dismay, victory and defeat. As we will see in the ensuing chapters, the grounds where soccer was played were also sites for the expression of a collective partisanship and pride that was a crucial element of being a member and supporter of a soccer club.

Among the most impressive sporting sites in this era were the various skating rinks. In Waterford, the skating rink, built to capitalise on the fashion for skating, was soon turned into one of the city's earliest cinemas. W.B. Stanford, student in Bishop Foy's High School and whose father was for a time Rector in Christ Church Cathedral in Waterford, in his memoirs recalls of this particular cinema:

> [E]very Saturday I went to the matinée in the Coliseum Cinema. There I sat in the front seat, for three pence, and saw some of the best and worst films made before 1922 . . . Express trains thundered down towards heroines tied to the rails. Indians surged over palisades. Sinister Chinamen threatened excruciating tortures. Masked figures emerged from secret passages. Ziggurats collapsed in ruins. Towers crumbled in flames. All this for three pence and a slight headache.[61]

The links between the skating rink and the cinema hall are well established; as Kevin Rockett has it 'when skating faded in early 1910 with hundreds of rink companies facing bankruptcy, the cinema industry stepped into the entertainment breech'.[62] That the relationship should eventually come full circle and sport, as part of the newsreels, become a significant feature of the cinema-going experience in many of these converted skating rinks is a powerful example of sport and leisure's increased commercialisation in the early twentieth century.

Cycling in Waterford was given a considerable boost by the inclusion of a cycling track in the People's Park, provided by funds from businessman W.G.D. Goff, an avid cycle and motor enthusiast in the city. The People's Park in Waterford is a particularly good example of a public space used for sporting recreation in the period we are concerned with. The Park's various bandstands are further testament to the place of the community in both sport and music at the time. A rare example of a municipally provided public space for recreation, typically the provision of the cycling track, the one sport-specific element, fell to the agency of a private benefactor. To have a piece of ground for a club or team to call their own was rare. There was something of a tug and pull in how sporting spaces were developed in Waterford, for instance, with a mixture of the municipal and private, as in the case of the People's Park above. Pitches were secured by a mixture of private landowners who were friendly or associated with the sporting organisations or occasionally in conjunction with the local government.

O'Sullivan's work on Cork readily notes the importance for GAA, rugby and soccer of the provision of land by private owners, and the sharing of land between the GAA and those who played football, as in the case of Turner's Cross.[63] The sports ground at Turner's Cross was used for a huge variety of sports, including rugby, cycling, athletics and Gaelic games as well as soccer from the 1890s to the 1930s. In Ireland, the evidence suggests the reliance upon patronage and individual or organisational endeavour, rather than relying upon local government, which came into being in Ireland in 1898, not much later than either Scotland or Wales, where it was instituted in 1894. Indeed as Curran puts it with regard to patronage in Donegal, '. . . many of these patrons saw it as their duty in the development in local society, with the donation of cups and medals and the granting of access to their fields being fundamental to the growth of competitive sport, long before clubs were able to own their own pitches'. This will be very important to understanding the development of soccer in Munster.

The Sporting Press

Recently, Tony Collins has written that 'it was print capitalism that provided the electrical charge that was to animate the culture of mass spectator sport'.[64] Ireland and Munster were no exception to this.

With rising literacy rates, sport provided newspapers with a continuous and changing source of material for their readers. General newspaper reporting of sport in Ireland in the 1870s was quite sporadic, with an increase in the 1880s and 1890s, until it became a firm fixture in many newspapers at the start of the twentieth century, aided particularly by the increased ability to provide photographic plates in the relaying of a news story. As well as the increased space given over to sport in normal daily newspapers, as Tranter notes, an important development was the 'many . . . specialist newspapers and periodicals launched to cash in on the demand for sporting news . . .' which were often 'also short-lived'.[65] The pattern is somewhat similar in an Irish context. The majority of papers were not hugely successful, but some were. As Paul Rouse puts it, 'in 1880 Ireland could not have supported a daily sporting paper, nor did it have the regularised sporting fixture list to warrant a "Saturday special". What emerged was a peculiarly Irish compromise: the "weekly special".'[66] *Sport* was the first major weekly sporting newspaper in Ireland and was to remain the biggest throughout the period. Rouse again notes, 'the style, content and price see *Sport* fit easily into the story of the popular press in the Victorian world'.[67] Not only that, but he further notes that 'cheapness alone was obviously no guarantee of success and apart from the obvious fact that it rightly identified an opening in the market – or, more properly, saw the potential to expand the market – the success of *Sport* was rooted in the quality of its content'.[68] As Eoghan Corry has also noted, as time wore on, sport 'played its part in the rise of newspaper circulation during the first third of the twentieth century. In the case of the *Independent*, already the best-selling daily in the country in 1906, this helped boost circulation more than fourfold, from 30,000 to 132,000, over a twenty-five year period.'[69]

There were a huge number of sporting newspaper ventures in the period from the *Irish Wheelman* (1894) to *Ulster's Saturday Night* (later *Ireland's Saturday Night*, also 1894). Similarly there was the *Irish Field and Gentleman's Gazette*. This was an important newspaper since it provided not just a dedicated sporting weekly, but was primarily for horseracing, hunting, coursing and other sports of the turf. A paper like *Gaelic Athlete* (1912) was an exclusively GAA-based newspaper. *Football Sports Weekly* (1925) was something of a mouthpiece for the soccer establishment in Dublin but was highly encouraging of the game elsewhere, particularly Munster. A similar venture was the *Irish Coursing Calendar*, a newspaper set up by the Irish Coursing Club in 1924. Although a largely coursing and greyhound racing centred newspaper, it also reported on other sports.[70] The proliferation of these titles shows, despite their sometimes uncertain existence, a real appetite for a sporting press among the Irish public. It is noteworthy too that in Munster, one such paper developed to satisfy the needs of a province where sport was flourishing. That newspaper was another which saw the opportunity to expand the market as *Sport* had done in the 1880s: the *Cork Sportsman*.

With a short lifespan of just three years, 1908–11, at the beginning of its final year of publication, the *Cork Sportsman* was widely distributed, copies available in some forty-eight different locations in Cork city alone. Along with twenty-three locations in the county, the paper was available in Kerry (in Tralee and Killarney), Dublin, Waterford and Limerick city and county. It could be purchased in the stations of Cork, Blackrock and Passage Railway, the Cork and Bandon Railway, Cork and Macroom Railway, the Great Southern and Western Railway and the Cork and Muskerry Railway.[71]

High distribution levels in the Cork region suggest that the paper was in high demand. The availability of the paper in all the major railway points in the region is important too. Much is often made of the link between the growth of railways and the ability for localised regional sports to become nationally organised, but the growth of newsagents in places like the new railway termini is crucial to the spread of cheaply produced newspapers. In its second issue, the editor notes that 'one thing has pleased us immensely in connection with our critics – they are united in saying that our paper is "too small", and . . . are "asking for more"'.[72] The early signs were good, with an editorial shortly after noting 'the enthusiastic support we have received from all classes of sportsmen coupled with the fact that advertisers have taken to us'.[73] The *Cork Sportsman* was, for part of its life, sold for a halfpenny, the price later rising to a penny, like its other sporting and general newspaper counterparts.[74] The anniversary issue was jubilant in its assertion that the paper had achieved its aim of providing more fulsome coverage than the more traditional press, with the editor recalling the first editorial and saying that 'our confident expectation of the co-operation of all classes of sportsmen has been more than realised.'[75] Similar self-congratulation was not to be found around the paper's anniversary in either 1910 or 1911, however. Indeed what was the third anniversary issue carried instead a rather bristling notice to contributors that 'the Editor wishes that he could invent some form of language which would really convince Contributors that unless "Copy" reaches the office by a certain date each week, there is no likelihood of it being included in the issue for which it was intended . . . we must impress upon our Correspondents that we have no option in the matter'.[76] This reliance on irregular contributions was not viable in the long run and stands in stark contrast to the editorial of the second issue where it was felt that, with the help of their correspondents, described as 'some of the ablest', the paper would be a success.[77] As well as relying on largely voluntary contributions of material, providing just one form of news for the same price, as newspapers providing everything from local, provincial, national and international news, not to mention sporting news, always meant that servicing only a small provincial area in a specialist interest was unlikely to remain profitable in the long term.

That it was in decline becomes apparent from early September 1911, until its final issue on Thursday, 19 October 1911. Up until this point the paper was coming out weekly on a Saturday morning. But from September 1911, the day and the intervals between the papers changed. An edition of the paper came out on 2 September, a Saturday, followed quickly by an issue on 6 September, a Wednesday. It then came out the following Wednesday, 13 September, followed by an issue on 20 September and another does not appear until Thursday 28 September. While this would appear to be a switch simply to publication on a Wednesday rather than a Saturday, the dates again become erratic. With issues coming out on Friday 6 October, followed by a Wednesday edition on 11 October and then the final issue on the following Thursday, 19 October, it appears that the paper is simply struggling to meet its old deadlines.

A further indication of the paper's decline was its increasing reliance on English sporting news that was used to fill out the pages, with reportage of the Football League and English horse-racing occupying a more prominent place over local reporting. There are also increasingly large ads for the paper's printers Landons, indicating that the *Sportsman* is not just printed by the company, but is intimately tied up with the paper. The *Cork Sportsman* was printed by Landon Brothers Printing. Their premises were situated at 16 Bridge

Street in the city. This was also listed as the office of the paper. This would suggest that the brothers owned as well as printed the paper. It is little wonder then that their going out of business would coincide with the decline of the paper. The premises at 16 Bridge Street was in the hands of another proprietor by the following year.[78]

Local competition came from the *Cork Examiner*, *Cork Constitution* or the *Cork Free Press*, all of which carried considerable sporting coverage. The *Examiner* was able to print photographs from matches, making it especially popular and difficult for the much smaller operation of the *Sportsman* to match. As Legg points out, 'new nationalist newspapers founded . . . were short-lived, finding themselves unable to compete against the well-established press in the area, which itself was changing over to nationalist politics'.[79] In the same vein, the specialist sporting press in Ireland, although many would have a brief flowering, in the end could not compete against the more established press.

Its short life as an organ for sport in Cork and the rest of Munster indicates that even in Ireland, the demand for a localised dedicated sporting press could be fulfilled, even if only briefly. The fact was that larger provincial and national newspapers increased their sporting coverage as time went on and were better able to absorb the costs of such expansion. The growth of the specialist newspapers alerted the bigger concerns to the value and necessity of dedicated sports coverage, which in some cases they promptly excelled in, surpassing their specialist counterparts. This milieu created a first celebrity sports journalist in 'Carbery' in an era just before Micheál O'Hehir. Of all the specialist papers to emerge, *Sport* was best placed to thrive since it was run as part of a larger parent company, the *Freeman's Journal*, rather than a self-sustaining business like the *Cork Sportsman*, which proved to be an unsustainable business model. The larger dailies benefited from economies of scale, something with which specialist enterprises like the *Cork Sportsman* could not compete.

Wray Vamplew has argued that sport itself underwent an industrial revolution in the period 1875–1914.[80] Of course, this same 'industrial revolution' would continue past 1914. To a certain extent, the evidence for such an assertion is compelling in the British case, though not necessarily for Ireland. Here, a more cultural revolution took place in sport. Certainly sport by 1930 would have been largely unrecognisable to a sportsman of 1830 or even 1860. We can state quite easily from looking at the elements investigated above that a part of what made the change to sport so significant was that it permeated society in a manner in keeping with other forms of entertainment at the time. Of course there were some novel particulars to the emergence of sport that made it different to other forms of developing mass entertainment and these deserve to be emphasised. First and foremost, unlike other emerging mass entertainments, the accoutrements of sport were available to buy in many local retailers so that individuals or local clubs could have all the appearances of a professional sporting outfit for relatively little cost. This is where the notion of the club itself is so important; subs money collectively could do more for a group of players and members than they could alone – buy jerseys and equipment maybe, or build a pavilion. In some clubs there was separate subs for playing and non-playing members, but undoubtedly the non-playing members must have felt an equally strong sense of investment in their club and its successes.

So in the Munster of the late nineteenth and early twentieth century, sport was many things to many people. To some it was an opportunity to expand into new markets in retail, for others it offered a change in the direction of a company; it saw the founding of many new companies as a result of the requirements of sport in its new form. It provided new work for building firms, stationers, was a boon to hoteliers and publicans, and the railway companies. It provided opportunities to expand the remit of the popular press; after all, few papers could claim to have any constant other than that they carried sport. It also created a demand, supplied with varying degrees of success, for a specifically sporting press. What is true for much of Britain and metropolitan centres such as Dublin and Belfast was just as true, in all of the same respects, for Munster.

But beyond providing new means of earning profit, sport helped, as part of a wider trend in associational culture across the province and across the country, to add to the social life of communities. This was achieved by means of the entertainment provided as a playing member, spectator or supporter. In the latter's case, the experience of spectating and supporting was buttressed by the inclusion of bands, and sometimes fireworks, in the sporting occasion. Not only that, but when clubs needed more money than could be provided by gate receipts and their annual dances, either for the benefit of their own coffers or for the good of the needy in their community, they further enhanced their role as cohesive centres in those communities. Through their smokers, Cinderella dances and whist drives, clubs engaged in the same social pastimes as were being provided by other organisations, be they religious, political or social causes in those communities. This confirms that they existed not outside their communities but were instead a significant and reciprocal part of the whole – as vital as the church, the school, the pub, the political party or any other civic and social institution that provided a sense of community to people. The sports club, whatever the sport being played, would eventually come to be the most enduring and widely popular form of associational culture in the country, at the heart of communities in both rural and urban Ireland.

Sport, then, had a lasting impact on both the psychological and physical shape of the region. Many grounds and stands were built with land sculpted and reshaped for a variety of sporting purposes, even if in most cases no one sport could claim them as their own. This is one of the most tangible inheritances that we have from the late Victorian and Edwardian sporting 'revolution'. But it was the psychological reshaping of the public space, one that put a team or a club at the core of what it meant to be from this place or that, to wear these colours or those, that was sport's greatest legacy in the region. Soccer, as we will learn later, was no exception to this process.

Commercial Leisure emerges

When soccer emerged in the new Free State as a hugely popular game, for the first time it got its very own newspaper, the *Football Sports Weekly*. This paper, produced, circulated and concerned in the main with soccer (though not exclusively), ran for three years, 1925–28. This newspaper has received little enough academic attention thus far, though Conor McCabe has written of it that it 'was not part of the establishment: it was much more important – it was part of the everyday'.[81] Like many other papers before it that focused solely on sport, it ran aground due to an inability to sustain itself. As well as the usual problems that plagued such specialist press, new media forms were emerging when it began publishing that had a profound effect on how people engaged with sport.

That everyday experience of which *Football Sports Weekly* was a part was changing with many new types of leisure finding their place in Irish society, following the end of the war, and the cities and towns of Munster were no exception. As noted in the previous chapter about the emergence of soccer in Ireland and Munster, the country and province had been open to influences from across both the Irish Sea and the Atlantic. As Ireland became an independent nation following the acceptance of the Anglo-Irish Treaty by the majority of the population, while many attempted to instil and impose a sense that it was time for the development of an Irish-Ireland, what actually happened was rather different.

Those influences that had brought soccer to Munster initially, that connectedness to a broader culture in the British Isles, now brought with it American influences in the world of leisure too – new musical styles in the form of jazz, thrillers in the cinema, and new commercial sports like greyhound racing. This was also the era when Ireland began to see new chain stores opening up, with an emphasis on cheap consumption and sales with ready cash rather than the traditional credit system operated by many smaller outfits. In her history of Woolworths, Barbara Walsh shows that such shops placed an emphasis on 'a bit of additional razzmatazz to create publicity for an advertised "preview" or "viewing day"'. This was 'one of their most successful ploys'. This included, at the shop opening in Clonmel in 1931, the free distribution of ice cream at this inspection-only day.[82] While the first shops were opened in Dublin and Belfast, the period 1919–31 saw shops open throughout Munster with Cork getting Woolworths in 1920, Limerick following in 1921, Waterford in 1930 and Clonmel in 1931.[83] With their cheap prices of 3d and 6d, these shops were emblematic of the new consumer culture which pervaded not just the Irish main street, but as we will see, was also part of the sporting culture of the interwar period. If the culture that was shared between Britain and Ireland in the Victorian era had paved the way for sporting codification, the establishment of sporting bodies like the Munster Football Association as well as national bodies, along with the rise of commercialised leisure and popular culture that came from America and Britain in the 1920s and 1930s, had an equally profound impact on how sport was played, understood – and now – consumed.

Beyond the pages of the daily or weekly newspapers like *Football Sports Weekly* that captured the action on the pitch, sport was also becoming a part of people's experiences in other spheres: publicly at the cinema and privately in the home, thanks to the radio. The growing medium of motion pictures saw sport become a part of the early cinema experience. According to Rockett and Rockett, by 1930 there were 265 cinemas on the whole island of Ireland. In the period 1928–31, cinema and film agents grew most among those entertainments, with companies registered under the Companies Act, 1908. The number of such companies went from thirty-eight down to twenty-six back up to thirty-eight in the period, but the nominal share capital rose steadily in the period from £351,850 among thirty-eight companies to £461,150, an increase of £109,300.[84]

As well as the masked figures and sinister Chinamen that W.B. Stanford recalled from that era of cinema, sport was often featured through the newsreel.[85] At the beginning of the twentieth century, enterprising cameramen like Mitchell and Kenyon captured Cork at play at the very beginning of the Edwardian era, when the city was the site of a major exhibition.[86] The archive of British Pathé also reveals that sport of a highly localised nature was part of the newsreels, before the feature film, at the time.[87] As Ciara Chambers notes, 'local newsreels were shown between the "big" newsreel and the main feature . . . they often depicted local sporting or civil events, and the more local people caught on camera, the higher the numbers likely to turn up'.[88] Just some of those that can be found include Cork Constitution versus Bective Rangers, the opening of the Waterford City Racecourse, Fordsons versus Shelbourne in the 1925 Free State Cup, Munster versus Ulster, QUB versus UCC, coursing in Clonmel, and a significant amount of GAA.[89] The cinema newsreel and the reasonably large amount of footage that survives from the 1920s especially show us the sporting world in vivid motion, as important for our sense of sport then as sports reports in the press in the same and earlier periods. It helped to make local heroes, and draw audiences to the cinema to catch the newsreels of events they may have attended themselves, to relive goals scored and chances missed.

Sport as a spectator-driven industry was a modern phenomenon, as was the motion picture, and the marriage of these two things was as natural as that between the press and sport, as noted by Rouse.[90] Mark Duncan has noted of early GAA photography: 'these early photographs underscored the reality that finals were as much social, cultural and commercial events as sporting fixtures. On-field action shots were coupled with images of the pageantry and social activity around the game, with marching bands, pressmen and important dignitaries sharing the limelight with the players and officials.'[91] Precisely the same can be said of the newsreel footage, and not just for the GAA but for all sports represented on that medium. Clubs were well aware of the cinema's power. For instance, the minute books of Cork Constitution RFC from the 1921/22 season show an outlay of 9/– for an advertisement at the cinema in March 1922.[92] Mike Huggins, analysing the impact of the newsreel on British sport, argues that 'unobtrusively, unnoticed, newsreels had become central cultural items, telling audiences of the symbolic place of soccer in British life. They offered a wide perspective, providing visions and images that contributed to soccer's later social and cultural power and to a national self-image in which sport in general, and soccer in particular, played an ever more prominent part.'[93] Similarly, the importance of the cinema to Irish life in this period can hardly be overstated.

By 1935 there were 190 cinemas in the county with fifty-five of those in towns of between 5,000 and 15,000 people; thirty-six in County Dublin; nineteen across Cork, Limerick and Waterford and some eighty in the rest of the country. Of that eighty, some thirty-six were in Dublin city alone.[94] The numbers employed in the industry across all six counties of Munster was 154. Unsurprisingly, Cork accounted for the largest proportion of the total.[95] It is entirely possible that cinema, and its representation of soccer in particular, had an effect on its popular perception in Ireland similar to the one it had on the game in Britain according to Mike Huggins; this is particularly true of the 1920s when people in Irish cinemas were more likely to see soccer, then at its most popular. Another strong indicator of the medium's power can be seen in the large amount of revenue earned through customs duty by the first Free State government. Between 1924 and 1930, this rose from £13,148 to £18,902; it also indicates the growing influence of non-Irish cinema.[96] Radio would lift off at the end of the 1920s and would develop into the 1930s. Eoghan O'Brien, presenting to the Social and Statistical Inquiry Society of Ireland, noted that 'the principal role played by electricity has been to offer an immense increase in the amenities of life: in most so-called civilised countries the applications of electricity enable the great majority of even the humblest and poorest to enjoy a luxury of life and a variety of pleasures undreamt of fifty years ago.'[97]

According to Terence Brown, the number of licences for the radio issued increased dramatically in the mid-1930s with 50,500 in 1935, 62,200 in 1936 and 100,000 by 1937. He also notes that a majority of these were in the Dublin area. Nevertheless, as he also acknowledges, many did not have a licence. Even if 40 per cent of those issued in 1939 were for the Dublin region, that still left 60 per cent for Munster and elsewhere.[98]

Maurice Gorham recollects of the job of 2RN, Ireland's first state radio service, that 'it was expected to revive the speaking of Irish; to foster a taste for classical music; to revive traditional music'.[99] Not just music, but sport was also a part of the early programming of 2RN. Sport would feature from radio's earliest days in Ireland. The first game broadcast live was the All-Ireland hurling semi-final between Galway and Kilkenny on 18 April 1926, the earliest broadcast of a field game in Europe. Irish radio, despite being a monopoly of the state, was still competing with outside broadcasters since radios could usually pick up the transmissions of the BBC, for instance. As a result, the sporting programming was varied, including not just GAA games but also soccer matches, with Cork side Fordsons game against Dundalk in the 1927/28 season being among the earliest soccer games broadcast in the state.[100] Rugby was also soon on the airwaves, with an international against Scotland broadcast from Lansdowne Road in 1927 among the earliest broadcasts of the sport.[101] The practical realities of finding the revenue to run the station mediated against sticking strictly to the kind of aims outlined by Maurice Gorham, and as well as spreading their wings in terms of the sports broadcast, the addition of shows with popular music, broadly denounced by some as 'jazz', were seen to be 'selling the musical soul of the nation' for the revenue generated by programmes sponsored by advertisers.

By way of contrast, as Diarmaid Ferriter notes, in time to come 'Fianna Fáil in the 1930s occasionally attempted to create the impression that traditional Irish music was second only to the Irish language in distinguishing Gaelic from Anglo-Saxon culture, though the standard of music on the Irish radio was rarely uplifting'.[102] Indeed, as Mary Daly has noted, electricity generally was regarded as a means, not to save labour, but to give leisure in post-1945 Ireland. She argues that 'electric radios were undoubtedly the first appliance bought by most Irish households. They meant an end to fears and uncertainties caused by batteries failing in the middle of important football matches or during evening music programmes.' It's difficult not to see similar thinking influencing choices to buy radios in cities and towns in the 1920s and 1930s prior to the post-war rural electrification that concerned Daly.[103] The more relaxed attitude displayed by programmers in the 1920s, where sport was concerned, indicates perhaps that it had more reach in terms of getting and keeping an audience tuned to their dial than music did. This development made the home into a sporting space too.

The success of sporting broadcasts was such that the Aonach Tailteann was broadcast over the airwaves of 2RN and by 1930 a sports magazine programme had been established on the station.[104] Like the appearance of sporting goods in the shops and retail outlets throughout Munster, the entry of sport into people's homes through the radio and its part in the newsreel that ran before the main feature demands our attention if we are to understand sporting culture in this period. They helped to widen the audience for sport. This increased commercialism in the 1920s manifested itself in other ways too. For instance, the volume of people betting on sporting events saw the Cumann na nGaedheal government introduce a Betting Act that legalised gambling, and brought with it the licensed betting shop, which would have a profound impact on how sport was enjoyed in Ireland. Betting had long been big business on the track at horse races, but betting on races and now soccer could be conducted just yards from your own home. To get some idea of just how big a business betting was, an estimated £312,000 was spent on betting in 1907, which by 1926, when the Betting Act was introduced, had risen to around £400,000 as part of £1.5 million in total spent on entertainment and sports, according to Kiernan.[105] This figure indicates on-track betting only, since this was the only legal way of betting in Ireland until the introduction of the Betting Act in 1926. There was illegal betting and bookmaking although by the very nature of unlicensed betting, a figure for this is impossible to quantify, though it was no doubt substantial.

Backing it Both Ways: gambling and commercial sport

Betting on horse racing had long been a popular activity in Ireland by the time Irish independence from Britain was achieved. Gambling, generally, was an important part of Irish male popular culture. And in the Free State era, the new Cumann na nGaedheal government sought to capitalise on this culture by providing legislation that legalised and regulated gambling in Irish society. Just before the Betting Act of 1926 was introduced, Irish hospitals were beginning to benefit from the newly developed Hospital Sweepstakes. Marie Coleman notes 'the immorality of legalising gambling and utilising its proceeds for charitable purposes emerged as a powerful argument against the bill [for the sweepstakes]'.[106] The eventual establishment of the Hospital Sweepstakes under law in 1929 would offer further encouragement to gambling via the Sweepstakes, especially on major horse races like the English Grand National, among many others. Commercial sport and leisure was growing in general in Ireland at the time. For instance, at the end of 1928, there were forty-eight different companies registered variously as racecourses, greyhound racing or other sports grounds, clubs and baths in the Free State with a combined total nominal share capital of £339,145. By the end of 1930 this nominal share capital had risen to £348,145 among fifty-five different companies.[107] This was part of a general trend of increased leisure commercialisation, indicated by the rising employment in that sector generally. Between 1926 and 1936, the numbers employed in entertainment and sport rose nationally from 4,325 to 5,470, while in Munster the rise was from 1,297 to 1,529. In Cork, the numbers employed this way rose from 549 to 639; in Tipperary, the rise was negligible, rising only from 198 people to 205; while in Waterford the numbers employed in entertainment and sport went from 166 people in 1926 to 212 by 1936.[108]

The success of horseracing as an industry in Ireland, fuelled by and fuelling an equally successful horse-breeding industry, ensured that the new Free State government, eager for sources of revenue, would seek to impose a taxation on the industry in the form of a betting tax. Not only that, but it would also insist on the registering and granting of licences to bookmakers in an effort to curb illegal street betting and to discourage chancers from entering the bookmaking trade who would welch on their debts. Betting was a central part of sporting culture. Historian Neil Tranter has noted that 'all historians would agree that the capacity of sport to generate pleasure had much to do with the opportunity it afforded to indulge man's passion for gambling' as anything else.[109] A handful of laws relating to gambling had existed under the union between Ireland and Great Britain, with Acts of Parliament for 1845 and a continuation of this legislation in 1892. But the Betting Tax of 1926 was to be the first Irish legislation to deal with the matter; coincidentally, similar legislation was working its way through the British Parliament in the same year. Munster had many horse racing courses. For example, Waterford at various times had three different racecourses: one in Waterford city, one near Tramore strand and a third one opened in 1912, also in Tramore but closer to the town and away from the sea to replace the first one. In Tipperary, the Powerstown Park racecourse was a site of important meetings throughout much of this period. In Cork, both the city racecourse and the track at Mallow were significant sites.

Due to the unregulated nature of betting before the introduction of the 1926 Act, it is impossible to know just how many were making their living, either through on-track betting or those making money illegally through betting in the street. Yet, given the desire to regulate and introduce licences, we can presume that it was a substantial number engaged in the practice, legally or otherwise. When the 1926 Betting Act came into law, there were many who objected, and on a wide variety of grounds. The sporting newspaper *Irish Field and Gentleman's Gazette* felt that 'a very undesirable feature of the Betting Tax is that it makes provision for the opening up of an unlimited number of betting shops all over the country'.[110] This was problematic mainly because it meant that 'women and children may wager away to their hearts' content in a State-sponsored betting shop'.[111] The author of the article hoped that 'every right-minded father and mother will protest against a facility of this kind being provided'.[112] The article was scathing, saying that 'there is not a single sound point in the Betting Tax as at present drafted'.[113] This was a crucial element of the commercial forms of leisure that had gambling at their heart. While sport was open to many middle-class women through the schools many of them attended – sports like tennis and hockey in particular – it was in this period largely denied to working-class Irish women. What they could not participate in, however, they could spectate and speculate on. Commercial spectator sports like horse and greyhound racing, and the gambling that went with it, provided working-class women in Ireland with one of the few opportunities they had of, in fact, participating in the new commercial sporting culture then emerging. Behind the moral panic regarding women gambling in the pages of the *Irish Field* was of course a fear of the detrimental impact the tax would have on the horseracing industry. This was a two-fold fear since the tax would have to be picked up somewhere, either by reduced stakes or in the odds offered by bookies. The other fear was that the focus of licensed premises for betting would be on English meetings since these were more frequent than Irish meetings, taking yet more money from Irish racing. On these matters the journalists of *The Irish Field* submitted that 'racecourse betting should not be taxed', and that nothing should be done 'to discourage people from attending race meetings . . . office bookmakers have not to discharge the heavy outgoings of their racecourse brethren . . .'[114]

The paper argued that in order to ensure that licences had been paid by on-track bookies '. . . a number of new officials would have to be found to travel from meeting to meeting to carry out their duties. We fancy that public opinion would not favour the creating of more jobs.'[115] In other words, people would not want it to seem as though jobs were being created by the government for their friends when unemployment was so high. Indeed, the paper also utilised the fact that the horseracing industry was one of the few successes of the early years of the Free State: 'the employment it affords is especially valuable when unfortunately so many people willing to work, are workless'.[116] In its turf column, *Football Sports Weekly* highlighted the negative impact the tax may have on areas where races are held, in a similar fashion to the *Irish Field*.[117] In June, the turf correspondent of the paper argued that 'it is not a question of bookies being made pay. It is a question of a business that gives employment to thousands of people and circulates an enormous amount of money in the state being ruined by an ill-considered and crushing tax imposed by a Minister who is apparently regardless of what evil consequences it might have.'[118] The oppositional nature of the debate is borne out in the above quotation and it appears that the minister, Ernest Blythe, was himself no great fan of the racing lobbyists, and was quoted as calling the racing lobby's arguments 'all cry and little wool', according to one report.[119]

Despite such opposition, the bill went through to become law. The new licensed premises could open between 9am and 6pm, on all days except Sundays, Good Friday and Christmas Day.[120] As it transpired, much of the trade would be done during the lunch hour and this would become a significant element of the debate about the law

when an Oireachtas Committee was set up to report the new legislation's impact. Its findings were published in a report in 1929.[121] In a
general rundown of the report it was said that the Act had 'wiped
out street betting',[122] and that it 'should not be repealed, but, rather,
amended'.[123] Stating that 'the gambling craze has affected all classes
down to persons in receipt of unemployment benefit and home assistance and the results are demoralising, disorderly, uneconomic,
thriftless',[124] the report conveys shock and surprise that what could
be broadly termed the working classes of Ireland had taken so much
to gambling with the introduction of the newly licensed premises.

The committee convened to deliver the report interviewed a large
number of people, including the Commissioner of An Garda
Síochána Eoin O'Duffy; the Revenue Commissioner P.S. O'Hegarty;
the Secretary of the Department of Posts and Telegraphs; the chief
justice of the District Court in Dublin; the Central Savings Committee; and representatives from the Catholic Church, Church of
Ireland and Presbyterian Church. These, along with the editor of the
newspaper *Sport*, representatives of the Turf Accountants' Protection
Association and the Irish Bookmakers' Association, were called upon
to offer their opinion of how the betting tax was impacting on the
horse racing industry, and the apparent proclivity of the Irish people
to gamble.

O'Duffy's testimony is interesting on two counts, particularly
since it provides us with a solid impression of the bookmaker's trade
as it stood in 1929, three years after the introduction of these
licences. We will deal with this aspect of his testimony first. According
to O'Duffy, in the time between the legalisation of betting and his
interview for the interim report, there were a total of 517 licensed
premises in the country for betting. Of those, just shy of half were
located in Dublin city, which had 220. The whole of Munster contained ninety-eight such premises.

Waterford city had the largest concentration, with twenty-nine
premises licensed and twenty-eight bookmakers running these. Cork
had some twenty-five premises, with twenty-three bookmakers and
Tipperary with twenty bookmakers and just nineteen premises.[125] By
1936, there were 418 people who made their living as bookmakers in
Munster, legally at least. Again, Dublin had the largest percentage of
the total in the business, but Munster had the next largest amount,
accounting for 26 per cent of the total. For Cork, Tipperary and

Waterford, the breakdown was 154 in Cork, seventy-nine in Tipperary and seventy-four in Waterford. In Cork the vast majority were inside the county borough, ninety-three men in all, with the remainder in the eastern and western halves of the county. In Tipperary, the vast majority of bookmakers were situated in the county's south riding where most of the county's major towns were, as well as venues like the Clonmel racecourse. In Waterford, the vast majority of bookmakers lived inside the county borough, forty-five in all. Meanwhile in Limerick city, there were some fifty-four registered bookmakers, forty-three of whom were men, while the county had another twenty-six, the majority in that case being women.

Neither Clare nor Kerry had anything like these numbers, at least not officially on the census. Not all of these bookmakers would have had premises, operating either at racecourses or dog tracks by then.[126] The higher number of premises in Cork city and Dublin indicates a stronger market for betting in urban areas, with greater populations and, a more substantial working class. These figures bear out the strong interest in horse racing in all three counties. In the case of Cork, it bears witness particularly to the emergence of greyhound racing as a popular sport, which was cheaper than horseracing to enter and the bookies were willing to take bets of much smaller amounts, thus encouraging a crowd of much poorer means than might be found at a race meeting.

Concerned about the moral impact of licensed bookies, O'Duffy was wary of the bookmakers themselves, given how 'some of the bookmakers boast that they have saloons capable of holding 500 persons'. He also seemed concerned about what the people in the bookmakers' offices talked about, saying 'the language that the police have heard is not always edifying' and that 'there is not much talk about athletics or any other form of manly sports'. Indeed, for O'Duffy the popularity of these premises and of gambling, he feared, might have 'very serious results so far as the physical development of our race is concerned'.[127]

O'Duffy and particularly the clerical representatives who were interviewed in the preparing of the report seemed most concerned about the gambling habits of the poor, especially those receiving home assistance benefits, and suggested that anyone in receipt of the benefit found to be gambling should have their assistance taken away from them, as a deterrent. Fr J.J. Flood, head of the Pro Cathedral in

Dublin, suggested a minimum bet of 2s 6d in order to discourage the poorest and prevent them by means of exclusion from betting.[128]

This system of minimum wager was offered up by all three clerics across denominations. However, the Presbyterian minister Rev. E.J. McKee stated in no uncertain terms that 'we would like to see the evil suppressed'.[129] McKee's opposition mirrors the apprehension of the Board of the Protestant-run Adelaide Hospital in Dublin towards the Hospital Sweepstakes.[130] Such an extreme position was never likely to be taken seriously by the Committee, however. The issue was certainly a vexed one. C.J. Thorpe, representing the Irish Bookmakers Association, with around eighty members, took a swipe at the government during his testimony, saying it was 'morally wrong to impose a tax, because you, gentlemen, and all governments have looked upon bookmaking as a reprehensible thing. When you look upon it as a reprehensible thing you should not accept any money out of it.'[131] The leader of the Labour Party, Thomas Johnson, also felt that the making of money for revenue purposes out of gambling was questionable. As it was, earning revenue from alcohol sales was already an element of revenue income the government was dependent upon, making it a regressive form of taxation.[132] Johnson recognised that it would be Ireland's (largely unemployed) working class whom this revenue would derive from.

> I think it is desirable we should discourage the setting up of betting houses in districts where they might lead to the inculcation or the extension of the habit of betting as a habit, and where as a consequence people would be encouraged to devote most of their thoughts to racing matters. One does not object to occasional betting, or even to frequent betting, but one does object to the habitual concentration on this feature of public life to which so many people in the country are addicted. I feel it is desirable we should frame this measure in such a fashion that we should, if we can, in some degree reduce the temptation to the following of betting as a habit. I simply repeat my request to the Minister that he will allow ample time for the preparation of amendments to this very complicated measure.[133]

Historian Richard Holt makes the point that those who were poorest in society were the more likely to engage in an activity they could not 'afford', in a certain narrow sense. He writes that 'the chance of a small windfall was a source of hope as well as amusement . . . Most working people did not believe it was possible to save enough to really improve their lives. The effort required would just make a hard life worse.'[134] Given the huge sums already discussed above being spent on gambling in the state, this suggests that the hope of winnings was something a lot of Irish people needed in their daily lives.

As Michael Byrne, editor of *Sport*, put it in his testimony to the Oireachtas Committee investigating the operation of the Act, 'those who want to bet will bet'. He made the following point, that 'to make it [a minimum wager] larger than a shilling and to say that a man must not bet in sums smaller than a half-crown, for instance, would encourage him to invest more money than he could afford, and it would be an inducement to him to spend more money. I see no reason why the working classes, say, should not be allowed to indulge in their relaxation. It may be foolish from a certain point of view, but if they want it they are entitled to it.'[135]

Although much of this testimony seems to have in mind the poorer parts of Dublin, the same kind of culture can be found in Cork and Waterford cities particularly, as the large number of betting premises would indicate. Tipperary was likely to be a different matter as a result of its lack of a single major urban centre, but the evidence for Carrick-on-Suir and Clonmel indicates that a similar kind of culture prevailed among the working classes in those areas.

The tax's impact on the horse racing and horse breeding trades was very real, but in many ways it compounded existing problems. In a depressed economy, with so much unemployment, it is hardly surprising that the numbers attending races at Ireland's thirty-two courses declined, especially now that you could get the thrill of the betting ring at a bookmaker's shop. Although not extravagantly expensive to attend, soccer, rugby and GAA were still undoubtedly cheaper, even with the Entertainment Tax.[136] It was far cheaper to wager a small amount in a licensed premises than it was to attend a day's racing and pay for the excursion train, drinks, dinner, your wagers and possibly a hotel.

The government's need for sources of revenue saw them capitalise on an apparently lucrative industry in horse racing and the developing sport of greyhound racing,[137] but their method of taxation – on wagers rather than on winnings, as was being proposed in the UK at the time – appears to have had a detrimental effect. The issuing of licensed premises for gambling seems to have encouraged greater interest in horses and gambling generally, but not necessarily in the Irish turf. Beyond this, the decision on the part of the government to legislate for betting, making it legal, also implies their acceptance of it as a part of Irish sporting culture, despite the evident misgivings of many constituent parts of Irish society. Huggins makes the point about betting in Britain between the wars that 'morality, respectability and reformist belief were unable to make a negative impact on gambling, despite the apparent power of such belief through its rhetorical volume in pulpit, press and parts of Parliament'.[138] As the racing correspondent for *Football Sports Weekly* put it in the summer of 1926, 'locking the stable door after the horse has gone is still the guiding rule in the Saorstát'.[139]

The first Irish greyhound race meetings took place in 1927 in Belfast and Dublin and, by the middle of the 1930s, a large number of tracks had been established, notably throughout Cork, Waterford and Tipperary. As for the government itself, the introduction of the Act certainly brought money in, as the following tables illustrate:

TABLE 3.1

Saorstát Éireann excise income
from Betting Act, 1926

Financial Year	Premises Reg. Fee (£)	Licence Fee (£)	Betting Duty (£)	Total (£)
1926/27	10,380	5,448	43,343.0.4	59,171.0.4
1927/28	11,500	5,494	211,461.13.8½	228,455.13.8 ½
1928/29	11,800	5,450	181,698.0.2	198,948.0.2
1929/30	10,940	5,016	204.148.8.5	220,104.8.5
1930/31	11,120	5,064	201,125.13.11	217,309.13.11
1931/32	192,011	4,973	11,520	208,504
1932/33	144,102*	5,380	13,080	162,562
1933/34	158,873	5,310	14,720	178,903
1934/35	164,372	5,070	13,760	183,202
1935/36	169,327	5,000	14,080	188,407
1936/37	193,711	5,700	16,040	215,991
1937/38	218,053	5,570	15,940	239,563

SOURCE: Finance accounts of Saorstát Éireann, 1926–38.

*Duty on betting only applies to bets made off-course. Levy of 5% (Finance Act, 1931)

TABLE 3.2

Greyhound Racing Companies registered
in Ireland, 1928–38

Year	No. of Companies	Nominal Share Capital	Paid Up Capital
1928	3	42,000	-
1929	3	42,000	-
1930	5	45,000	-
1931	7	47,800	-
1932	9	51,800	-
1933	11	55,800	-
1934	12	59,000	-
1935	13	49,000	-
1936	15	56,000	-
1937	15	56,000	38,844
1938	15	56,000	46,883

SOURCE: Company registration reports, 1928–38.

To put this intake into perspective, in the same period, entertainments duties brought in a total of roughly £783,904; while the only excise duties more valuable to the exchequer during the period after the Betting Act was introduced were those on beer and spirits.[140] As well as that, these tables indicate that if not exactly depression-proof, then the new sport of greyhound racing was certainly resilient in the face of economic downturn. Undoubtedly, the hope of a quick win on the dogs, horses or the pools will have appealed to those for whom these were especially straitened times. These figures, and in particular the betting duty figures, give a clear indication of the level of betting in the Irish Free State. Introducing the Betting Act proved quite successful in terms of raising revenue for the state. According to one source, in the first three years, it raised some £436,503 through duties on betting, along with £34,180 in bookies' registration fees. All told, that was revenue in three years of £470,683.[141] The table above shows the rapid rate of expansion of the new spectator sport of greyhound racing, a sport open not just to working-class men but working-class women as well, an important facet of its new popularity.

The first greyhound tracks with the electric hare in Ireland were established in 1927 at Belfast Celtic's ground and at Shelbourne Park in Dublin. Almost immediately this was followed by the establishment of a Cork greyhound racing track and one in Thurles and Limerick as well. When the first night meeting passed off in Belfast, *The Irish Times* described it as a 'most spectacular' scene.[142] The opening night at Shelbourne Park was just as enthusiastically received by the newspaper, which estimated that roughly 10,000 people turned out to see the dogs.[143] Only months after the first races at Belfast and Dublin, a group of businessmen in Cork were agitating the university in the city to sell off a portion of the remarkable acreage it owned to establish a greyhound racing track, recognising it as a prime location for just such a business venture.[144] In the end, a site called the Lower Park, belonging to the Munster Agricultural Society, was agreed upon as the site for the introduction of greyhound racing in the city.[145] This would in 1932 become home to Cork Bohemians FC, of which more later.

The introduction of the Betting Act just as greyhound racing – a sport centred around betting – got off the ground raised significant questions about the extent to which the behaviour of the population ought to be regulated by the state, especially in terms of how their leisure hours were spent. There were men like O'Duffy, who took a distinctly dim view of the practice of gambling since it was out of sync with quite common notions of sportsmanship and its moral benefits. In a new state, where a moralistic view on personal conduct was encouraged, it also reveals a deep contradiction between the desire to discourage gambling while at the same time encouraging a monetarily significant industry in order to benefit from its considerable revenue. The evidence suggests that it was ultimately a socially regressive tax as well as detrimental to the horse racing industry, if not the greyhound racing industry. Finally, if, as Mike Huggins has argued, in interwar Britain the government's attitude there made gambling a more acceptable practice;[146] in the new Irish Free State, the legislation on betting, the establishment of the tote, and the establishment of the Hospital Sweepstakes collectively strongly institutionalised gambling as a central part of Irish sporting culture during the period.

Indeed, soccer was party to this craze too. As a small notice in the *Limerick Leader* attests, illegal betting on the popular football pools was taking place in Ireland with betting slips related to the pools being seized in Waterford port by the customs authorities in 1934.[147] Obviously, given the clandestine nature of the engagement, it is hard to know just how popular betting on the pools was in Ireland, though given the fact that such a seizure as that in Waterford was possible, it suggests it was indeed a popular part of people's gambling habits.

Such commercialism, though it was the hallmark of the interwar sporting world in Ireland, was not the whole story. In the same era, sports clubs began to hold dances, called 'Cinderella dances' because they ostensibly ended at midnight (though rarely actually did),[148] and organise card nights, usually playing whist, as a way to help raise the balance in the club coffers.

Lovers of the Light Fantastic

Over the course of the 1920s the country and in the south-east especially, the Cinderella dance was a popular pastime. Jazz and other forms of popular music from Britain and the USA had made their way to Ireland and were immensely popular, not alone in cities and towns, but throughout the countryside. As an article in the *Limerick Leader* noted, 'foreign dances are all the rage; the Fox-Trot and the Goose Step hold sway'. Dancing enjoyed huge popularity as a pastime during the 1920s and into the 1930s, until the activities of many dance halls were curtailed under the Dance Halls Act of 1935, which required a licence to hold a dance. Those who danced the night away were frequently referred to in the press of the day as 'lovers of the light fantastic'. As an entertaining night out for teams, the club dance had been around before the craze of the 1920s, but it was in that decade that things really took off. The Clonmel Workman's Boat Club were organising them as early as 1910.[149] Subscriptions from dances and money made from the sale of minerals were an important part of the income generated.[150] Whist drives and Cinderella dances formed a large part of the social aspect of clubs. The annual dinner, and smoking concerts too, formed part of this social milieu in which club members took part. When revellers made their way to the Cinema Hall in Carrick-on-Suir in County Tipperary on the night of 24 November 1922, they were informed that the planned Cinderella dance to be held was cancelled on account of the death of Erskine Childers.[151] The organisers of the dance had been informed of the death by a member of the Irregulars.

These dances were most often held in the run-up to Lent and around Christmas and New Year. Unfortunately, detailed descriptions of what they involved are apparently no longer extant, though their popularity during the period can be in no doubt. In all likelihood, they were some kind of fancy dress ball. Examples of clubs that engaged in Cinderella dances as a means to raise money from Waterford city and county included Waterford City RFC, Waterpark RFC, Waterford Boat Club, and the Dungarvan GAA club. In south Tipperary, Carrick-on-Suir Boat Club held a Cinderella dance when hosting London Provincial Bank Rugby Club after their match with Carrick-on-Suir RFC.[152]

The Cinderella dance was equally popular around parts of north Tipperary too, though mainly towards the latter end of the 1920s. Borrisokane junior hurling club, Toomevara junior hurling club, the Toomevara Sports Committee, and the Nenagh Ormond RFC, are just some examples of clubs in that area of the county who put on Cinderella dances to aid their social standing in the community as well as the clubs' purses.[153] In west Cork, we see similar patterns and trends – Bandon GAA, Clonakilty GAA, Skibbereen Cycling and Athletic Club, Doheny Football Club, Clonakilty RFC, and Kinsale GAA were among those who utilised this popular form of entertainment to buttress their clubs' coffers.[154] In the same decade, ex-pat Irish in Wales were using Cinderella dances to similar effect, with a Cinderella dance held by the Cardiff branch of the Gaelic League to establish a hurling club for its members.[155] Likewise, Limerick saw its fair share of such nights, like when North Wales University were guests of Bohemians Rugby Club in 1927, to take just one of hundreds of examples from the period.[156]

It is also worth recognising that these activities were ones in which the wives and girlfriends of club members could also engage; since many of the sports which used these methods of fundraising were not necessarily open to female membership, these activities may have been a way to engage the partners of members. After all, as historian John Tosh notes, the club, sporting or otherwise, had a role to play in the declining domestic role of the male in Victorian England and the same certainly goes for the Irish male too.[157]

Whist drives, often preceding a Cinderella dance, were used in a similar way and are equally interesting. The card game, which is played in tables of four in huge numbers, was of course itself a sport of sorts. Its popularity seemed to wax and wane, but for the early part of the twentieth century in Ireland it was certainly a popular means of socialising in sports clubs and raising money for a club's coffers. Examples of it being used for fundraising either for clubs or by clubs in aid of other organisations abound. In Waterford, for example, the Civil Service Sports Club held a whist drive in aid of the Sisters of Charity poor relief fund, Dungarvan Golf Club likewise held whist drives, as did Dungarvan GAA club Brickey Rangers. In south Tipperary, whist drives were especially popular. In Carrick-on-Suir, examples of whist drives held by sports clubs include the boat club, and the Christian Brothers Boys Athletic Club.

In Cork the newspapers point to the annual dance as being a fixture of the soccer clubs, including Cork Celtic and Southern Rovers, both of whom made use of the Ancient Order of Hibernians' hall on Morrison's Island for their dances.[158]

That these two particular forms of entertainment were so widely utilised is significant. They appear to be two of the most popular pastimes in the 1920s, not just for fundraising among sporting clubs, but also to raise funds for nursing and child welfare organisations, bands, and entities such as Distributive Worker's Club, and even the INTO National Congress.[159] Their use by sports clubs, either for their own coffers or in some cases to help charitable causes, is a clear indicator of the importance of the sports club, whatever the sport, to local community in this period and their interaction with it, beyond the merely sporting.

But even this could not escape the clutches of commercialism, to some degree. The music that drove them, the new popular music, generically and often wrongly described under the umbrella term 'jazz', was one more product now made more readily available thanks to prices that were considerably more affordable, even if the record players themselves remained something of a luxury item. As Barbara Walsh has noted, when Woolworths arrived in Ireland during the jazz craze of the late 1920s and 1930s, they sold these modern pop records, seven-inch double-sided vinyls, for 6d apiece in comparison to the ten-inch double-sided records sold by more respectable music shops for 3/.[160] As shops like Woolworths began to make their presence felt in Munster in this period, the popularity of gramophone records of the cheaper variety led to customs duty being placed on them at a rate of 33.3 per cent. During a Dáil debate, as part of the wider debate on the 1932 Finance Bill, the whole notion of whether gramophones and cheap records which could be bought in Woolworths were indeed a 'luxury' item was contested by some, including Cork West Cumann na nGaedheal deputy Eamonn O'Neill and his fellow party member Margaret Collins-O'Driscoll, Cumann na nGaedheal deputy for Dublin North. When an amendment was tabled to have gramophone records exempted from a planned duty by Ernest Blythe, deputy Collins-O'Driscoll showed her support, arguing that 'in some of the poorest houses the people save their pennies in order to purchase gramophone records. It would be inflicting a great hardship on them to tax records.'[161] It was argued by Sir James Craig that this would disproportionately affect working-class children, and for Eamonn O'Neill of Cork West, his view of the proposal was that,

> With regard to gramophone records, it is disgraceful to put a tax on them. You can, at any rate, remedy matters by eliminating the tax on the lower-priced records which are available for the homes of the poor. It is ridiculous to class gramophone records as luxuries. The gramophone is the only sort of musical entertainment the poor can have. They buy reasonably good gramophones and records cheaply. That is the only way they have of getting into touch with some of the master minds in the musical world; that is how they acquire the more popular airs and songs. Any form of culture as applied to the lives of the poor ought not to be taxed. Their lives are drab enough and these gramophones are the means of bringing them some brightness. If you go through the smaller towns and cities you will find gramophones installed in the houses of the poor. They cannot afford expensive wireless sets, pianos or violins. Gramophones in their cases are essential and I do not think the Minister should define them as luxuries.[162]

As we will see in the next chapter, similar debates raged about the imposition of a tax on entertainment, one which would disproportionately affect soccer, and by extension, many of its more working-class adherents. Similarly, this proposal from Seán MacEntee to impose a tax on the sale of gramophone records was going to disproportionately affect the young, working and lower middle-class children and young adults who were so caught up in the popular music craze of jazz and dancing. Interestingly of course, MacEntee would be accused in years to come, when the anti-jazz campaign emerged, of 'jazzing every night of the week' by Fr Peter Conefrey, even though during this debate MacEntee insisted that 'I am not going to give away money, which is absolutely essential in order to balance the Budget, simply to make it cheaper for people to inflict this music upon them'.[163] 'This music' being in MacEntee's eyes little more than a nuisance:

> As soon as one jazz tune becomes popular they buy the record with that tune and make the lives of their neighbours a misery, playing it daily to the end of the week. Then they go and buy another one. The proportion of really good class music which is recorded on the cheaper records as compared with music of the ephemeral kind is insignificantly small.[164]

Whatever the views of the Minister for Finance in 1932 about jazz and the gramophone records on which many people heard it, the popularity of the Cinderella dances at which people were also introduced to it as fundraisers and charity events meant that before long such dances were being held weekly, and not always with a benevolent goal in mind. Such a development did not precipitate a decline in their use as a form of entertainment among fundraisers, a point worth remembering. In the New Hall in Kilmacthomas, County Waterford as the 1930s progressed there appeared to be a Cinderella dance every Saturday night. These nights became so popular that eventually a bus was provided for people who wished to go from Waterford city. As the *Munster Express* advertised, the bus would leave from the Clock Tower at around 7pm on a Saturday night and the fare was 2/6, the same amount as entry to the dance once they got there. This was scarcely a cheap night out, yet remained very popular.

The entry price of 2/6 seemed standard enough in many places, although women were usually admitted for less, often 1/6. Given that entry to the average GAA, soccer or rugby game at the time stood usually between 6d and 1/–, or that cinema tickets varied widely from as little as 4d and up, we can get some perspective on just how much saving might go into these nights. As such, it's likely that the Cinderella dances of the more commercial kind will have appealed to younger, single men and women and those of a charitable nature more than to those living settled lives. And of course, given that sports clubs were usually especially popular among young, single men, it is no surprise that Cinderella dances would form part of the entertainment the clubs would provide.

The price of some of the bigger charity balls was often close to a pound, those patronised by the Marchioness of Waterford for instance. This may be partly in order to cover the cost of their more lavish set-up but also to ensure good remuneration for the charitable cause. Perhaps, just as importantly, to make sure that those who were attendees at the regular dance nights, in the halls like those of Kilmacthomas, were not permitted to these affairs.

Not that it is likely that many of those attending the regular Cinderella dances in places like Kilmacthomas would have cared a great deal, their continued staging the clearest suggestion of their overwhelming popularity. These nights contained a mixture of dances, from the old waltzes to traditional Irish dancing and most probably some of the pop hits and 'jazz' dancing of the day. The dreaded jazz was seen as such a pernicious influence on the young Irish people at the time, certainly in the mind of the commentator who stated in the *Nenagh Guardian* in 1923 that 'The Black and Tans have left a legacy behind them in Ireland, and their followers never fail at any function avoidable to exploit that foreign dowry to the detriment of Irish morality and nationality. The jazz is one item of that infamous legacy that youth of Ireland must uproot and eradicate.' Such language was quite typical of the views of many in this period as regards the developing taste for jazz among the younger people of Ireland. This formed yet one more part of the tussle to assert cultural dominance in the newly independent state.

There seemed however to be no such inclination among either the young or the organisers of the dances. Indeed the jazzing was so troublesome to some in the community that on one occasion in 1930, at a court hearing, a member of the Gardaí asked the sitting judge that the playing of jazz music be prohibited at GAA-organised dances. The judge was suitably flummoxed and threw out the request. The attitude of the garda in this instance was a clear indicator of the outlook shared by many in officialdom in Ireland. It was just such an outlook that led to the Public Dance Halls Act of 1935 which it was hoped would greatly curtail the more unseemly aspects of the Irish youths' love of dancing.

It is worth recognising too that such commercialised ventures as those in the New Hall of Kilmacthomas, County Waterford would have been quite impossible if there wasn't a steady supply of bands who knew the popular standards of the day to keep the crowds interested in going. So just who was it that provided this often-incendiary music? Local bands provided the music for these dances usually but occasionally a treat would be provided in the form of a band from outside the locality.

The names of these bands are as good an indication of the type of music that they might have played for their audiences as anything else. For instance, it is hard to imagine Louis Lee and his Radio Dance Band or The Swingsters not playing quite a few of the jazz and pop standards of the day. There is also a kind of faux-sophisti-cated big band feel to the names of several of the bands who were doing the rounds at the time, such as these bands from north Tipperary and across the south-east: The Bohemian Band; Griffin and his Waterford Band; Mick O'Shea and his band; The Fethard Twilight Serenaders Band; Dick Walsh and his Premier Dance Band. There is a charming incongruity between the names of the band-leaders and the band names. That more than anything is indicative of a desire to imitate what they surely perceived as American glamour, and by such imitation, even if for a brief few hours at the weekend, embody some of that same glamour. This is backed up by the assertions of Austin, who writes that 'Geographic and economic isolation had encouraged homogeneity in the character of rural Ireland's dance and music, but after the First World War, outside influences entered the country with a rapidity alarming to many. Aided by mass media, international dance vogues had a strong effect on the dance and music of the country.'[165]

As Ireland moved from its position in the United Kingdom to independence as the Irish Free State, in Munster and elsewhere people began to enjoy themselves dancing and sporting, in a world where the cinema and radio were becoming an increasingly central part of life, exposing young people in independent Ireland to yet more outside influences, not just from Britain but from the United States of America as well.

All of these developments pointed to a kind of amateurism that may seem at odds with the increasing commercialisation of people's leisure time, but as historian Stephen G. Jones noted of Britain in the same period, 'it is clearly wrong to depict the working class as impo-tent consumers, having little or no say in the form and content of the leisure product. In fact, working people had the capacity to resist and contest attempts at social control. There was, in short, a great deal of ingenuity in workers' leisure.'[166] The sheer number of card drives, dances and other similar entertainments to be found all over Munster at that time is ultimate testament to that ingenuity. Not alone that, but as Jones further notes, it was in the interwar period that both the voluntary and the commercial forms of leisure grew, and the same can be seen to be true of Ireland generally, and Munster specifically.[167] And so on the one hand the interwar period saw the emergence of mass spectator sport like greyhound racing coupled with increased leisure produced by people themselves voluntarily in the form of Cinderella dances and whist drives among other things. The sport which best exemplified this apparent paradox in Munster at the time though was soccer: at once a grass-roots game increasingly embedded in many urban communities, it was also a sport with a top tier run as a commercial business enterprise. In Munster, the antagonism between giving over leisure time to being a spectator at Free State League games while also being a participant in the playing and running of clubs, leagues or regional associations could be a drain on the potential success of the game, as either a locally run grass-roots voluntary form of leisure or as a commercial leisure business. This was working- and lower middle-class amateurism in full swing. Here were all the confluences of those British and American ideas which had come in film stock, on the airwaves, on wax discs, and through good old-fashioned print culture, which had made their way into Irish life and been repurposed for the specific situations of each locality across the country and throughout Munster, to create a vibrant, and diverse, social and popular culture of leisure and sport in which those who played soccer would share. The important thing is this: soccer, or any other sport, was just one of a variety of activities in which people engaged during their leisure hours: they read, sang, danced, gambled, shopped and watched; many may have been members of a brass band, a political party, or both. People played too, but it was not the sum total of their persons or their experience of this new commercial world of entertainment. A world moreover into which soccer fit so neatly as something experienced in a multiplicity of ways, from live action to print to moving image. As we will learn in the next chapter, however, not everyone felt such a mixture of influence was to be welcomed in the new independent state.

4

BASE FOOTBALL PLAYERS? SOCCER
AND CONTESTED IDENTITY

*We are daily importing from England not only her manufactured
goods, which we cannot help doing, since she has practically stran-
gled our own manufacturing appliances, but, together with her
fashions, her accent, her vicious literature, her music, her dances,
and her manifold mannerisms, her games also and her pastimes, to
the utter discredit of our own grand national sports, and to the sore
humiliation, as I believe, of every genuine son and daughter of the
old land.*

Thomas Croke, Archbishop of Cashel and Emly, in a letter
to Michael Cusack, 1884, *Freeman's Journal*, 24 December 1884

Probably one of the most famous letters written in the late nineteenth century in Ireland, Archbishop Croke's words of support for
the nascent GAA sum up not only what was for many its role as a
cultural force in Irish life, but also helped to frame the way in which
those who 'imported' English culture were viewed in the public discourse during this period. We have already seen how soccer began to
emerge in Munster from the last years of the 1890s and the
momentum the game picked up among civilians by the outbreak of
the First World War. We have also seen in the previous chapter how
sport was but one more way to enjoy your leisure time alongside
bands, dances, listening to music, reading and cinema-going.

In this chapter we will explore soccer's relationship with Gaelic
games in the province from the point of view of those who felt that
each sport represented in its own way potential visions of the future
of Ireland. Many press commentators saw Gaelic games as the ultimate manifestation of a hoped-for Irish-Ireland, while soccer, and the
new modern 'jazz' music and various other popular cultural outputs
represented not just a continued Anglicisation of Irish culture but
more troublingly for some, a sign of moral decay and emasculation of

the Irish race in the face of greater exposure through mass mediated forms to new popular cultural trends.

The momentum of the pre-war years indicated an evident change in the shape of Munster's sporting landscape – now as well as Gaelic games and rugby having a significant presence, soccer too had its presence and its supporters. But how was the playing of soccer viewed by others in the province? In this chapter we shall explore reactions and responses to the game both before the First World War and following the establishment of the Irish Free State. As the period following the establishment of the Free State saw soccer take off in a manner which those involved pre-war might have only dreamed of a good deal of the chapter will consider this post-independence reception of the game. By then, with soccer played on the streets by young boys as well as in more formal settings, the popularity of the game gave the lie to the notion of soccer as merely a garrison game.

If the military had some role to play in the spread of the game, then as we've already seen in the first chapter, theirs was not the only influence – local people throughout Munster organised and, in the case of Cork, re-organised the game after 1921 just as rugby was organised in small rural towns and villages in the same era. This was problematic to many who wished to see the development of the Irish Free State into an Irish-Ireland free of foreign influence. In the decade that followed the separation of Ireland and Britain politically, there was a battle for dominance of the direction of Ireland, its politics but also its culture. Part of that battle was informed by the rise of soccer as a popular participatory sport, but also as a commercial venture. For many of Ireland's nationalists, this newfound popularity for a game so strongly associated with the British presence was unthinkable. A debate raged in the provincial press, in the committee meeting rooms of GAA clubs, and in the new national chamber, about sport and its role in shaping national identity in the newly independent state.

As a driving force in society, nationalism came into its own in the late nineteenth century.[1] Ireland's nationalism was no exceptional development, but part of an international trend that saw the nation become the basis for statehood on a scale never before seen.[2] Beyond the overtly political sphere, Irish nationalism was marked by a cultural revivalism that saw the formation of the GAA, as well as the Gaelic League, coupled with renewed interest in Irish dance and traditional culture and custom.³ John Hutchinson argues in his work that the aim of cultural nationalism was not to integrate the community and the state but to relocate the moral centre to the historic community instead of the legal rational state, in this case that of the United Kingdom. He argues that as a result of this, cultural nationalism in Ireland arises 'out of a crisis of identity'.⁴

In sport, this crisis of identity manifested itself in the representation of soccer as a garrison game, a foreign import that sapped national spirit and feeling, and the imposition of a ban on playing those games by people who were members of the GAA from 1905 onwards. The ban and particularly, the entrenchment of the position following the failed attempts to remove it in the period 1924–26, was not solely a result of anti-British sentiment following independence. It was of a piece with the general anti-modernisation that characterised late nineteenth-century nationalism throughout Europe, which in its more strident form gave rise to right-wing politics and later fascism. In the Irish case, its emphasis was largely on reviving the Irish language, dance, dress, customs which were largely invented, romantic and idealised versions of Gaelic culture, brought to the public through several mediums. The role of the ban on foreign games was best understood in this broader context of nationalism, invented tradition, and anti-modernism. The extensive public discourse outlined below shows how the imagined Ireland of the late nineteenth-century Gaelic revivalists was threatened by modern popular music, mass commercialism, but most of all by soccer.

For Douglas Hyde, 'the work of the [Gaelic Athletic] association in reviving our ancient national game of *camán*, or hurling, and Gaelic football, has done more for Ireland than all the speeches of politicians for the last five years . . . the physique of our youth has been improved in many of our counties; they have been taught self-restraint, and how to obey their captains; they have been, in many places, weaned from standing idle in their own roads or street corners.'⁵ As R.V. Comerford has noted, however, echoing Hobsbawm's invention of tradition, when talking about Archbishop Croke's railing against foreign influence in Ireland, 'it is important to observe the process of invention at work here. Tennis and cricket were no more foreign than tea-drinking, train engines, rosary beads, the Italianate glory of Croke's cathedral in Thurles, or numerous other things that the archbishop felt no need to renounce.'⁶ Here

Comerford latches on to an important element in the debate that raged in Ireland about foreign influence, especially in the era of independence – that what was 'foreign' was largely that which it was politically expedient to declare as such. Foreign was still shorthand for English.

There is a considerable literature on Irish nationalism, both political and cultural, much of it conflicting about the ideological underpinnings of cultural revivalism and its level of success. What is certain is that a particular conception of 'Irishness' was seized upon, frequently combining an imagined pastoral idyll of the Irish before their corruption by English custom, with notions of Celtic racial purity and strength. Amid the development of such an understanding of Irish identity, sports, without the imprimatur of such revivalists, occupied an unusual place, as did those who played those games. The complex interrelationship between Irish identities and sport has been considered, especially in relation to Northern Ireland.[7] Mike Cronin has also written about the topic and he is of the opinion that soccer had to work 'twice as hard' to prove its nationalist credentials as did the GAA. He also notes that despite initial favour for soccer as an apolitical space, it soon became contentious and very much 'the property of the outsider'.[8]

This, despite the reality Brian Hanley notes when 'even at the highpoint of the independence struggle from 1919–21 there were republicans who either had little interest in the GAA or who followed what [the GAA] considered "foreign" games'.[9] The very survival and even expansion of rugby and soccer in the interwar years reveals a substantial group within Irish society for whom sporting cultural nationalism was anathema. Some defied it; others were apolitical while some simply, actively ignored it. The core point is that there was a large constituency whose cultural and sporting preferences have been occluded by the historiography concerning cultural nationalism.

Hobsbawm acknowledged that 'what has made sport so uniquely effective a medium for inculcating national feelings, at all events for males, is the ease with which even the least political or public individuals can identify with the nation as symbolised by young persons excelling at what practically every man wants, or at one time in his life has wanted, to be good at'.[10] Over the course of this chapter we will examine a number of key issues in the interwar period relating to 'foreign sports' in Ireland. The same period saw Ireland compete for the first time as an independent nation in the Olympic games; it also saw the setting up of Aonach Tailteann, a kind of Irish Olympics that was held in 1924, 1928 and finally in 1932.

A sporting event in the main, Aonach Tailteann was a celebration of literature, art and commerce too.[11] It was a public display of an image of an Irish Ireland; at once highly traditional in its programme of sporting events and pageantry (witness the opening ceremony with Irish wolfhounds), while simultaneously being utterly modern, including as it did speed boat racing among other things. If, as Comerford wryly noted, Croke could enjoy many foreign things from tea to rosary beads, then it seems that the organisers of Aonach Tailteann could stomach foreign sport too if it was sufficiently modern, despite the contradictory nature of such a position given its dim view of a range of sports, including rugby and soccer, and the anti-modern sentiment of the Gaelic revival generally. Louise Ryan notes that 'the case study of Aonach Tailteann illustrates the many complexities and tensions involved in the "revival" or reinvention of national traditions'.[12] The key figure behind its inception, J.J. Walsh, wrote in a letter to sports journalist 'Carbery' in 1948 of why, given his vehement pro-independence political stance, he voted in favour of the Anglo-Irish Treaty:

> Our revolution was a partial one only. Eventually I came to the conclusion that if we included 3/4 million West British cut-throats [sic] that had dominated the Country and claimed they owned 2/3 of it, they would again influence our national policy. The Irish language and all that pertained to it would go by the board. They even boasted that in such circumstances, all efforts at National Culture and everything we have fought through 800 years would be smashed to atoms and swallowed up in the British Empire.
>
> The alternative to that position was partition which would at least give us a chance of [sic] to re-establish our own language, games and culture, and enable us to bide our time, no matter how long, in removing partition by the removal of the partitionists, having utilised their position within the ambit of the 32 counties until such time as we should have established our Irish Culture.[13]

This vision of Walsh's – that a free Irish state would be able to develop fully its own sport and culture – was shared by many and was to him and many others no less realisable for all its heady aspiration.

Such views are borne out in the manner he performed the role of Minister for Posts and Telegraphs, particularly in relation to Aonach Tailteann and programming for 2RN. The key issues around this outlook and how they relate to foreign games, with their special emphasis on rugby and soccer, must be considered as follows: the place of the ban on foreign games in the GAA, the opposition to its continued existence from within that body itself, and the insistence upon maintaining it; the language of race and masculinity that was espoused in both the provincial press and the radical press and the focus on the physical and moral degradation that some insisted came with the playing of rugby and soccer; the views of the members of the Dáil on these issues; the language of 'West Britonism', 'foreignism' 'shoneenism' and the place of all these things attempting to undermine the popularity of rugby and soccer in the new Free State.

Terence Brown has noted that in Ireland, following independence, 'much of social and cultural life was markedly similar to that in the United Kingdom'.[14] He insists 'the policy of Gaelic revival might be pursued in schoolrooms across the country, but the language of daily intercourse in most regions remained English'.[15] Once again, as it had been for Douglas Hyde and Archbishop Croke in the late nineteenth century, the playing field was a hotly contested space of identity; in the new state the contrast was between those who were 'racy of the soil' who played Gaelic games and their modern, and apparently foreign, counterparts who played soccer.

The Ban: battling the new popular pastime of soccer

The ban on foreign games has received some scholarly attention, notably from Paul Rouse. His broad outline of the ban's history is vital to understanding the peculiar history of this rule.[16] But we must ask, how did the ban operate at ground level in Munster during the period when soccer was at its peak and what were people's attitudes towards it? An important point that ought to be noted about the ban is this: generally speaking it was not hugely popular with many within the GAA's membership. The ban, as it came to be enacted after 1905, was driven in part by the experience of the Parnellite split which nearly caused the GAA to collapse in the 1890s. On top of that, as was noted earlier about the playing grounds in Dungarvan, divisions were not so pronounced before, but as McElligott argues convincingly, the GAA was transformed from the playground of, to a player in, the separatist politics of the War of Independence, following a radicalisation of membership post–1916.[17] The focus in the Free State era on the ban by many commentators comes largely as a result of soccer's increased popularity in Ireland in the 1920s, especially its spread and cementing in much of Munster. As a result, it tended to attract the ire of far more commentators in the press than did rugby, which saw some expansion in popularity, particularly in places not known as strongholds of the game.[18] This was a key element of the concern: both sports spread into or were revived in areas not normally associated with them. Soccer was the main target however of the various diatribes launched by a variety of columnists.

The implementation of the ban varied of course and in the universities at least, was not enforced owing to the nature of the environment, or overlooked in the case of local clubs.[19] At the 1928 convention of the Munster Council of the GAA, Dr E. O'Sullivan of Killarney, and head of the Munster Provincial Colleges Council, a subcommittee of the Munster Council, gave a speech to the assembled delegates in which he proposed that 'schools playing foreign games may take part in GAA competition provided the constitution of the teams in the latter competition complied with Rules 12 and 13 [the ban rules]'.[20] Several of the province's colleges refused to accept the ruling – some no doubt because it still imposed the ban and others because it did not impose it sufficiently strictly. Sensible approaches to the ban like that displayed by O'Sullivan and his subcommittee were too often drowned out by the extraordinary invective that could be found in the pages of the provincial press, however little it might have reflected the desires of the greater mass of GAA members.

Ten years earlier, in late July 1918, a special meeting of the Central Council of the GAA was held. Among the topics reported on in the *Nenagh Guardian* was the 'large number of letters received from persons hitherto identified with other forms of sports, especially rugby and soccer, against the "banning" of the national pastimes, asking to be admitted as members, and promising whole-hearted support to the Association in future. It was unanimously decided to accede to the requests, and all such requests are to be made to the secretary of the local County Boards on or before 1 September 1918.'[21]

A common notice for the time but, as we shall see in this section, the place of the ban was not always so secure in convincing people who were against it that the solution should be 'whole-hearted support' for the GAA as it stood currently on this highly contentious issue. Reporting a violent incident after a hurling match between Ballymackey and Ballywilliam in May of 1919 in the *Nenagh Guardian*, the reporter wrote that 'discipline and order must be maintained and whoever sins against good conduct be driven from the society of the decent young manhood of Ireland. In rugby and in soccer, which is practically altogether played by the riff-raff of Irish society, these things do not occur.'[22]

The reporter felt it was an inherent 'sin' of the offender in GAA that was at fault here, and not the players in general themselves, since after all rugby and soccer 'is . . . played by the riff-raff of Irish society'. Such strong views inform the reasons for the continuation of the ban. The North Tipperary GAA only a few short years later seems to be struggling to meet the demands of its fixtures list, and worried about the impact this would have on the popularity of Gaelic sports: `

> Chairman – We must take the matter up at the Convention and decide once and for all whether we will go over. Rugby and Soccer are obtaining a hold on this country, and unless we make a determined stand now we may give up trying to run a GAA in Tipperary.[23]

Clearly the inroads being made by rugby and soccer were being felt, especially in Tipperary. The rallying call from the Chairman of the North County Board would have a way to go before being sure of the safety of the GAA as it stood. The following year, the ban was once again up for discussion at the Convention, where a Mr R. Stapleton said this:

> He played football as hard as any man twenty-two or twenty-three years ago, and they in Clonmel at that time had to contend with three or four rugby clubs. Some of their best Gaelic men, including their captain, were trained by rugbyites. He thought it developed their men and made good footballers of them. In Tipperary there were some of the best men in Ireland at that time. His honest opinion was that if they amended the rule it would open the association to some of the best and leading Irishmen that ever lived.[24]

This is a competing view of masculinity within the new Irish state, one that does not equate foreignness with being necessarily effete, advocating a more tolerant, pluralistic outlook. When the motion that the rule banning the playing of foreign games was put to the Tipperary men, it carried thirty-three votes to twenty-nine against. It was felt they now had a mandate to vote for the deletion of the rule at National Congress. A similar vote against the ban was moved at the Cork County Board Convention.[25] Probably the most significant thing to take away from the speech of Mr Stapleton was that he saw the opening of the GAA as being beneficial to it from a sporting perspective, that there would be a crossover in styles across the football codes that would serve to make the Gaelic code better.

As soccer extended its reach out from Dublin to the provinces and, in 1924, two 'provincial' sides contested the Football Association of the Irish Free State (FAIFS) Cup final for the first time, there was hostility towards the Cork-based team of Fordsons FC. In the pages of Ireland's most popular sporting weekly, *Sport*, there was incredulity that 'a silly idea has gained currency to the effect that the Fordson players are not Irishmen. Every one of them is an Irishman. All of them are local lads with the exception of Buckle, O'Hagan and Miller. I suppose the idea sprang from the astonishment created by a team of Irishmen from the provinces reaching the final of the national senior cup competition after an existence of two years.'[26] The feeling was that these must have been well-versed foreign imports, rather than locally produced players with a high degree of skill and knowledge of the game. Only a month later, the same newspaper reported on that year's Annual Congress of the GAA saying that 'the latest Gaelic congress did not think that "Irish-Ireland" is yet in a position secure and strong enough to throw down all its defences'.[27]

As the new state moved away from the initial elation of victory, through the turmoil of the Civil War, the insistence on holding what it had in sporting terms became ever more important; giving leeway to the 'foreign' games was not an option for many who desired to finally create the nation they saw as the natural development following independence from Britain. Within the GAA, which was split badly by the Civil War, opposition to foreign games may have provided a means to unity for some of its membership. Interestingly, much earlier, and admittedly in a period prior to the rise of the Volunteers in 1913, the Munster Council of the GAA gave the go-ahead to Cobh to use soccer players in a Gaelic football match against Macroom, yet another example of the malleability of these rules.[28] When no such agreement existed of course, the playing of 'illegal' players was hotly disputed, with clubs demanding replays. One such example was a match between O'Briens and Clonakilty in Cork where the secretary of the Clonakilty club laboriously laid out the occasions on which O'Briens' players had flouted the ban, listing who they played for and the teams against whom they played soccer and on what dates these matches took place.[29]

On 26 April 1924 at National Congress, the *Nenagh Guardian* reported that the motion to abolish the ban on foreign games was defeated. It was defeated fifty-four for and thirty-two against. Mr Dennehy of Cork felt that 'the rules . . . were being evaded. If they were to be rigidly enforced, a large number would be rendered illegal players. The season for playing Gaelic games did not coincide with that for others. A number of athletes wanted some form of exercise during the winter months, and the Rules deprived them of that.'[30]

Another man was quoted as saying at the meeting that 'the retention of the rules was, in his opinion, an insult to Gaels'.[31] Such language suggests that the perception of what it meant to be a true Gael in newly independent Ireland was not so rigidly bound to viewing other sports as inherently 'foreign' and, therefore, bad. In Limerick, a member of the Commercials Gaelic Football Club brought a motion before the county board that the ban on foreign games be removed. The Commercials had some players who were also members of the Dalcassian Soccer Club at the time. Mr Lenihan, who was representing the Commercials team, was told by Limerick's county board chairman, W.P. Clifford, that he could not agree with Lenihan's view on the foreign games ban, saying it would allow those who wished, to continue Anglicising Ireland.[32] In 1926, at the Waterford GAA County Board's annual convention, the ban was retained by a slim margin, twenty-two in favour of retaining and sixteen against.[33] Meanwhile, at the annual convention of the Tipperary County Board there was an initial attempt to stymie debate on the issue of the ban, with the Chairman, Mr John Leahy, particularly keen that the debate not take place. A Mr Duhy had this to say regarding the ban, and what lifting it would mean:

> [It] would create a more healthy exercise and tend more to the moral and physical well-being of the Irish race. When the GAA was formed, it was to be non-political and non-sectarian. Some twenty-two years later the ban was brought about. He [a third

party not named elsewhere in quote] had been a member of the GAA and also a player for years before the ban was put on and he knew the conditions that prevailed then. He also knew that the greatest men he ever knew played rugby and soccer football at that time, and he could not see where it interfered with their nationality, and these were as good and true Irishmen as were in that room to-day . . . The crowd that had entered the Association a few years ago were full of patriotism and they wanted to lessen the Gaels who took to the field years ago and made it possible for them to play to-day.[34]

Mr Duhy's feelings about what made a true Gael were not predicated on a narrow definition, as might be expected of someone whose involvement in the GAA stretched back so far. Instead he saw the re-iteration of the GAA as a sporting organisation first and foremost, and one self-consciously 'non-political and non-sectarian'. The army of the new state even weighed in on the issue, with General O'Duffy declaring strongly that he felt the ban should not be repealed. At the same meeting, the President of the GAA, Daniel McCarthy, stated that 'his belief was that the men who now played "foreign" games could not be held as shoneens. A Frenchman was not made a worse Frenchman because he took up Rugby or Soccer – nothing of the sort.'[35] Such a note of conciliation from the Association's President was not heeded by many, with one particularly vehement outburst reprinted in the *Southern Star* under the heading 'Lame Excuses' in 1925 remarking that 'surely, if the GAA that has lived and fought down all the foes that have tried to sap its principles and undermining its mission for the past forty years, is now recruited from a stock of degenerated Gaels . . . it would be about time that the obituary notice of the GAA were written'.[36] For the GAA-only weekly newspaper *The Gaelic Athlete*, the prospect of the 'ban' being up for discussion at National Congress in 1925 was not one to be welcomed. Their edi-torial line was perhaps predictably not in favour of its repeal:

Some of the men who are to-day either consciously or uncon-sciously trying to Imperialise the Association could much better employ their energies in working inside the organisation for its development and perfection. The Association exists to-day because these rival sporting organisations utterly failed, after continuous and bitter opposition to wipe it out. These rival games were founded to propagate foreign sports in Ireland to the detriment of national pastimes and national aspiration, and because of these qualifications they were used for all they were worth – and a great deal more – to subvert the games, pastimes and ideals which were racy to the soil.[37]

Similarly, just as the GAA's Annual Congress was about to take place, the same paper's editorial that Saturday stated:

> The devotees of Rugby, Soccer etc. have no wish to encourage Gaelic football in Ireland; they prefer exotic imitation and if the preservation of hurling and Gaelic football depended upon them then these games would be long since as dead as the dodo. We have nothing but admiration for the Englishman who developed the game of Rugby College and the Soccer code to their present attractiveness and influence. These are the games of the Englishman and the Englishman is perfectly right to keep them foremost as the games of England, but also as the games of his Empire.[38]

In the eyes of that author, Ireland was no longer a part of the British Empire and therefore had no more need for the games of that empire. Mr Duhy is to be found making life difficult for the Tipperary GAA once more late in the summer of 1926. This time a player, a G. Casey from the Templemore club, was looking for re-instatement to the GAA after being barred for taking part in foreign games. His ban stretched back to October 1925. Mr Duhy became engaged in an argument with the chairman, saying that there was much talk of 'the advisability of keeping it on [foreign games] and some of these [GAA members] had been at several rugby and soccer matches'. The chairman dismissed this as idle gossip without proof, which he asked Duhy to produce. Duhy said that 'if everybody who witnessed these matches was to be debarred from the GAA, then your GAA would be very small'. Mr T. Ryan weighed in behind Duhy commenting that 'it is rather strange that most of these applications do not come in until the soccer or rugby season is nearly over'.[39] Carbery noted in an article in 1926, when the ban came under serious discussion at that year's Annual Congress in Dublin:

> Arguments for and against 'the ban' were seriously and lucidly argued. Messrs. Fleming and Beckett (Cork) led their respective camps, and the conversative [sic] idea once more won. When everything is said and done, we are very much against 'new departures' in Ireland, much as we are written and spoken of to the contrary . . . The Munster men were at great strength. Indeed, soft Southern accents dominated the debates. The crisp

Easter and sharp Northern speech to get little space [sic] from those effusive and enthusiastic Cuige-Mumhain men. The proceedings ran late into the night.[40]

Tipperary was not alone in dealing with reinstatements. At a meeting of the Waterford GAA board in 1929, two men applied for reinstatement. One was admitted and the other was not. The one who was refused was Jason Morrissey, whose expulsion resulted from playing foreign games, in this case soccer. He stated that he had to play the match or else he would be fired by his employer. As he put it, 'Portlaw were playing the toffs.'[41] However, this was not sufficient to see him re-instated. A week later a letter from the Portlaw AFC stated that 'members of the Portlaw AFC are at liberty to play any game they wish and, to our knowledge, are not compelled by any employer in this district to play foreign games through fear of loss of employment'.[42] Realistic attitudes of this kind were not shared by everyone, even outside of the GAA. At a concert in early 1928, for example, a Fr O'Flynn implored 'do good to yourself and to your fellow man, work for the perfection of another especially in culture. Support your own games. Don't mind the skulker and miserable kind of fellow who says, "There's no game like Soccer", "No game like Rugby" – in fact, "No game like the game that is my own". Be men. The skulking slave spirit has got into our people – that is the reason for slavishly following foreign games and customs. Let us be strongly national – that is not bigotry.'[43]

Such talk clearly still drew an audience and had many supporters; what we have seen above from Duhy and many others is that within the GAA and among its ordinary playing members, the identification with being nationalist was not necessarily tied up any longer with playing the 'national' games over the 'foreign' ones. Evidently both soccer and rugby, since they are the most frequently cited, were the main benefactors from this shift in identifying games as being more nationalistic than others. In an article entitled 'Irish Dances; Irish Games' the author tells us that 'foreign games are not by any means as unhealthy as foreign dances, but foreign games create a foreign atmosphere, and while the struggle for supremacy is going on between our own Gaelic culture and foreignism we cannot afford the luxury of propagating anything foreign'.[44] A similar attack is to be found in the *Southern Star* on 5 June 1926 with an article stating that 'There is grave danger of a big land-slide towards West Britonism as exemplified by the Jazz-Soccer-Golfstick mentality which is on the increase in this country today.' Such insecurity seems misplaced when contrasted with an extract from an article in the same paper earlier in the summer which stated that 'Soccer, which had a great run for a few years, is practically dead in Tipperary towns.'[45]

In 1929, the *Nenagh Guardian* re-printed an article from the Dublin-based *Star*. The article was written by a 'prominent Irish-Irelander' who went by the name of 'K.O.' The *Guardian* printed it to hear the views of its own readers on the situation, since clearly the battle over this, outlined above, was of great public interest to the people of Tipperary. Talking about the good sense of initially inventing Gaelic football, he felt as 'a compromise between rugby and soccer, it is perhaps, as a game as good as either'. For him 'its great fault is that no one plays it except members. The GAA are not allowed to play . . . any other kind of football, or even associate with those who do in other branches of athletics.' The 'bad results of this exclusiveness were perhaps compensated for in the pre-Treaty days by the definite barrier it established against the RIC and the British Army'.

Continuing on to say that another result of the GAA's inward policy had been that our two main national games were no use on the European stage, he instead argued not just for a repeal of the ban, but for the widespread adoption of rugby as a national game:

> We should lose absolutely nothing at all by removing the ban on 'foreign' games, or, in fact, by going further and adopting rugby as our own, and we should gain enormously in international pres-tige . . . We must learn to distinguish between the national and the narrowly parochial before Ireland can take her proper place in the growing communion of inter-European civilisation.[46]

In the same period, 'Moltóir' of the *Munster Express* saw it as an issue of the GAA not being allowed to govern itself, saying that '[rugby and soccer associations] are at liberty to run their respective games on their own lines and to shape their rules and regulations as they deem advisable. While claiming these advantages for themselves, our opponents in effect say the GAA should be restricted . . .'[47]

Yet another similar letter was written by someone under the name 'An t-iomanuidh' in the *Nenagh Guardian*. This along with the letter of 'K.O.' clearly sparked the debate the editors of the Nenagh paper were looking for. In a letter with the headline 'This

Ban, That Ban and Bans in General' in November of 1929, one reader had this to say:

> Personally, I believe that 75 per cent of those who play rugby do so because they like it, just as the majority of those who jazz do so because, they too, like it, not because it is danced in London . . . That 75 per cent don't care a jot under whose control they are, given that they get matches and the excitement of the game.[48]

Regarding the GAA's willingness to accept tennis and golf, because of their inclusion in the Aonach Tailteann and because they were not team games, the author of the letter wrote that 'the atmosphere surrounding tennis and golf was never too redolent of advanced Nationalism . . . if you can nationalise the atmosphere of golf and tennis, why, in the name of common sense, can't you do likewise with the others'.

The author seemed incredulous at the apparent hypocrisy of the GAA and its ban. An argument can be made too that, because these games were solidly middle and upper middle class, they were of little concern to the GAA. The other ban which perplexed the author was that ban recently issued by the IRFU with regard to playing rugby on a Sunday. This time the letter writer contends that '. . . both this ban and the GAA ban, rightly or wrongly, have the same aim – the creation of a certain atmosphere around that particular game'. He wonders would it not be a 'merciful change that as a result of this attempted ban of Sunday rugby, we raised the standard of revolt by taking rugby and those other ostracised games into the happy family'.[49] Such voices for conciliation and amalgamation were few and far between, however. Evidently, from the end of the First World War up to the beginning of the 1930s, even though the GAA's rules were steadfast, the application of them had indeed become loose, honoured more in the breach than the observance, through the reinstatements we have seen and the open opposition among many in the Tipperary and other GAA boards regarding the usefulness of the ban.

The consistent and strong-worded attacks on soccer and rugby indicate the popularity of the games in the county; also that some within the GAA chose to use the ban as a means to maintain a foothold on the grass roots of Irish sport in the face of soccer's growing popularity. This is hardly surprising when one looks particularly at the growing strength of soccer in these years, which will be done in the chapters that follow.

Soccer in Cork for example had some thirty-nine clubs by 1926, a tremendous number considering it was in a parlous state not too long before. Waterford had a similarly large number of clubs in the period, around fifteen or twenty, and while there were only seventeen GAA clubs in east Waterford in 1926, it grew to thirty the following year, suggesting a real battle was on between hurling and soccer in Waterford city and its hinterland. This is a further reiteration of the fact that the battle ground in which the new war for cultural dominion was being fought was in the urban areas and less so in the rural areas. In large part this may be due to the fluidity of urban life, where mobility was more likely than in the rural context.

The debate about foreign games was not confined to just the newspapers and the GAA conventions. In the Dáil, during the debates on the Finance Bill in June 1930, it was also an issue. In the Finance Act of 1927, section 8 contained an exemption from income tax for organisations which supported Gaelic games. In 1930, it was asked that this be amended to include all sports, since it was seen to be giving unfair advantage to the GAA otherwise. One deputy stated that:

> I desire to support this amendment moved by Deputy O'Connell. I do so in the interests of sport generally and of health. I think that when there is an unfortunate spirit evident in some parts of the country to more or less break up sport and divide various forms of sport by barriers that it would be decidedly unfortunate if the Parliament operating for all the people, in the interests of all the people, were to discriminate in favour of some sections of athletics and against others. The carrying of this amendment does not in any way worsen the position of Gaelic football.[50]

The amendment was defeated but not before there was a serious debate about whether the GAA's role in promoting a national identity was sufficient to offer it an exemption. Although the deputies who debated it were at pains to distance themselves from linking one's sense of patriotism from the games one played, there was a strong indicator that the GAA deserved a special exemption. Soccer's professionalism was seen to be against it:

> Let us consider soccer. The one objection I have to the soccer game is the spirit of pure professionalism which is extending wherever it is played throughout the Twenty-Six Counties. When a game becomes a business, then I think that game, and

those who govern it and make a livelihood out of governing it, should pay income tax in the same way as any person deriving an income from any other occupation. Therefore, prima facie, so far as the Association game is concerned, I do not think, in view of the spirit of professionalism with which it is imbued, that any case could be made for its exclusion.[51]

Deputy MacEntee felt that rugby's access to a wealthy patronage stood in its favour:

Take the case of Rugby. There, again, the great majority of clubs are well established, in wealthy circumstances and well able to pay out of the revenue they enjoy from the game. There is no man debarred from playing Rugby by virtue of the tax imposed, but certainly the clubs should surrender some part of the profits which they derive from the public, and not all of which are used, in the Twenty-Six Counties, at any rate, to advance Rugby merely as a sport.[52]

Others saw it as an issue of class, with Deputy O'Higgins saying, 'it merely, to a very slight extent, betters the position of other forms of football and we cannot forget, particularly members who have any association with the City, that the very poorest people in our cities are followers of Association football, that possibly the brightest couple of hours or the only bright couple of hours, that they have in the whole week are when they get off on Saturday afternoon to see an Association football match'.[53]

After independence, people no longer felt they were hurting the national cause by playing games that were not 'national'. For some in the GAA there was probably a surprise at the suddenness in people's willingness to tolerate non-Irish sporting endeavours. Indeed the popularity of soccer in this period in Cork and Waterford, as well as Tipperary, may well have caught many in the GAA by surprise. From the Dáil chamber we see that the commercialism of soccer and the presumption that rugby clubs are 'in wealthy circumstances' was held against them.

Challenged by the rising popularity of soccer just after independence, there would be a fight on the hands of those in the GAA for whom its primacy was paramount. It also indicated for those who desired to see an Irish-Ireland come in to being that it would not be won easily, and that there would be a strong challenge to meet. It further points to a deep anxiety and insecurity among many who, having secured political independence, found much Anglophone culture which was far less easy to extirpate. The GAA's ban on 'foreign dances' as well as 'foreign games' occasionally saw from members of the Association very bizarre diatribes. A quote from the *Nenagh Guardian* in the late 1920s will be sufficient to show the disdain in which jazz was held by some members of the GAA in the country. At a public lecture, a 'Mr J. Cawley (BL) said that 'the leanest time in Ireland's athletic achievements followed the Great War' and that he had 'little hesitation in putting down the first cause to jazz life and its concomitants'.[54]

This supposedly corrupting influence – which was according to some both morally and physically debilitating – was lumped in with the degenerative effects of playing foreign sports. There is an under-lying accusation that engagement in these activities was essentially effete and un-masculine. The ultimate aim of the ban rule would be to strangle the playing of non-Irish games. The difficulty arises that, much as the GAA might have liked, these games could not be outlawed outright. As a result, they were left over from pre-Independence, an undesirable cultural residue that had sufficient remaining voluntary support after British withdrawal that could not be totally eradicated. They had to be stifled in as strong a way as pos-sible instead. This nationalist cultural revolution was not left solely to the GAA and its ban. The Finance Act of 1927 and the defeated amendment of 1930 show a clear support for the GAA even if not in an explicitly anti-foreign games fashion. Ernest Blythe, Minister for Finance during the debate, had this to say: 'I do not agree, of course, with the point of view that would make adherence to these games an article of faith or would brand a person who played another game as being a bad Irishman or anything of that sort.' In later years the intro-duction of the 1935 Public Dance Halls Act would see a prohibition on foreign dancing and dances that were not strictly under the control of some organisation. A concerted attack on the newly popular foreign games seemed to come from many corners of the Irish press throughout the 1920s; to this we will next turn our attention.

Political Newspapers and the Language of Race

Away from the chambers of the Dáil, the increasing popularity of soccer particularly was noticed in the press of radical nationalism and was especially to raise the ire of the Gaelic games correspondent for *An Phoblacht*, 'Mutius'. From 1925 right through 1926, the journalist writing under this name used his column frequently to launch invectives against the 'emasculation' and 'decadence of spirit' that he saw as prevalent in Ireland as a result of a turning away from Gaelic games in the new Free State. As Louise Ryan notes of the gendered symbolism of Aonach Tailteann, 'the Irish race is . . . not only constructed as distinct, unique and ancient but also as masculine'.[56] Of course, for 'Mutius' writing in *An Phoblacht* this betrayal of our distinct and masculine culture was simply a part of the wider betrayal of public acceptance of the Free State over a thirty-two-country Republic. In the very first issue of the new *An Phoblacht* 'Mutius' quotes William Rooney:

> It is the mongrel spirit of the sycophant that despises its own, and servilely and soullessly imitates the fashions and fads of the foreigner. No nation ever yet rose to power and influence by any way other than the development of its own genius, characteristics, and resources.[57]

Republicanism and soccer were not necessarily utterly estranged, however. Brennan has shown that links between the two were occasionally quite strong in some settings. He writes:

> The presence of so many different sports in the programme was only limited by the exclusion of sports subject to 'The Ban' by the GAA; soccer, rugby, cricket and hockey. The irony here was that 'English' sports, especially soccer, were also sometimes used as vehicles of Irish nationalist identity. Republican Todd Andrews recalled that soccer was the most popular sport for anti-Treaty internees in the Curragh camp after the Civil War. The O/C of the Anti-Treaty IRA in Dublin, Oscar Traynor, was a professional soccer player and had toured Europe as the goalkeeper of Belfast Celtic. He later became President of the Football Association of Ireland and served as a minister in numerous Fianna Fáil administrations.[58]

Such credentials were used, notably in the *Football Sports Weekly*, to insist that soccer was no impediment to nationalism – something followers of the game clearly felt, even if some commentators in the provincial press did not. The resource to which 'Mutius' most often turns is hurling, of which he insisted 'the best of modern games can be mustered by the physically fit by practice – hurling requires some "afflatus" that is begotten only of inheritance and inspired only by Fianna ideals'.[59] Nonetheless, those who espoused republican ideals, wore the Easter Lily but played soccer were still decried by some as not truly being Irish, as was the case in Waterford in 1935 during the county convention there.[60]

By framing things this way, 'Mutius' makes the suggestion that one's playing of soccer or rugby can be learned and is something one imitates, but hurling is something that is inimitable, accessible to those 'inspired only by Fianna ideals'. There is a striving for purity in this language and this purity is not possible with the contamination of foreign games. When reporting on matches, the language of vigorous but fair play, of true Gaelic virtue, can also be seen. Take this example from a match between Cork and Tipperary in a junior hurling final where we are told that 'there was something like ten thousand people at the matches, which was good for the Munster Council and inspiriting for those who hold that native games have lost none of their appeal to Gaels. The contests were played and applauded in a manner worthy of the reputations [of Munster]'. They lost nothing by being clean and vigorous, keen and earnest.'[61]

Using words like clean, vigorous, keen and earnest, suggested two things; first that the game was played in a manner that was moral in its spirit and competitive; secondly, its vigour and keenness suggest it was physically tough and thus played to a masculine tempo that did not shy away from hard playing. Of course, this kind of masculine idealising is just as prevalent in Munster rugby's self-perception of itself as a tough and vigorous brand of rugby.[62] In its way, the above quote is a conflation and reusing of the concept *mens sana in corpora sano* now being applied, not just as being muscular and Christian, but nationalist and republican. By the end of 1925, 'Mutius' felt the GAA were to be excoriated for their lackadaisical attitude toward the increasing West Britonism of their organisation, fearing that 'the foundation purpose of the GAA – the promotion of native pastimes' for Ireland's good – has been jettisoned, and it will only be a little while till even the remnants of Gaelic character which the Association possesses, follow'.[63] The New Year appeared equally bleak to 'Mutius', who wrote that 'a new calendar never brings a change of responsibilities. Duties take no heed of passing years. The instincts of true manhood remain inviolate through all changes of time and clime . . . Is it not possible, also, that for Gaels, individually and collectively, the times call for alertness of mind and firmness of purpose.'[64]

His views are expanded upon the following week, leaving us in no doubt how he feels about the membership of the GAA, of whom he says 'if the GAA submits to racial emasculation, it will be the result of the supineness which is being so heartily denounced and so docilely tolerated. Anything is better than sham and self-delusion; and if hurlers and footballers lean towards the enlightened customs and melt to the clemency and pretended self-ostracism of English influ-ence in Ireland, let them do it openly, not covertly, as now. When the choice comes between embracing alienism and smashing the Association, they will not hesitate to be wreckers'.[65] In February of 1926, 'Mutius' continues his tirade against what he sees as a 'pacified Irishry' which displays what can be best described as the slave spirit, when he writes that:

> 'Rugby and Soccer', says another 'are played all over the world.' Even were this so, were they played in also in a score of the nearest planets it would be no reason for their encouragement here. But they are not. Outside 'Mother England' these games are cultivated only where the Colonial mind prevails, and else-where by little coteries of Anglo-maniacs only . . . The only consistent side the advocates of secession show is their abject devotion to the aim of Anglicisation.[66]

The language that 'Mutius' applies to the GAA as an organisation and body, their 'supineness' – elsewhere he calls them the 'apostles of apostasy' – indicates his feelings that the effect of the acceptance of the Free State, which he describes as 'dope', has been to hasten a racial and masculine decline of the Irish stock that would have been inconceivable had the Irish people, and especially Irish men, remained loyal to the notions of Irish republicanism that the paper he wrote for promoted. By comparison, another radical newspaper of the 1920s, this time James Larkin's revived *Irish Worker*, took rather a different view to the dim one offered by 'Mutius' in *An Phoblacht*. Throughout its pages in the same period, soccer is not excoriated for its deleterious effect upon the male population of Dublin or Ireland; instead there is an active attempt in the pages of the paper to involve soccer and soccer clubs, as well as GAA clubs, in the lives of the Irish working class. An attempt is made to get Shelbourne FC to host a benefit match in aid of the striking dock workers in 1923.[67] This is an acknowledgment, like that of Deputy O'Higgins above, of soccer as not merely a game that is contemptible for its Britishness but also for its popularity among an urban working class in Ireland. As we will see in greater detail when looking at Fordsons FC in Cork, the game's ties with industrial Ireland rather than a rural, Gaelicised Ireland was problematic for many. More than a sign of Britishness, it was a sign of an emergent global economy, a sign of modernity.

The language 'Mutius' employed was not confined to papers that wore their political colours strongly on their sleeves. In many of the provincial papers already quoted, terms such as 'West Britonism', 'Shoneenism' and the wider lexicon of cultural nationalism were equally prevalent. Thus, for these commentators, one's choice of sport was not merely an engagement with something you enjoyed but was instead at the core of your conception of your national identity. For many such commentators, there could be no making your own of rugby or soccer. A letter appeared in the *Irish Independent* in 1930 which makes explicit the link made by many regarding being a 'Rugbyite' or a 'Soccerite' and ideas of 'shoneenism'. The letter, written under the pseudonym 'Soccerates', is quoted below in full:

> Sir – In the *Irish Independent* of 10th. Inst. I read where Ald. Corish, TD refers to the Rugbyites and Soccerites as the 'Shoneens of Ireland'. I am a Soccerite and the remark amuses me, and I am prompted to ask boldly if the able representative for Wexford knows what he is talking about. As I have more regard for the usefulness of facts than for the usefulness of wild, sweeping statements, I will recount an experience I have lately had, which may open the optic of the innocent and esteemed alderman.
>
> Some Sundays ago I went to a dance, held under the auspices of a club which is a branch of the GAA. There was a band of four, and the music was ragtime. There was a gathering of some sixty couples, and they were all very proficient in the wraith-like contortions of the fox-trot, one-step etc.
>
> At length an Irish dance was announced – the 'Siege of Ennis'; the band struck up appropriate music and the MC asked those assembled 'to take to the floor' and dance. But not a single person in the hall got up for that Irish dance. The band played; there was no response, and at length the music was changed into a tear-ahead one-step. Practically everyone then got up, and so the 'Siege' was a failure and 'Ennis' fell. I am afraid the Alderman must now give me a definite definition of the word 'Shoneen'.

I could further acquaint the Alderman with how Soccer has helped the poor of Dublin, and has willingly helped other such worthy institutions, by the organisation of charity matches, but I am assured that the consensus of public opinion is against the application of the title 'Shoneen' to Soccer. I will conclude, satisfied that Ald. Corish TD is more learned now than he was before.[68]

Here we see 'Soccerates' pointing out much of the obvious hypocrisy of the ban and its distinct lack of understanding of public desire in the new Free State. *The Star* was a political newspaper that acted as a mouthpiece for Cumann na nGaedheal, and its often conservative outlook shared more with *An Phoblacht* where Gaelicism and sport were concerned than its readers might have liked. In an article headed 'Gaelic Games Losing Ground!' in January of 1929, a major point of concern for the function of GAA clubs is honed in on where the author argues that a 'Gaelic club is really a misnomer. The members turn out in a match when called upon; but in no other sense do they constitute a club. Not one Gaelic club in a hundred engages in any social activity except, perhaps, to hold foreign dances to fill the club's coffers; not one in a hundred owns playing grounds as most of the more important Rugby and Association clubs do.'[69]

An interesting point was being raised in the article. For a sports club to thrive, ultimately it must show itself to be more than merely a sports club, but also a place of conviviality and community. It seems unusual to think of GAA clubs as failing in this particular regard, but yet it was a failing evidently felt: the article also says that a Gaelic club 'is kept alive by one man or two'.[70] Where *The Star* differs quite strongly from *An Phoblacht* and 'Mutius' in particular is in the views the paper expressed on the ban on foreign games. 'Padraig' writing in the paper's 'Playing the Game' column notes that 'the one thing generally overlooked in the discussions is that those out for the repeal of these rules are not concerned for the progress of the foreign games; their concern, like those who stand by the rules, is solely the welfare of the GAA'.[71]

In another article in *The Star* later that year 'Life-long Gael' wrote about his expectation that the ban should remain in place; he describes it as 'senseless' but proposes instead that the game of Gaelic football should be replaced by rugby in order that an international element be allowed to exist in the GAA. He writes of having been on the tour to Belgium in 1910 – organised by J.J. Walsh as part of the Pan-Celtic Congress – and what little effect it had in spreading Gaelic games. This outlook was likely to carry little real currency within the GAA, since the impetus for the article – the 43,000 who attended the recent final between Kerry and Kildare – would suggest a healthy state of affairs to most in the organisation.[72] Indeed such an outlook and such a proposal could have only furthered the feeling within the GAA and given voice in public through articles like those of 'Mutius' that the opposite of what 'Padraig' wrote was the truth: that those opposed to the ban were less interested in advancing the foreign games than protecting the GAA.

The Provincial Press and Shoneenism

So how were these views expressed at a local level in the province of Munster? Moving on to examples of this language of 'West Britonism', 'foreignism' and so on, the local newspapers serving much of Munster abounded in a more restrained version of the language to be found in *An Phoblacht*. Take this example from the *Nenagh Guardian*, from a report on the Clare GAA convention and the foreign games ban when someone from Kilrush 'said that the object of the ban was to keep the young manhood of Ireland away from the Saxon and the shoneen'.[73] A decade previously an article on 'Our ancient game of Hurling' had said that 'it's [sic] milk-and-water imitations are good enough for the physically defective, or those who love to ape the customs of the Sasannach or who prefer the atmosphere of the Shoneen and the place beggar'.[74] The diluted 'milk-and-water' imitations refer specifically to hockey most likely, though the sentiment is equally applicable to the rugby and association codes of football, about to begin their new ascent. A few years earlier, in his manual *How to Play Gaelic Football*, published in 1914, multiple All-Ireland-winning Kerry captain Dick Fitzgerald writes of other football codes that 'Everyone knows that the tendency of outdoor games of the present day is to reduce the individual player to the level of a mere automaton. How dry is the description one often gets of those great matches, in which perfect combination is the only thing commended! In them there is no hero – no great individual standing out from the whole field.'[75]

Fitzgerald even posits the argument in favour of playing Gaelic football by insisting that 'Gaelic football is what may be called a natural football game'. He continues on to say that 'Truly there is no artificiality about our game. There is no such thing as the artificial "forward", "off-side" "knock-on" &c. rules, hedging the player about in all his movements.'[76] One writer in the *Nenagh Guardian* is certain that the GAA must not be complacent in promoting Irish games in the new state, for 'unless those associated with the GAA are alive to the necessity for keeping a firm grip on the feeling of the country, there is every danger of a grave setback for our national games. A lot of specious propaganda is abroad at present; that one game is as good as another; that good Irishmen play foreign games and so on.'[77]

It should be noted, by the way, that the verb 'to ape' is no mistake, and appears elsewhere in similarly themed articles in the same newspaper. For instance, in 'Finnerty Talks' in 1924 we are told 'Shoneenism is thriving mightily. There seems to be something irresistible in the smell of a shoneen. With all our Irish teaching, we are growing less Irish. We are aping and imitating the so-called "superior people".'[78] Here in the first quarter of the twentieth century we see a language and imagery used against the Irish by many British cartoonists reverted and recycled in an attempt to encourage a wariness of seductive shoneenism, lest we fulfil these cartoonish stereotypes. To make the point more explicit we have this quote from the *Southern Star* in 1928, where it is said that 'It is true that Seoinin Irish Catholics and Protestants have their inferiority complex, those children of tyrants who disguise their nationality and are always kowtowing to the English garrison and aping English ways, propagating English games and dances that come to us from darkest Africa in England.'[79]

A fear of slavishness is particularly prevalent in this language too. From the *Nenagh Guardian* once again, this time in 1924, we see 'our national games and native customs are despised by those who are nothing, but want to be something. Cheek, clothes and accent (of a kind) pass current as good breeding . . . the fact is that all the shackles of slavery have not yet been got rid of – hence the servile herd of imitators.'[80] In the *Southern Star* in 1925, we are informed that 'the slave mind has not been completely eradicated. We find persons with good blood in their veins running and racing after, and toadying to the sham and mushroom "grandality".'[81] *Football Sports Weekly* insisted that the popularity of the game must give these commentators some pause for thought, insisting on one occasion that 'the crowd at the Drumcondra-Fordson match must give these people a rude awakening – and this in Rebel Cork'.[82] The journalist goes on to mock the thinking of the game's detractors, saying he is 'surprised that on their methods of reasoning they dare allow and [sic] Olympic team out of the country. To what awful temptation these poor innocent Irish boys will be subject! I would [sic] be surprised if they returned semi-Bolshevik.'[83] When the Munster Football Association petitioned Cork City Council about the possibility of erecting an advertising hoarding in order to help cover the costs of maintaining the ground, objections were raised on the basis that the advertisements may not have been of Irish-made goods, or worse, 'the display of indecent fixtures'.[84]

In Waterford, in late November 1930, when the city's premier club had just begun its first season of Free State League soccer, a streamer was run along the bridge into the city which read 'Irish games for Irishmen. No importations. No ex-Black and Tans'.[85] Meanwhile, a report of Gaelic games by 'Thomond' in the *Limerick Leader* in August 1932 wrote of how rarely 'we have occurrences that take from our games' saying that on the rare occasions when these things do happen, it is the shoneen who jumps on such instances, and for that reason alone, 'Thomond' suggests, young players shouldn't engage in foul play that would give shoneens ammunition.[86] Back in February, 1932, Limerick had been host to that year's annual convention of the Munster Council of the GAA. The chairman of the council in his speech had noted the arrival of professional soccer teams 'dumped upon the cities' in order 'to carry on foreign games', a sentiment those who displayed the banner in Waterford will no doubt have agreed with.[87] Despite this, Limerick, of all the counties of Munster, with its strong tradition of junior rugby, saw many more sensible views, often with less sharp division, prevailing on the question of the ban on foreign games. Surveying what we have seen thus far, it is quite evident that those writing in these newspapers saw a real threat from soccer's increasing popularity. Evidently, they were worried that a complacency had set in among the Irish population with regard to maintaining an outlook commensurate with nationalist politics and ideology. In a humorous article on the introduction of the electric hare to greyhound racing, a journalist writing for the *Nenagh Guardian* stresses:

. . . we have no doubt that in time greyhound racing will be denounced as a cause of national degeneration as fiercely as were in the past such unmanly pursuits as cycling, roller-skating and professional football. Fortunately the public goes its own way in these things, and the electric hare has as little to fear from its critics as the greyhounds it eludes so easily.[88]

This is a crucial point. For all these concerted campaigns on foreign games conducted in the press, they did not act as preventatives. Not everyone was convinced of the arguments made against soccer, other sports, or foreign dances for that matter, in the newspapers – despite the sheer volume of them. The author of 'Dungarvan notes' for the *Munster Express* in 1929 lamented the moving of the rugby players from the Gaelic pitch, recalling there was a time when 'differences were not so pronounced as now, when cricket, rounders, and even rugby were played in the Gaelic field'. For our author, 'however one may incline to one side or the other, it must be said that all the games are excellent physical exercise and have the beneficial tendency to promote muscular development and the attributes of health'.[89] There is a key lesson to be drawn here about the gap between the commentators in the press and the reader of the paper. People, we have seen already with soccer and plenty of other entertainment, went their own way in these things. For a sizeable minority of the GAA's membership in this period, these rules were anathema.

Mike Cronin has argued that 'historians who have explored the emergence and growing popularity of the GAA have always examined the Association through the medium of political upheaval, emergent nationalism and state building. As a result, a consensus history has emerged that places the GAA at the heart of Irish nationalism, thereby instilling the game with a definite and specific identity.'[90] By comparison both rugby and soccer have been occluded from the conversation about cultural life in Ireland at this time. Of course, as is evidenced by much of the push here by the GAA's own membership to rid themselves of the ban – after all only they could insist on it – the narrowness that prevailed in the words of many commentators was not necessarily reflective of the great body of GAA members; it must also be acknowledged of course that the GAA was hugely popular at this time in Munster, with crowds at peak levels in the body's history – in such a large mass of support, an overzealous and vocal fringe was bound to present itself.[91] In a strong period for Cork, they won All-Ireland hurling titles in 1926, 1928 and 1929. For Tipperary meanwhile there were All-Ireland successes in 1925 and 1930. At junior level in the period 1923–30, Tipperary won three All-Irelands, Cork won one and Waterford won in 1931; finally at minor level, from its inauguration in 1928, the All-Ireland was won successively by Cork, Waterford and Tipperary to 1930. The attitude of the Munster Council of the GAA in the period when soccer was emerging as a strong force in places like Limerick and Waterford is telling in its own right, however. When the council decided to pay grants in 1928 to each of the province's six counties, it is worth noting that both Limerick and Waterford – two counties where, in the urban areas, sports other than Gaelic games were strong – were given £50 each in contrast to the £25 received by the other four counties, where the GAA was much stronger. This was followed in Waterford with another grant of £50 that December and the annual convention of the Munster Council was held in Waterford in March 1930. By the end of 1931, another £125 had been given to the Waterford County Board in an attempt to encourage the GAA there. All of this can be seen as an attempt by the GAA not only to improve its own standing, but also, in a city like Waterford where soccer had gained such a foothold, to ensure the Gaelic games thrived.[92]

Yet, soccer (along with rugby) had the unique ability to represent the nation at large in international competition, representing the new Irish Free State first at the Paris Olympics in 1924, and then in their first international against Italy in 1926. This marks them out from the GAA in terms of representing the nation, and as expressions of nationhood. Their use of their Irish name on official correspondence, *Cumann Peil Saorstát Éireann*, was an indication too of how they viewed themselves.

Sport then was a central part of the debate about how Irish identity in a post-independence setting was to be constructed. The focus of such discussions to date have largely been in relation to the Gaelic revival and the literary arts, although it should be clear by now that the same issues affected the conversation around sport. P.J. Mathews has written that 'any student of Irish cultural history will be aware that the first decade of the twentieth century was marked by an intense and at times heated debate over attempts to define the essential nature of Irish identity. Interestingly enough, it was in the theatre that the debate became most animated, as objections to plays . . . bubbled to the surface.'[93] He notes that, 'clearly, the various cultural disputes which surrounded the inaugural production of the Irish Literary Theatre . . . were symptomatic of a wider contest beginning to erupt within nationalist Ireland over who should do the constructing'.[94]

Indeed, as literary critic Declan Kiberd has written, 'there was, if anything, less freedom in post-independence Ireland, for the reason that the previous attempt to arraign the enemy without gave way to a new campaign against the heretic within'.[95] Soccer was one such heretical practice in the eyes of many press commentators. Likewise, we see that, post-independence, the site of this debate is not just taking place in the theatre, but in the club committee room, in the newspapers and on the field of play as well; the heretic within did not just wish to watch foreign films or read foreign books but also to play foreign games. Liam O'Callaghan, writing about rugby in Munster, notes that 'the reality on the ground . . . was much more fluid and localised than the propagandised perception promoted by the GAA allowed'.[96] So too was it the case for soccer. What much of the language deconstructed here shows is a kind of language of race, masculinity, athleticism and morality that was present in a whole range of discourses, not just in Ireland or Britain, but throughout Europe. It was a language discourse that had developed in the nineteenth century which sought to classify different races in hierarchical terms. All the evidence suggests that the cultural habitat for the 'foreign' game of soccer was, if anything, expanding in independent Ireland during the interwar years, despite their denouncement by those holding Irish–Ireland viewpoints. As we've seen in Chapter Three, people had become exposed – thanks to a variety of media and a new commercialised leisure culture – to a whole world of popular culture and sport. In such a climate, the polemical stance of many writing in the newspapers during the 1920s and 1930s was always likely to be a loud but ineffectual voice of opposition, especially in those urban centres where soccer was able to gain a foothold. The chapters that follow will tell the story of soccer in those parts of Munster where it took a foothold and became a significant part of many people's leisure hours.

5

SOCCER IN CORK, 1918–1937

A few years ago I scarcely anticipated seeing a Soccer club running two trains in a single morning from Cork to the metropolis.

Evening Echo, 12 March 1926

Soccer Revived: the Munster Football Association and the Munster Senior League

As we saw in Chapter Two, in 1900 there were at least eight civilian teams in Cork. There were ten a year later, with eighteen teams having played at least once by the end of the decade. This indicates a proliferation of the game over a twenty-year period. However, teams seemed to come and go at a considerably greater rate than was the case in rugby, even after independence. This was true across Munster. This may be partially explained by the fact that there was no school-oriented structure for soccer acting as feeders for teams that existed in the adult population. Although the league and cup structures that were present had the effect of maintaining the sport, the number of clubs did not decline visibly over a long period; instead the sport itself ground to a halt between 1914 and 1918 on the orders of the Munster FA, as a result of the hostilities in Europe, the feeling being that the civilian teams alone could not carry the game in the province. As we saw, though, this decision was probably taken as much because of the huge military involvement in the MFA as any true reflection of the popularity of the game among civilians or their ability to continue it in the military's absence.[1] The period from 1918 to 1922 was too fraught, especially in Cork, and across most of Munster, to reasonably conduct the business of organised soccer. However, with the resolution, more or less, of much of the conflict by 1922, the organisation was set into gear once again and this time the population seemed willing to provide the kind of support required to keep the game going in that initial difficult phase of consolidation.

Soccer was almost non-existent in Waterford in the period 1918–23, or if it was being played, it certainly was not featured in the press of the time, though probably still popular with young boys. We have seen there was soccer activity in the city nonetheless in the run up to the First World War, and those young pre-war players, coming of age after independence, were probably responsible for putting the game on a stronger footing.

Likewise, prior to the First World War, little enough in the way of association football was conducted in Tipperary, with Cahir Park AFC, founded in 1910, being probably the sole significant club to emerge into the new era of the Munster Senior League. Their case will be treated in Chapter Seven, since they were one of the few really significant clubs to emerge from Tipperary until after the end of the Second World War.

In 1921, when the split from the IFA to form the new Free State bodies for football – the Football Association of the Irish Free State (FAIFS) and the Free State League – occurred, all of the teams involved in the league in that first season were from Dublin. This situation was soon to change, however. In the initial period following the end of the First World War, when the IFA sought to put soccer back on its pre-war footing, the Munster FA had made an application for £200, and received nothing. Yet, from the beginning of the 1920s, soccer moved beyond its old confines, and in Munster particularly, it blossomed. Over the next fifteen years, from 1922–37, the shape of soccer in Munster would change greatly. Despite the often difficult economic conditions in which the game sought to grow, both in terms of participation and commercial viability, the game in the province was in a surprisingly healthier state than might be reasonably expected by 1937. To understand these developments, it might be as well to see the regional development of the game in Ireland as part of a broader trend then taking place in Britain, where the game was unevenly affected by the onset of economic crisis and depression. In some parts of England, the increased leisure time many unemployed men were presented with saw a rise in participation in soccer, even if gates at the big professional clubs were down.[2] So in the interwar era in Munster there was increased participation leading to the foundation of many local teams for all-comers, while the success of the game on a participatory, grass-roots level encouraged the establishment of Free State League clubs, despite the less than propitious circumstances of the day.

Central to that healthy state was the development and formation of leagues at grass-roots level in Cork, Waterford, Limerick and Tipperary. Cork, which had been the main centre for soccer prior to the political upheavals experienced in Irish life in the period 1914–23, resumed its position as the game's main provincial centre, with the re-establishment in 1922 of the Munster Football Association. Although the MFA was victim at times to the disinterest of the Dublin-centric FAIFS, nevertheless the big crowds, increased gates and high affiliation rate would seal over, more often than not, the cracks created by the sometimes myopic organisation that emerged, stretching from local district leagues to the MFA right to the national body, the FAIFS.

The newly reconstituted Munster Senior League, without its previous military base of teams, included Fordsons, YMCA, Barrackton, Clifton, Tipperary, Tipperary Wanderers, Cahir Park, Clonmel and Limerick. In 1922/23, the South Munster Senior League included Barrackton, Shandon, Bohemians, Fordsons, YMCA, Tramways, Clifton, Cork City, Cobh Ramblers, Parnell Rovers and Blackrock Rovers. The junior affiliates in that first season were YMCA, Tramways, Ramblers, Barrackton, Fordsons, St Vincent's, Exchange United, Shandon, Clifton, Victoria Cross, Turner's Cross and Ballintemple. As Tom Hunt has noted in his work on the GAA's social structure, in its formative period 'The evidence presented . . . suggests that when territorial units formed the focus about which a club was organised smaller units than the parish were more important.'[3] The list of teams noted above for the revived Munster Senior and Junior Leagues shows a similar trend of micro-networks helping to establish clubs in Cork soccer circles. The territorial units in this case were streets or groups of streets, locality, work, religion, friendship; all tight-knit, micro social networks that found a mode of expression and collective purpose on the field of play.

In this chapter, and those that follow, by considering the development of a number of specific clubs, namely Fordsons FC, Cork Bohemians, Waterford FC and Limerick FC, alongside the development of the grass roots, we will better understand the shift soccer underwent, from being a moribund game outside of Dublin and

Belfast in 1918, to 1937 where there were three Free State League clubs and a strong Munster Senior League in the region. While soccer had survived relatively intact in Dublin and Belfast, and recovered in both cities in reasonably good time following the war, the game was in a far different state in Munster. The remaining chapters of this book will show soccer going from an underreported game to one that drew huge crowds at all levels, sometimes matching and overtaking those of the GAA, when it might have been reasonably expected for the game to disappear, given the depletion of its old base. Soccer was decried throughout the period as the garrison game, a foreign import, as we saw in the last chapter, yet it was never as popular in Ireland, and especially in Munster, as it was in the 1920s and 1930s. So how are we to account for this explosion?

Fordsons FC and the changing fortunes of Soccer

Important as the re-establishment of the MFA was for the game's expansion in Cork, just as important was one of the new clubs formed at the game's grass roots: this club was founded by workers in 1922 and was to leave an indelible mark on the game in the city until after the interwar period. In 1917, Henry Ford & Sons built a factory in Cork city and five years later, just three years after production began, Fordsons Football Club, established by Harry Buckle, were playing locally. Buckle, born in Belfast in 1882, played for a large number of clubs. He began his playing career with Cliftonville before moving to England where he played for Sunderland, Portsmouth, Bristol Rovers and Coventry City. He later played for Belfast Celtic, Belfast United and Glenavon, as well as for Fordsons, with whom he finished his career.[4] The factory, located along the city's marina, was built on the site of the old Cork Park racecourse, thus industrialisation took from Cork one of its main open spaces and sporting grounds – the trade-off, which, as well as giving the people of the city employment gave them a triumphant soccer team, was no doubt considered a good one by many in the city.

The impact of a successful works team, such as Fordsons, cannot be overstated for soccer's development in Cork. Fordsons FC provided Cork with something which it had until then lacked: a team set up around a place of work, giving it a huge support base, that

118

rose through the divisions to play at the top level like other works teams in Dublin and Belfast had done before. Here was a team that thousands of people in the city could rally around as their representatives on the field.

So how did the new Ford factory end up with a football team? It was quite common during that era and earlier for large companies to provide welfare for their staff through a variety of means, and this often included providing sporting facilities for the workers. In Britain it was a part of worker welfare, developed most famously by Cadbury's at their worker village, Bourneville.[5] The industrial paternalism that informed the provision of the football team at Ford in Cork was nothing new. Importantly, in the case of the Ford factory, the choice of soccer suggests that it was decided by the workers themselves rather than being imposed on them by anyone within the company.[6] Remarkably, in 1922 there was an Irish Baseball Commission established in Cork by a Mr Johnson of the Ford factory, according to an article in the *Irish Independent* in February 1922, but nothing much seems to have come of the idea. A baseball league was due to commence that April but the establishment of the football club more than likely put an end to any hopes of this taking off in a serious way. As well as the soccer club, there was also a general social club that held whist drives offering prizes in their club rooms on the marina.[7] There was nothing unusual in their choice of game: Ireland was full of teams that originated in industry, such as Jacob's and St James' Gate (Jacob's Biscuits and Guinness brewery respectively) in the South and Distillery and Linfield (Dunville Distillery and Ulster Spinning Company) in the North. As Garnham rightly points out, 'such industrial paternalism was not unusual'.[8] In the same period in Wales, the works team of Lovell's sweet factory in Newport, Monmouthshire began playing football professionally, joining the Western Football League in 1923.[9] This club, Ian Pincombe notes, was important 'because it symbolised the aspirations of the firm's workers – and bosses – among whom the players worked and lived'.[10] The same thing can be said about the team from the Ford factory.

A paper presented to the Statistical and Social Inquiry Society of Ireland in 1923, not long after the club was founded in Ford, entitled 'What the Workers Should Know', about developing adult education in Ireland, recognised the need for sporting activity to be part of workers' welfare. The author favoured the encouragement of basketball as it could be played both indoors and outdoors, making it especially suitable to the Irish climate. He even contends it had the ability to hold the attention of men in Jacob's factory, where the emphasis was on the football team.[11]

The level of involvement from companies varied from place to place, and though it is difficult to know the level of help received by the club at Ford from the management, the relationship between the two seems to have been strong. In Cork, the club took the name Fordsons, after the tractor model which was the main output of the plant for the Russian market, and thus they were known by the nickname, the 'Tractor Boys'. This name, and nickname, extended their association, not just to Ford, but to local production and the output of local workers. Fordsons' fortunes rose rapidly after their foundation in 1922; they were admitted to the new Free State League after only a few short years playing in the Munster Senior League. The new Free State League was founded in late 1921 out of necessity, since the split with the Irish Football Association, and with the exception of Athlone Town FC was exclusively Dublin-based. Fordsons joined the Free State League in the 1924/25 season. This came on the back of reaching the FAI Cup final in which they lost 1–0 to Athlone Town. Fordsons were replacing Midland Athletic in the Free State League. Their stint in the league was relatively brief, lasting until the end of the 1929/30 season.

Figure 5.1: *Fordsons FC in the Munster Senior League, c.1923*
Reproduced with kind permission of Plunkett Carter.

Although they had their own ground at Ballinlough, they frequently made use of the university-run athletic grounds at the Mardyke for fixtures, as the UCC Finance Committee's minute books reveal. In that brief period in the late 1920s, as the table below bears out, they were enormously popular with the people of Cork. When they won the Munster Senior Cup against Barrackton in April 1924, the *Cork Examiner* report of the match reckoned 5,000 people were present to witness the game at Victoria Cross.[12] At the Mardyke, the figures indicated below are only 85 per cent of the total gate receipts of individual matches. A taking of 15 per cent was given to the Athletic Grounds Committee for hosting the club at the Mardyke. Below is a table giving some indication of the level of gate receipts received by Fordsons FC in the period up until they were re-constituted as Cork FC. Although it is possible to extrapolate attendance figures from these gate receipts, it would be at best guesswork. A good guide to the strength of the gate money below is that Fordsons were to take about £220 from their FAIFS Cup final in 1926.

TABLE 5.1
Gate receipts of Fordson FC
1926–1930

Cheque No/Date	Details	£	s	d	100% gate estimate*£
6956	Fordson	126	2	5	148
6968	Fordson	158	2	10	186
7010	Fordson	262	17	11	309
7126	Fordson	91	6	2	108
7188	Fordson	10	5	4	12
9530	Fordson	159	12	-	188
9649	Fordson	148	-	3	174
10352	Fordson	178	-	10	210
10692	Fordson	115	11	7	136
11747	Fordson	140	-	10	165
11869	Fordson	128	-	9	151
11963	Fordson	126	4	-	149
21/1/29	Fordson	100	12	-	118
Do.	Fordson	111	10	3	131
10/5/29	Fordson	28	8	8	34
18/11/29 (summer)	Fordson	175	7	3	206
Fordson	97	3	-	114	

TABLE 5.1 (cont.)

Cheque No/Date	Details	£	s.	d.	100% gate estimate*£
18/11/29	Fordson	163	5	6	192
Do.	Fordson	124	17	3	147
Do.	Fordson	117	11	5	138
10/12/29	Fordson	177	6	-	209
7/2/30	Fordson	20	10	-	24
Do.	Fordson	34	6	-	40
Do.	Fordson	273	8	4	322
26/5/30	Fordson	108	10	5	128
Do.	Fordson	46	11	5	55

SOURCE: UCCA: UCC Finance Committee minute books 1926–1931.

*To the nearest pound. This figure is based on the fact that UCC took a 15% cut of gates.

Over the course of this five-year period, the club came third in the league on one occasion, fourth on four occasions and reached their lowest ebb in 1928/29, finishing seventh. From their foundation, they won the Munster Senior Cup a total of five times, with four of those wins coming during their time in the Free State League. They also had their remarkable victory, winning the FAI Cup in 1926, beating Shamrock Rovers 3–2.

In eight seasons, Fordsons FC did more than any other club, player or person to promote soccer in Cork had previously done. Here we are going to examine the club's rise and re-shaping, looking especially at how the club was received in the press of the day. Due to the team's near-immediate success, mention was occasionally to be found in the pages of the national press, including *The Irish Times*, from early on. The earliest mention came in 1923, when the Cork side played against Alton United of Belfast in the FAI Cup. On that occasion the Fordsons team was described as:

> [displaying] a sound knowledge of the game, but their combination was not so finished, and the passing was at times erratic, particularly that of the wing players, while their defence with the exception of the centre-half and right-full was disjointed, a weakness which Alton took every advantage of. It was in this division that the Southerners failed and it is safe to say that had their backs been as reliable as the winning lot the result would have been different.[13]

Later during the 1923/24 season they would make their mark by reaching the final of the Free State Cup. This game was played against Athlone Town FC and was noted as the first time this cup was played by two 'provincial' sides.[14] The game was played in front of 22,000 spectators 'which included large contingents from the midlands and the southern capital'. Again we hear that 'little was known of the southern side' although they had beaten St James' Gate soundly by four goals to nil in the semi-final. The *Cork Examiner* described a scene where 'notwithstanding the counter attractions at Baldoyle, Lansdowne Road and elsewhere, there was an enormous attendance. Half an hour before the kick-off, 14,000 people were present and crowds were still pouring in. Fordsons had many supporters with them by the excursion train, and in addition their colours were sported by many in the huge crowd.'[15] Fordsons could not reproduce any such heroics on this occasion, with their defence and midfield coming in for particular criticism. It seems likely that, but for the goalkeeper O'Hagan, the score might have been much worse. We are told that '. . . the Southern halfbacks were very feeble in dealing with the persistent efforts of the Athlone attack, and when O'Hagan was beaten by Hannon, as the result of twenty minutes' play, after he had cleared several good shots, it was only the smartness of the reply that caught him by surprise'.[16]

Despite the disappointment, Fordsons were invited the following season to play in the Free State League, when Midland Athletic failed to gain re-election to the league. Among the earliest games the club played that season was against Bohemians. The game was to be a drubbing, however, the Cork men being beaten by four goals to nil. Such disappointments were offset by how the club finished that year. They came fourth at the end of that first season, a considerable achievement given the club's origins only a few short years previously.

In 1926, they were back in the running for the FAIFS Cup. This time, they would prove to be the victors. On the day of the final, St Patrick's Day, the *Cork Examiner* was anticipating a huge spectacle, saying that 'it is expected a record crowd will witness the game, and elaborate arrangements have been made to cope with the gathering'.[17] The *Examiner* was not alone in its anticipations. The *Evening Echo* was talking about the match a full week before, with the author reminding us that just 'a few years ago I scarcely anticipated seeing a

Soccer club running two trains in a single morning from Cork to the metropolis. I have not yet met the "fan" who is remaining at home on St Patrick's Day.'[18] The very idea that there were indeed soccer fanatics in the city was novel enough in itself but this usage of what was effectively an American import is further proof that this was an important era for the emergence of spectator sport. The day after the game, the *Cork Examiner* ran an extensive column covering the game. The introductory remarks of the piece are especially interesting:

> The most important event in the Soccer world of the Free State, namely the final of the Senior Challenge Cup, took place at Dalymount Park, Dublin to-day the teams engaged being Shamrock Rovers and Fordson. Since the inception of this competition, four years ago, no final has aroused anything like the extra-ordinary interest in to-day's battle. At the moment Association is the most popular game in the Free State, and the teams engaged to-day represent the cream of its talent.[19]

An exciting contest for spectators, it finished 3–2 in favour of the Cork side, bringing the FAIFS Cup down south for the first time. The *Examiner* described the scene vividly saying that 'the climax was reached when after escaping from the penalty Fordson secured the winning goal. Then hats, caps, sticks, flags, etc. went into the air, and some of the spectators actually rushed on to the ground to congratulate the scorer. When the game ended, the overjoyed spectators swarmed over the ground and carried the victorious team shoulder high off the ground.'[20] Were you eager to relive the day in print, you had to wait until the edition of the Saturday following the game to finally get the take of 'Observer', then one of the main soccer correspondents in Cork, in the *Examiner*. Describing the anticipation of the morning, he noted that 'a train timed to leave the Glanmire terminus at 7.35 was full one hour earlier; but, notwithstanding the discomfort involved, hundreds took up their position in the corridors. The scene at St. Patrick's Church was amazing, hundreds being unable to gain admittance to the special Mass which by the kindness of the Dean was celebrated at 6.45.'[21]

With the game over, the crowds made their way back from Dalymount Park to the train station, the scene one of pandemonium. 'Observer' notes 'the Fordsonian following swelled the number to big proportions, traffic being completely held up at the station premises for some time'.[22] He writes that the victory 'was

Figure 5.2: '*Fordsons on Top*'
Source: *Evening Echo*, 18 March 1926.

certainly unique for Cork soccer' before noting that 'being one of the old contemptible, I felt glad to have been alive to see the day a Cork club win[s] the blue riband of Association Football'.[23] The *Football Sports Weekly* reported after the victory that 'never since the days of the old political leaders has such a vast throng turned out to give a spontaneous welcome to a man or a body of men'.[24] This coverage indicated quite a shift for soccer within Cork people's imagination.

In Cork, a city and county which had been the centre of much of the War of Independence and the resulting Civil War, such a shift was significant. 'Observer', having a few short years before been 'one of the contemptible' for playing soccer, now celebrated very openly with thousands in the streets. That the FAIFS held the Cup on St Patrick's Day at that time is significant too. This suggests a moving away of the sport from its distinctly military origins and aligning itself with the new, and distinctly Catholic, Free State, to say nothing of a shrewd business move to hold the final on a major public holiday. Even the holding of an early mass before the match in Cork for the purposes of the game suggests a shift from a hardline anti-'foreign games' mentality to one that was more accepting of soccer's place as one of the most popular sports in Ireland. Of yet further significance was the size of the crowd who attended the game: roughly 25,000 people. In the same year, only marginally more attended the All-Ireland hurling final, Cork winning for the first time since 1919.[25]

> It's worth pointing out that the dances to be played at the celebration were old, new and Irish, making this a celebration that encompassed many traditions, including those of a nationalist hue. At the victory ball in the Arcadia, the link to the factory was strongly acknowledged. Mr Jack Kelly presented the managing director of the plant, Mr Edward Grace, with the match ball. Mr Grace said that 'he felt very proud of them and so did the firm, whose hearty support the Cork factory would always have.[26]

The victory photograph of the team from that year shows them in front of the marina plant. This photograph helps to reinforce the relationship between the players, the management and the factory in a striking fashion – the interdependence of all three in the cup-winning adventure is insisted upon in this image. A little over a week after the victory a rumour about the benefits of the win appeared in the *Football*

Figure 5.3: *Fordsons 1926 FAIFS cup-winning team*
Reproduced with kind permission of Plunkett Carter.

Sports Weekly, where 'we heard a great deal about the Ford boys each getting a new car and the possibility of a trip to the big factory in Detroit, Michigan if they won the cup. You can take it from me there is no likelihood of them being presented with a new "Henry"; but the directors have under consideration the trip to USA.'[27]

Both cup runs in 1924 and 1926 were worth a substantial amount to the club, if the cut they received from both finals is anything to go by. When Athlone Town beat them in 1924, the total gate for the game was £1,074.16.0. Of that, both the clubs got about 10 per cent, each coming home with £101.18.0. The Free State Association took £407.12.9 while the duty on entertainments imposed by the Cumann na nGaedheal government saw the exchequer take £222.16.1.[28] The take-home sum for Fordsons more than doubled two years later when they beat Shamrock Rovers in 1926. From a total gate of £1,601.18.8, both teams took £219.1.6 home with them.[29]

An important force in Cork footballing circles, they brought the city its first real success in the game, and made the game more popular, more acceptable. Although difficult to quantify directly, the strength of the Munster Senior League throughout the 1920s must have been helped by successes such as those of Fordsons FC. Indeed, the minute book of the committee in charge of the Mardyke provides one of the strongest indicators of Fordsons' impact. A statement of net revenue for the period 1926–30 shows that soccer, with Fordsons the main team, was worth more to UCC's coffers than any other sport played at the Mardyke. For instance, at the end of the 1927/28 season, soccer had earned UCC £316, compared to £241 earned from gates at rugby matches. Similarly, in 1929/30, soccer was worth £470 to the college compared to £247 earned from rugby. Only in one year, up to 1931, did rugby earn more for UCC than soccer. That was in 1928/29 when rugby brought in £346 to soccer's £316.[30]

Fordsons Football Club were perfectly well aware of their worth too, and they were less than happy with giving a 15 per cent gross cut of their gates over to those in charge of the Athletic grounds. It may well be one of the earliest examples of the clash between town and gown where sport was concerned in Cork city. A letter from the club's secretary indicates their willingness to move, even though they were loath to do so, if terms did not improve with regard to gate receipts:

> If your committee could see their way to alter the charge to even
> a 10% basis we would have a strong argument to put up those I
> mentioned to allow us to continue to engage your ground and as
> none of my committee would willingly make the change of their
> own choice I trust your Grounds committee will give our appli-
> cation their favourable consideration.[31]

The issue was not fully resolved by the time the club had lost their
affiliation with the Ford factory to become Cork FC.[32] Such success
in the provincial capital made the parent body, the FAIFS, take note
of the development of the sport in Munster. Indeed a month before
the cup win of 1926, *Football Sports Weekly* noted that, thanks to the
Fordsons club, 'things are vastly different today in Munster ... the
quality of Munster football has developed most rapidly, and the
players have reached a standard of proficiency within the past four
years exceeding all expectations. Unquestionably the inclusion of
Fordsons in the Free State League has contributed largely to the
growth and popularity of the game in the Southern Province.'[33]

The Munster FA was not shy to come forward to claim its dues
either on the occasion of the 1926 final. A letter from the MFA secretary Fitzgibbon was written to the FAIFS on March 3rd for free
tickets and train expenses for the night before the match so that the
FAIFS could 'in this way recognise the work we are doing for the
game in the south'.[34] In eight seasons in the Free State League,
Fordsons played a good deal of exciting football. The club's relative
success in the period ensured their popularity. During their six seasons
in the Free State league, they scored a combined total of 233 goals.
This was across eighteen games a season; until 1930/31, there were
only ten teams in the league. That averages out at just over two goals
a game, which is a reasonably high scoring rate. A number of those
who played soccer for Fordsons gained international caps for Ireland
in the 1920s. Those capped included Frank Brady, James 'Sally'
Connolly, Jack Sullivan, Paddy Barry and Frank McLoughlin.[35] In
fact, for Brady, Connolly and Sullivan, the victory over Shamrock
Rovers in the cup in 1926 was not one they got to celebrate. On the
same day as they won the cup, there was an 8.10pm train to be caught
in Dublin as they embarked on the journey to Milan for the Free
State's first ever fully recognised international match. For reserve
player Sullivan, the prospect of taking part in the history-making tie
had to be tempered by economic reality. As an amateur, he wrote to

the FAIFS saying he could scarcely afford the expense of losing eight days' wages without some guarantee of reimbursement from the FAIFS. For Connolly and Brady, two professionals, there was a guaranteed £5 each from the FAIFS.[36] And despite commitments in the league, the team continued to be involved in inter-firm competition, like the one announced in 1927 with the winners getting a set of medals provided by the management.[37]

In a controversial move, a Drumcondra versus Fordsons game was broadcast over 2RN on 19 February 1928.[38] It is uncertain if this was the first soccer game to be relayed by radio in the state, but is among the earliest. This was not well received by those who wished to see 2RN used as a means to promote Irish 'Gaelic' culture. One correspondent for *Football Sports Weekly* rebuked them saying, 'as the night follows the day – according to them – we must all come away coated in a thick varnish of Shoneenism should we enter Dalymount or Lansdowne'.[39] Nonetheless, the debate about soccer in the Free State would rumble on.

The club was to end its association with the Ford factory after the 1929/30 season to become Cork FC, just as things were souring in the plant with the opening of the new factory at Dagenham. As Nyhan notes, many workers moved to Dagenham with the jobs, and were referred to locally as 'Dagenham Yanks'.[40] This was also when the Free State League expanded to twelve teams, including for the first time, Waterford FC.

Beyond the most obvious fillip of success on the pitch, another element that helped soccer attendance figures was the price. Matches in general had an admission charge in the 1920s of 6d, or 3d for schoolboys. If available stand and enclosed stand could reach up to 1/– or even 2/– at a match, but by and large 6d and 3d were normal match-day prices and those availed of by the majority of attendees. The price was identical for GAA matches at the same level. Compared to other popular entertainments at the time, in particular the cinema or dances, attendance at a sporting event was quite cheap. Cinemas in Munster had prices ranging from as little as 2d or 4d for a matinee to 1s 6d for evening shows, although the most frequent price was 9d.[41] Cinderella dances, as we have seen, usually cost men 2s 6d, or 1s 6d if you were a woman. So for the price of a single night's dancing and refreshment one could attend up to five soccer matches. Another indicator of the low cost is the gate receipts for games. Although the gate amounts and crowd figures are usually rough estimations, they do provide a strong indicator nonetheless. Cheaper still was to see a team training, to which the public were welcome for free, and many, as the photograph below shows, availed of this chance.

Figure 5.4: *A Crowd watches on as Cork FC train at Turner's Cross c.1936.*
Reproduced with kind permission of Plunkett Carter.

Some training sessions, however, were not for public viewing, as the photograph below shows Cork FC players running the road in Blackash circa 1934.

A Free State Shield match Fordsons played in Dublin saw over 1,000 people coming up from Cork to offer support; a later Free State game saw a gate of around £300 for them. A Free State Junior Cup match between Cork side St Vincent's and Brunswick of Dublin attracted around 4,000 spectators, making the gate somewhere in the region of £240, if the vast majority paid an entrance fee of 6d, which

Figure 5.5: *Cork FC players put through their paces
at Blackash circa 1934*
Reproduced with kind permission of Plunkett Carter.

was usually the case. For instance, for a Cork City versus Waterford FC league game played in December 1938, of a total gate of £124.17.0, the bulk of that, £78.7.6, came through turnstiles charging 6d. This was undoubtedly the trend throughout the 1930s.[42] An interprovincial match between Munster and Leinster at the Mardyke saw an attendance of over 3,000 at the game with a gate of around £276. Revenue, its creation and its availability was a serious issue for the game in this period. In late August 1926 the southern correspondent of the *Football Sports Weekly* was critical of the newly elected Munster FA committee over a variety of issues, including that of turnstiles at the grounds of Victoria Cross which were then their headquarters:

> [F]our turnstiles arrived in Cork last June and their destination was Victoria Cross. They are on the ground certainly, but instead of being placed in a position at the various entrances, are reposing contentedly in one of the dressing rooms – probably resting after their strenuous labours 'clicking through' at Wembley.[43]

Such barbed statements indicate that the slowness of the organisers of soccer to adopt an approach to gate income like that of the GAA was a considerable concern to followers of the game, especially given the obvious public interest shown in soccer. Given the general upward trend in commercial leisure from betting shops and the cinema to the greyhound tracks, soccer was, provincially as well as nationally, in a strong position to capitalise on the unprecedented public attraction to the sport for its long-term success and financial health. Although there was an undoubted and important overlap between those who were to be found at the weekend attending Free State League soccer and those involved in and responsible for the game's new-found strength at the grass-roots level, not everyone who watched also played. Certainly, if the figures attending games from the region are to be taken at something like face value, than many more people were watching the game than playing it, at least in affiliated and organised teams and clubs. This is important in under-standing soccer in the interwar period in Ireland. As with all of the other commercial leisure practices emerging in Ireland at this time, which we have discussed above in detail in Chapter Three, soccer was for many Irish people a novel experience – a new leisure good to be consumed for a relatively low price.

Unlike either Gaelic games or rugby, most local soccer clubs, and certainly the senior sides in Munster, were all a product of the post-independence era. Therefore, the new Free State League sides slotted particularly easily into this new popular culture of commercialised leisure. Soccer matches after all provided high drama and excitement on a par with any movie at the local cinema. It was possible now in Ireland to be a soccer fan without necessarily being a member of a local club or to have ever so much as kicked a ball. As such, it did not exist in Munster in the form it had done since the 1880s in either Belfast or Dublin. The prospect of a local side beating counterparts from Dublin or elsewhere in Ireland was a new feature of soccer in the 1920s and 1930s in Munster and this was undoubtedly a part of the game's new-found appeal. For those who enjoyed the game but for whom local rivalry would have been meaningless, the potential of having a team based in your locality beating off a more established Dublin club would surely have appealed to many in all parts of Munster, not just Cork alone. As a form of entertainment in this way, soccer was one more sign of modernity in popular culture and its novelty factor was an undoubted part of its success for spectators in the province at the Free State League level among those who did not also play the game. Of course, this also left soccer open to the vagaries of a roving public who might indeed decide it a better use of their spare cash to watch the latest talkie at the cinema than see a match at the Mardyke.

Success on the field of play then was vitally important to many clubs' financial health. Cup runs were an important source of funding for the game and the big gates, which a good cup run could muster, were of huge importance, especially to smaller clubs. For example, the money earned from the Burkley Cup was pooled together at the end of the season and divided between senior and junior clubs, 75 per cent in favour of the senior clubs, a practice from before the First World War. Likewise the Lee Cup was used to fund the game in Cork. In 1926, for example, when the final went to a replay between Cork Celtic and Cork Bohs, it was hoped that the money from the game could go towards erecting a pavilion and dressing rooms at the Victoria Cross grounds.[44]

The other significant development for soccer in Munster at the time was a revived Munster Senior League, which operated as a league for the whole province, taking the best senior sides from Cork, Waterford, Tipperary and Limerick and allowing them to play against each other, as well as in their own district leagues. There was a gradual development available to clubs in this way, since they would be elected to play in the Munster Senior League from their district leagues and then, as happened to Fordsons, and eventually Waterford, they could be elected to the Free State League and become a full-time club; because the Munster Football Association was headquartered in Cork, so too was the Munster Senior League. This meant that there was a strong bias in favour of Cork amongst the clubs in the league.

Using a trade directory from 1925, we can begin to see the difference in the makeup of the game and those who ran it compared to those involved in the organising of the game before the First World War in Cork. In that year's trade directory for the city, fourteen clubs as well as the MFA were listed under clubs, societies and associations. Among the men involved in organising some of these clubs were Miah O'Donovan of Green Street, a van driver, and Patrick Fitzgerald of Mary Street, a coachman. Although it is difficult to be sure who the rest of these various secretaries were, many of their addresses were in working-class areas of the city, north and south of the river. In 1926, for example, only two of fifty-three teams playing across five leagues were from outside Cork city or county. Given that there were fifty-one teams playing soccer in Cork city and county in 1926, this is testament to the strength and popularity of the game in the county. The five league divisions were as follows:

1 Munster Senior League
2 Reserve League
3 Junior League
4 Munster Minor 'A'
5 Munster Minor 'B'

The fifty-three teams were made up of a total of thirty-nine individual clubs. This means that there was a total of thirty-seven clubs playing soccer in Cork by 1926. It is also significant that they dominated the league in all but the top tier, which contained Cahir and Tipperary Wanderers. In 1927, Cork teams won, among other things, the Free State Cup, Munster Senior Cup, Munster Junior Cup, and were runners-up in the Free State Junior Cup. No wonder then that this article should appear in the 'Soccer Review' section of the *Evening Echo* at the close of the season:

> Last Monday saw the close of the most successful season yet experienced in the history of Association Football in the South. In the matter of finance and public support the success achieved has eclipsed that of any previous season, and at the moment the game is one of the most firmly established pastimes of the nation. The first and most important was the success of the Fordson Club in Free State tourneys . . . Cork teams have won All-Ireland championships in other branches of sport, but the joy of the people was never expressed in such a singular manner.[45]

This dominance is reflected in the top division of the Munster Senior League just two years later. Take for example the list of clubs who were numbered in the Munster Senior League for the 1928/29 season: Barrackton, Bohemians, Cahir, Cork Celtic, Cork City, Cove, Fermoy, Fordsons, Victoria and Waterford. Only two clubs are not from Cork and its hinterland; this was an accurate reflection of the standard of soccer in Munster in the middle to late 1920s.[46]

Cork was more populous and had more clubs than Waterford, Limerick or Tipperary. This is proven by the strength of junior football in Cork especially at that time. Significantly though of course, the top league was the one with the clubs from outside of Cork. In 1928, when the draw was made for the FAIFS Junior Cup competition, twenty-six teams entered in the Cork section, making it the second biggest in the country behind Dublin, while Tipperary saw four entries and Waterford eight.[47] It makes sense therefore that there would be a significant number of teams from Cork who could justify their place in this 'intermediate' league between the local leagues and the Free State League. In 1926, there had been two Tipperary sides in the Munster Senior League, Cahir Park and Tipperary Wanderers. The Munster FA managed quite well in the period, if the few cheques paid to them by UCC's Finance Committee are anything to go by. Below is a table showing payments to the Munster FA in the period 1926–28:

TABLE 5.2
Gate receipts paid by UCC Finance Committee to MFA 1926–28

Cheque	Details	£	s	d
7454	Munster FA	210	6	5
7549	Munster FA	173	6	4
10595	Munster FA	79	18	-
Summer	Munster FA	88	16	8
Summer	Munster FA	102	5	8
11746	Munster FA	19	3	8

Source: UCCA: UCC Finance Committee minute books, 1926–1928.

This is yet further confirmation that the game had considerable support in Cork city and elsewhere in Munster since these receipts are most likely to derive from Munster Junior and Senior Cup ties hosted at the Mardyke grounds, suggesting that significant games between junior or senior sides could be as big a draw as a game in the Free State League. Yet, despite the kind of financial health that both this table and the gate receipts of Fordsons FC showed, little of this money appears to have found its way back into the infrastructure of the game at either senior or junior level in Munster.

However, as teams prepared to enter the 1930/31 season, the news that the new Cork side, Cork FC were about to secure the grounds at Turner's Cross for both themselves and the Munster FA was seen as a positive for the game in Munster as a whole. Likewise, the news of a new junior club in Cork, the Victuallers, was heralded in the same article as a sign of the healthy state of the game as was the expectation that the MFA would have five new affiliates from Tipperary.[48]

Cork Bohemians FC: Free State League club, 1932–34

The good health, and the optimism, regarding the development of soccer in Cork at the time continued with the election of Cork Bohemians to the Free State League in 1932. Cork Bohemians had emerged in the middle of the 1920s, and their ascension to Free State League status came as Waterford FC exited the league due to insufficient support, a topic which will be discussed in the next chapter in more detail. Cork Bohemians, not unlike Fordsons before them, came first to provincial and then national attention thanks to a number of big cup runs at the end of the 1920s that saw them winning the Intermediate Cup on two occasions, first in 1928 and then again in 1931. In the period 1927–33, they won the Munster Senior Cup on five occasions, with Fordsons and Fordsons 'B' the only interrupters of that run in 1929 and 1930. Given such form, it is hardly surprising that the club was able to mount a serious challenge to enter the Free State League when Waterford FC made their exit.

Cork Bohemians further benefited from Waterford's demise as the summer editions of the *Cork Examiner* show the club signing a number of players from that recently-exited club including Tommy Arrigan, O'Brien and the goalkeeper Harris, the former Manchester City player being brought in as player-manager.[49] In early August 1932, a few weeks before the season began, the *Evening Echo* looked forward to the new season's preparations and was especially excited about the prospect of local derbies between Cork FC and newcomers Cork Bohemians. The reporter, casting his mind back to the days when the Irish League included the southern teams of Bohemians and Shelbourne, wrote of the 'immense fillip to the game which was imparted by the glorious rivalry between the clubs', hoping that the same would one day be said of the coming derbies in Cork. While Cork FC's season got off to a bad start away to one of those illustrious Dublin clubs, Shelbourne, being beaten 3–0, Cork Bohs began their own season against the other half of that rivalry, Bohemians of Dublin. The first home game of the season for Cork FC was to be a grand affair at the Mardyke, when they took on Bohemians of Dublin, with the game being kicked off by Cobh-born boxing star Jack Doyle, soon to become British champion. Cork FC won this game, in the words of the *Evening Echo* correspondent 'making amends for their defeat to Shelbourne', while shortly afterwards Cork Bohemians took a draw away from St James' Gate in Dublin.[50]

Things initially looked bright for the newly elected club, but with the reintroduction of the entertainments duty which took a significant portion of clubs gate receipts, Cork Bohemians were always likely to struggle. The club had a ground, although like Cork FC, the ground was not their own, but on lease. Cork Bohemians had a similar deal with the Munster Agricultural Society to Cork FC's deal with UCC, playing their soccer on the greyhound track at their site in Ballintemple. This pitch had been offered to Cork FC but, as outlined above, they had decided to stick with UCC and the Mardyke, which opened up the ground for use by Cork Bohemians. Not all of their opponents were terribly enamoured of the ground, with Shelbourne's management apparently complaining that the pitch was not regulation size, though the *Evening Echo*'s 'Shandon' resolutely denied the veracity of the claim pointing out that before their recent game 'the ground was paced and acquitted of short measure'.[51]

'Shandon', author of a weekly column for the *Evening Echo*, which appeared in the Friday evening editions, focused his writing on a general discussion of the game in Cork, Munster and in the league more generally. Through this column, we can get a clearer idea of the key debates and stories within Cork soccer in the 1930s. Given that sports-only newspapers like *Sport* and *Football Sports Weekly* were both defunct by 1930, columns like those by 'Shandon' offer us a now invaluable insight into the game's development at the time.

Some early indication of the problems which would come to plague Cork Bohemians during their time in the Free State League can be found in 'Shandon's' column, where even early in their first season, he writes that 'Cork City is doing wonders to be able to keep two teams in the Free State League but if it is to continue it follows neither can be expensive, and aspiring amateurs will do well to keep this in mind', relating the signing of a player at the club as a professional, finishing the item by saying that 'this is not the day of big gates and big money, and, for the sake of Soccer, sacrifices must be made all round'.[52]

This was a prescient note by 'Shandon', yet things did at first not seem so bad, with the newcomers clocking up crowds of between five and six thousand at games. The prospect of a local derby game was highly anticipated, and the people of Cork hadn't too long to wait for the first. On Sunday, 16 October 1932, the Cork public got to see Cork FC take on Cork Bohemians at the greyhound track. According to a report the next day, 'a crowd conservatively estimated at 15,000 people saw Cork FC defeat Cork Bohs, their sister team of the Irish Free State League, by two goals to one'.[53] According to the match report, people filled the ground early in the day in an attempt to get the best possible vantage points, while 'along the route by the Blackrock Road buses laden with passengers, and private or hackney motor cars hooted their way through a long crush of pedestrians who preferred to foot it rather than risk missing a conveyance. The turn-stiles have rarely clicked to such an immense gathering.'[54] It was a sunny day, and the Butter Exchange Band, adding to the sense of occasion, provided the music.

Such occasions were a reprieve from an increasingly harsh reality, however. Ireland's unemployment rate had increased by 40 per cent earlier in 1932, and the state of the economy could not escape the notice of 'Shandon'. Only a few days after the first Cork derby, 'Shandon' wrote an item in his column entitled 'Au Revoir'. It ran:

> In addition to the toll taken by unemployment, a transfer of Fordson workers this week has further depleted the ranks of Soccer fans and players of Cork.
>
> With general regret leave was taken of Mr. Robert McClaverty, a popular referee at the meeting of referees last weekend. Mr. McClaverty has gone to Dagenham. Before he left he paid tribute to Soccer players and followers in Munster for their general sportsmanship, and said he was sorry to be leaving the country ... Four junior players have also left this week for Dagenham.[55]

Indeed 'Shandon' notes, not without a certain sense of pathos, that 'there are almost sufficient in the Ford Works there now to form a Cork team'. He goes on to encourage this by suggesting that 'this would not only keep them fit, heighten their lives in their new sur-roundings, but help to keep the name of Cork to the fore, and forge a further link with their native city'.[56] The topic was not one which the column dropped either. A fortnight after this initial mention, 'Shandon's' column wrote that 'football is going to play a part in the meritorious work of helping the unemployed in the sad times we are now going through'. The two Free State League sides, Cork FC and Cork Bohemians, were being encouraged to play a game to help raise funds for the city's unemployed in a one-off match for a set of medals to be presented by a local city firm.[57] Shortly afterwards it was reported that 'it is gratifying to find that our two teams in the city have come forward to help the excellent cause'.[58]

The game was set to take place on Wednesday, 23 November, with an afternoon kick-off time of 3.30pm. The match was once again obligingly kicked off by young champion boxer Jack Doyle. The game seemed to have been something of a mixed bag in terms of its fundraising efforts, with 'Shandon' noting that while both teams 'displayed the true spirit of sportsmanship in offering to help the unemployed of the city, and the public backed them up generously', it was 'not overgenerously, for, unfortunately, many more could have found room in the enclosure'.[59]

Given the timing of the match, that they managed to do as well as they did in raising funds for the city's unemployed is no small wonder. Similar endeavours were undertaken by other sports too, with UCC and Dolphin playing a challenge rugby match for the benefit of the unemployed, while the city's hurling teams played in a tournament in the same period in aid of the city's Sick Poor Society.[60] This particular tournament raised £78.17.3, a tidy sum.[61] The Able-Bodied Men's Unemployed Association and another Cork Relief of Distress Fund group also ran matches at the Mardyke, though these raised the considerably smaller sums of £9.18.3 and £6.18.4 respectively. This may point to a gap between people's willingness to support charity as opposed to the city's organised unemployed.[62] When in 1934 UCC applied for a grant for the building of a new pavilion for the Gaelic pitch at the Mardyke, the Office of Public Works granted £125 on the condition that the bulk of the labourers be hired from among those on unemployment assistance, and of those, 75 per cent were to be married men and 25 per cent single.[63] These were unpleasant times for many Cork people, with many living in slum conditions, their problems compounded by the rise in unemployment. According to one source, 18,645 in the city were living in unsatisfactory tenement or other housing conditions in 1925.[64] Yet they had reason to be hopeful of some improvement in the quality of their lives since, as J.C. Saunders noted in his annual report as Medical Officer of Health to the Cork Corporation, housing was improving in many parts of the city thanks to 'the attack on slum conditions begun in

1933'.[65] Similarly, the Cork Town Planning Association's survey from almost a decade before had noted that the loss of the Cork Park racecourse to Henry Ford's needed to be balanced out with the provision of more open spaces and playing fields.[66] In such cramped conditions, naturally the prospect of playing soccer out on the street was appealing to many young boys and men, and must account at least in part for the large number of teams that sprung up in the post-independence period. Of course, the unemployment crisis, which as we will see below was to have such a detrimental effect on Waterford FC, was not going to be solved by charity football matches alone, however good the intention.

The unemployment crisis experienced in Ireland was in large part thanks to the depression caused initially by the stock market crash in the United States in 1929. As Emmet O'Connor has noted, despite the creation of extra jobs thanks to Fianna Fáil's policy of protectionism that encouraged the establishment of home-grown industry, these extra jobs 'were insufficient to absorb rural depopulation, whilst the worldwide depression discouraged emigration, severely so in the case of America', if not it seems to Dagenham.[67] Around the same time as Cork FC and Cork Bohemians faced off against each other to raise money for the unemployed, the Cork Trades Council continually noted in its meetings the extraordinary levels of unemployment in the city, need for greater welfare provision from the government, and hiring out their hall to mass meetings of the organised unemployed, while long-term unemployment was a factor in the requests of some families' attempts at securing extra relief from the Cork Sick Poor Society at the same time.[68]

The city was not wholly impotent in its response to the unemployment crisis and its effect on people's access to leisure, even during this enforced idleness. The *Irish Press* reported a plan by Cork's city manager in August 1933 to give the grounds recently used for the Irish Industrial Fair over for the use of the unemployed following a request by those in whose trust the land was that it should be used for a public purpose.[69]

Something approaching a more realistic solution to the problem of unemployment was the introduction in 1934 of unemployment benefit under the Unemployment Assistance Act. This brought to an end, at least in part, the previous official view of unemployment and poverty as a moral failing of an individual that required charity only for those deserving of such charity. Although, as labour historian Emmet O'Connor has noted, here again 'there were limits to Fianna Fáil achievement, and basic differences with Labour would surface before the decade closed'.[70] Yet Labour could not take advantage of the emerging unemployment crisis in the elections in February 1932, where they lost five seats, going from twelve down to just seven deputies in the Dáil, though one of these seats was in Cork.

Unemployment was clearly having a detrimental effect on soccer in Cork and this is further illustrated by clubs' attempts to create yet more reasons for people to click through the turnstiles. With the purchase of a matchday programme, punters were automatically entered into a prize raffle to win the match ball of a game early in the 1932 season between Cork FC and Drumcondra.[71] Cork Bohemians were soon following suit with a prize of a six-month double ticket to the Pavilion cinema up for grabs in their prize draw.[72]

However, like charity matches, such prize draws relied heavily on novelty factor and were not sustainable solutions to the problems facing Free State League teams. Cork Bohemians had a Supporters' Club established at the end of that same November. As was noted in the *Evening Echo* announcing the Supporters' Club's inaugural meeting, 'Shandon' had previously 'referred to the difficulties of keeping a team in the Free State League, and the financial question looms largely in the outlook of the promoters'.[73] Of course, it is worth noting that attendances were often no reflection of gates. Frequently many attended games without ever paying a penny, which was often just as troubling for the Cork clubs as actual low numbers attending. As much is alluded to in a letter sent by M. Cohalan, the secretary of Cork FC, to the UCC Athletic Grounds Committee in November 1933. Cohalan notes in the letter that:

> Another serious loss of revenue to this club, and incidentally to your good selves, is the free 'Grand Stand' at the Mardyke. I refer now to the railings running along the Mardyke Walk. At least hundreds I would say, and some judging from appearance, who could well afford to pay, avail of these railings, thereby getting an uninterrupted view of the whole game.[74]

Cohalan suggested that something be put up to prevent people from using the railings in this way.

Cohalan's letter also points to an important change in the revenue for clubs like Cork FC and Cork Bohemians: those who were going

141

Figure 5.6: *The free 'Grandstand' at the Mardyke, c.1930s.*
Reproduced with kind permission of the *Irish Examiner*.

were opting for the cheaper entrances. Cohalan's letter points out that at a recent game it took a long time for the three 6d stiles to clear the queues entering, the cheapest end of the ground. He also reckoned that many went away, admittance taking too long. Cohalan suggested the addition of two extra stiles at the 6d entrance in order to ensure people got in quicker. This and the suggested measure regarding the railings were both approved by the Athletic Grounds Committee, the two new turnstiles being installed, including labour, for £63.15.6.[75]

At the Mardyke there were other novel ways of making it to the ground without paying entry through a turnstile, as well as the railings; some used a small boat at low tide to cross over to the other side of the pitch. This was a perennial issue, still being mentioned in 1937, especially the vantage point from high across the river in Shanakiel.[76] What is important to take away from this is that this period highlights the connection in Ireland between soccer and the Irish working class: relying so heavily upon the urban working class to play, referee, manage and watch the game, the trouble of unemployment was trouble for the game of soccer too.

Yet, soccer remained an important facet of working-class life. As a TD for North Dublin, Pat McGilligan, noted during a Dáil debate that saw the reintroduction of the entertainment tax on soccer in 1932, 'if there is any game which, as I said before, destroys the tedium of work for the working man, it is Association football, the game to which he looks forward on Saturday and Sunday'.[77] As the principal sporting entertainment of the Irish working class, soccer provided an important reprieve for an increasingly desperate population. The cost of the entertainment tax was to be borne by the paying spectator as entrance to matches went up from 6d to 7d, a penny too much for many who instead invested time in inventive ways to catch the game for free, especially in Cork.

If soccer at the senior, national level of the Free State League was on shaky ground, then the impression from coverage of the local game as the 1932/33 season began was of a vibrant participatory soccer culture. There was the Munster Senior League, composed of eight teams: two Waterford sides, the recently demoted Waterford FC and seasiders Tramore Rookies, both Cork Free State teams, 'B' selections, along with Cobh Ramblers, Rockton, Fermoy and Southern Rovers.

Below them were Munster Junior 'A' and 'B' divisions, with ten teams apiece. There was even a Munster Minor League, with fourteen teams competing at that level. There were also new teams emerging in the city, including one that affiliated to the MFA, IOC FC. This new club was just one of many work-based teams scattered throughout the leagues in Cork at the time. As well as Fordsons, whose example we have detailed previously, there was also a team of Butchers in the Junior 'A' League, while the Cork Steampacket Company had a club playing in the Junior 'B' League. This last club was particularly enterprising in bringing in touring teams, including a team from Fishguard as well as from the London office of the Steampacket Company, whom they played for the Read Cup, a trophy donated by the company's managing director.[78]

Despite the prevailing problems with unemployment and declining gates, which was worrying those involved with both Cork FC and Cork Bohemians, 1932 saw work-based soccer get a considerable boost. An inter-house league was established in the city by the end of 1932. The impetus came from those who worked in the city's warehouses. The warehouses had formed teams and had begun playing each other, and the MFA was keen to organise them into a proper league. Proposed names for the league included the Warehouse League or the Wednesday League, as this was when the games took place.[79] As has been noted already, the benefits of such workplace sport were not just health-giving, but as 'Shandon' himself astutely notes, 'it is surprising what a spirit of camaraderie a football team in a factory or workshop produces among staff and helps to make better employees of them'.[80] A happy workforce in a time of uncertainty and unemployment would of course have been no bad thing in the eyes of many employers. The league was due to begin in January 1933, and there was sufficient interest beyond the city's warehouses to establish a league with two divisions (one to play on Wednesday, the other on Saturday) teams included those from Cash's, Roches Stores, Cork Chemical and Drug Company, Fishmongers, T. Lyons & Co., Munster Arcade, Dwyer's, Lee Boot Co., Buckley's, Lunham's, Eustace, *Cork Examiner* and the ESB.[81] When this league transformed into the Inter-House League in 1934, there were teams too from Bedford's, Sutton's, a group of turf accountants, a team from Eagle printing works, the civil service, a grocers' team and a victuallers' team. Tom Hunt has argued in his examination of the GAA's social structure that 'In urban areas, the key socio-economic network of functioning hurling and football clubs was embedded in the retail trade and included shopkeepers, shop assistants, clerks and sales personnel.'[82] In the Warehouse League, and its successor the Inter-House League, we can see that in Cork, groups of men also connected to the city's retail and commercial trade used this workplace proximity as a means of organising teams to play against each other in their spare time, building on and extending the camaraderie of the workplace. Lunham's was a bacon-curing factory situated on Kemp Street; Cork Chemical were based on Cook Street; Eustace's were based on Leitrim Street; T. Lyons shirt makers had their business on South Main Street; the Lee Boot Factory was on Washington Street; while Cash's, Roches and the Munster Arcade were all major department stores on Patrick Street. By and large, the teams for this league were drawn from the island between the two channels of the River Lee, but again it's worth noting the range of workplaces that took part from factories to retail and many points in between. Unfortunately, only these few fleeting notices of the league exist so it is difficult to say who precisely within each of these businesses was involved in playing, but the kinds of companies indicates that more than likely it was mainly single men in their twenties, who were likely to be clerks, assistants, floor workers and of similar standing in the businesses. A good number of the games were to be played at Lunham's grounds, which may mean that it was Lunham's who were the main instigators of this particular league.

This was one more realm of masculinity which was touched by soccer, and the roles afforded women in soccer in this period are perhaps best summed up by the brief note regarding the Ladies' Committee of Cork FC, described as a 'very useful adjunct' who in an effort to fundraise for the club had up for raffle two prizes of a trip away: first prize was a trip on a cruise to the Canary Islands aboard the SS *Esperance Bay*, with all meals included; second prize was a trip to the Isle of Man; while third prize was a season ticket to any ground in Britain or Ireland. At 6d a ticket, this raffle was considerably more enticing than those we saw above. Interestingly, and perhaps most enticingly of all, the money value of the prize could be had by the winner if they so chose. But the key point to take from this brief notice is that it was rare in hundreds of column inches about soccer in the pages of the *Evening Echo*, and all of the other provincial newspapers that reported the goings-on of soccer enthusiasts, to explicitly mention women and their role in the world of soccer in Munster. The role assigned to women was that of organisers of a fundraising committee, a job that they appear to have taken to with considerable enterprise.[83] A rare game of football played by women in Ireland was that between a Dublin selection and a Scottish women's team, Rutherglen. This was watched by 12,000 people in Milltown, Shamrock Rovers' home ground, in 1927. The Scottish side came out strong winners, 9–1.[84] Aside from this apparent once-off, and though there is photographic evidence of women attending soccer matches in this era, their place in the game was, thanks to highly gendered notions of which sports were appropriate for women and men, largely left either on the sidelines or on a specially designated club committee.

Further signs of the good health of the grass-roots game was the acquisition of new grounds by clubs, a problem which had plagued soccer, not just in Cork, but throughout Munster and the rest of the country since the game's earliest days. Now, along with established venues like Victoria Cross, the college's grounds at the Mardyke, Turner's Cross and the greyhound track in Ballintemple, other smaller clubs began to get their own grounds, clubs like Cove Ramblers, which was, according to the newspaper, a costly enterprise.[85] This development came at the same time that the Organising Committee of the FAIFS was about to begin undertaking their task of providing grounds in those areas where soccer was growing but where, unlike in Cork or Waterford, there was not an abundance of playing pitches for the game. This was an issue flagged even in the middle of the 1920s, with *Sport* making noise about the subject in an article entitled 'Plans for the Future', with a subheading of 'Tapping Provincial Talent', as far back as April 1925.[86] The idea behind this was that with financial help from the FAIFS, these emerging areas would be able to acquire grounds on a more permanent basis for use by the local soccer clubs.[87] Like so many good ideas about how to stabilise and capitalise on soccer's popularity, however, little concrete appeared to emerge in the intervening years and many clubs still struggled to share the handful of grounds that soccer could call its own in Cork.

Of course, everything wasn't perfect at the junior level of the game in Cork. Although there was an abundance of playing pitches for those involved in soccer, another familiar problem hadn't gone away: referees. The problem lay not with the men in black, but in time-hon-oured fashion, in how they were treated by the rest of the footballing fraternity. Referees in Ireland were perhaps the most ill-treated members of soccer's family in the period from the beginning of the Free State Football Association to the beginning of the Second World War. Not alone did they have to contend with threats, but the Association which on the one hand wished to see them come to no physical harm, did not always rate the abilities of homegrown referees. Throughout the period, referees from Britain were frequently utilised for bigger matches such as finals and important league games. Unsurprisingly, this caused a strike action among referees in 1925, but to no avail. If anything, the use of cross-channel referees only increased in the years ahead, a prime example of this being Harry Nattrass, the Durham-based referee who as an out-of-work miner, ref-ereed the 1936 FA Cup final.[88]

In 1932, the Irish Referees' Association, the Dublin-based organ-isation for referees, looked to take strike action again, though this was not followed by everyone. As 'Shandon' reported in his column for the *Evening Echo*, 'it was decided not to affiliate with the Dublin body, though reports in the morning Press stated help from outside areas was promised in the strike of referees reported to have occurred'. However, the piece goes on to point out that 'The Munster Association rightly pointed out that they had agreed with the Munster Football Association to referee their matches this season, and intended to stick by that agreement'. This suggested that although they would not join the Dublin referees in striking, neither would they interfere by acting as scabs.[89] Certainly to judge by a court case in November 1932, the Munster-based referees had almost certainly made the right decision. On 1 November a case appeared before the Dublin District Court that saw three men, one of whom was chairman of the Irish Referees' Association, bound to the peace after the court heard that they door-stepped another man who intended refereeing a game on 15 October, the day a strike was declared.[90] It wasn't the end of things for the Munster referees, though, with a rumoured schism between the referees and the MFA, reported late in November. 'Shandon' felt that an agreement could be reached over the issue of inadequate sustenance allowances for the referees, though he noted that referees had other concerns at present, chiefly the manner in which they were treated outside of Cork.[91]

If referees had found 1932 a troubling season, then they might perhaps have been glad not to have been a part of the set-up of either Cork FC or Cork Bohemians. Although the latter club had victory in the Munster Senior Cup over Waterford FC on St Stephen's Day to boost their confidence as they entered the second half of the season, any lift to their spirits over the festive season was soon brought back down closer to earth.

Cork FC seemed to be in especially dire straits in the New Year, with the question being raised about whether or not the club would be in a position to fulfil its fixtures for the remainder of the season. The club needed a good cup run to see them to safety financially, but it never came, being beaten by Shamrock Rovers, in an upset that was against the odds. However, the club being a limited liability company meant it could not be dissolved on a whim but would require a vote at their AGM, which wasn't due to take place until April at the earliest.[92] Indeed, the minute books of UCC's Finance Committee, which was in charge of paying out to the club their portion of the gate receipts, noted in November 1932 that the club had applied for a £50 advance on future gates in order to stay solvent.[93] The same minute books also indicate that by renting the grounds from UCC, the club were at the mercy of the Finance Committee of the university, having to wait until payments were approved by the committee before they could see the money from their gates. This was a parlous state of affairs for Cork FC as the Finance Committee often met irregularly and sometimes there were gaps of months, even during the college term, which coincided largely with the Free State League season. It was suggested by some that a solution to Cork FCs troubles might be provided by moving from the Mardyke to Turner's Cross. It was estimated that the club lost £400 a year in gates, after what was owed in taxes and to the league, and to the owners of the ground, UCC. It was further estimated by one builder that to do Turner's Cross up to the standard required would cost in the region of £1,000, which could be recuperated in three seasons.[94]

Cork Bohemians were equally distressed financially and with the end of the season in sight, and money running low, they unburdened their expense account by getting rid of the professionals on their books, with only two players saved from this cull.[95] This move seemed to be the lifeline the club needed. However, Cork FCs attempts to steady their ship were less well-publicised due no doubt in part to the club being a limited company. This quietness on the part of Cork FC aroused more interest than acting transparently would have done, with one correspondent quoted by 'Shandon' as saying that 'the public are as much concerned in the welfare of the club as directors, and I think that they would be only too inclined to share the burden'.[96] Cork FC were planning something to buttress their income, and in mid-March 1933, the plan was revealed: the club was to start running a regular dance and whist drive, on Wednesday and Thursday nights respectively, something which people were encouraged to patronise in the *Evening Echo*'s soccer column.[97]

The following season saw things unravel for Cork Bohemians, while Cork FC bestrode new heights. 'Centre-Half', the *Evening Echo*'s other main soccer correspondent, reported on 9 December 1933 that Cork Bohemians were suspended from the Free State League because of the club's inability to fulfil their obligations. The club's game against Bray Unknowns fell victim to the suspension, though sense appeared to have prevailed in time for the Cork derby that took place the following week, with Cork Bohemians re-instated. The derby was won emphatically by Cork FC with a score of 4–1, a hat-trick being scored by Tim O'Keeffe. Embattled Cork Bohemians were charged £25 payable to Bray for the loss of a gate as well as seeing the two points for the game awarded to Bray.[98] The New Year saw Cork Bohemians end its agreement with the Greyhound Track and move from there to Turner's Cross.[99]

Cork Bohemians were suspended by the league, changed ground mid-season and lay bottom of the league table, while their local counterparts Cork FC were topping the table and about to begin a momentous cup run that would end in remarkable victory for them. The cup run began against Cork Bohemians, ending in a surprise 1–1 draw, with Cork FC winning the replay, setting a precedent that would last right until the final. Remarkably, Cork FC would beat Cork Bohemians, Bray Unknowns and Dundalk on the way to the final only after drawing and then replaying each match. The semi-final against Dundalk went to a second replay before Cork FC could best them in a game that ended 2–1. The replays congested the fixture list meaning this second semi-final replay took place just ten days prior to the date fixed for the final, St Patrick's Day. In a near repeat of what had happened eight years previously between Fordsons and Shamrock Rovers, Cork FC beat Dublin side St James' Gate 2–1 on the day. The club missed out on a magnificent double that season, finishing out the league second, a single point behind eventual champions, Bohemians of Dublin. The game was reminiscent of the 1926 final, with arrangements made for mass-goers either before or after the game, in Cork and Dublin, since it too was on St Patrick's Day.[100]

On the Monday night when the victorious team returned, an estimated crowd of 20,000 people greeted them: 'emblems, favours, and colours were plentiful, while tar barrels cast a glow over the animated scene, and four bands joined an enthusiastic medley of sound'.[101] Such were the crowds that the crush became too much for some and two people were actually hospitalised for injuries sustained during the celebrations. The *Evening Echo* reported that 'so great was the crush that many people fainted and were passed out over the shoulders of the crowd'.[102] Success was sweet, but money was still tight. According to figures released through 'Soccer Notes' in the *Evening Echo* the club only earned from its cup run, from the semi-final, through the replays and the final itself, marginally more than the Free State Government did from entertainment tax. According to the report, the total that Cork FC received was £523, while the Free State earned £520 3s 3d.[103] Here is the table in full as it appeared in the paper:

TABLE 5.3
Cork FC Gate receipts from
1934 FAIFS Cup Run

Matches	Total Gate (£)	Tax	Sum Received by Club (£)
1st Semi-final			168.0.0
1st Replay	935.17.1	148.14.0	152.3.6
2nd Replay	279.6.4	43.3.1	56.10.6
Final	1,429.7.3	321.6.2	146.6.0
Total	2,644.10.8	520.3.3	
Grand total			523.00

SOURCE: *Evening Echo*, 4 May 1934

This provides us with as good an example as can be found to show how hard it was to do well in Free State football in the middle of the 1930s. The tax was rescinded at the end of that season, a welcome reprieve for many clubs, but too late for Cork Bohemians, described in a season round-up as 'dead and buried, even if the bones do rattle now and again'.[104] If things were moribund for the Free State League clubs in this period in Cork, to the extent that one club folded and the other underwent a name and personnel change, then things at the grass-roots level, though far from perfect, could at least be said to be in a more stable condition than for those playing at the national level.

In January 1934, the report of the FAIFS commission into the state of the game in Munster revealed that there were around 100 clubs in the region affiliated, the bulk of them in Cork, with ten in Limerick, five in Tipperary and sixteen in Waterford. The report did note that financially at least the two Free State sides, while not adversely affecting the game at the junior or minor level, were having a detrimental effect on the Munster Senior League, the league from which the MFA drew the majority of its own revenues;

it did not receive money from the junior or minor leagues, and with that in mind, the FAIFS granted £50 to the MFA to help cover 'pressing debts' and a revision of the provincial council was considered to bring all of the senior, junior and minor Munster leagues under the control of the MFA.[105] Although there was concern in 1933/34 over the state of the senior league particularly, the rude health of the game at other levels in Cork indicated that soccer, if not the MFA, was in fine fettle.

As well as the continuation of the Munster Senior League and the other leagues below it, this same period saw the beginning of a new initiative: the Inter-House League. In its first season, the new Inter-House League was an unmitigated success. The league ran smoothly from the off and was sufficiently popular that even after entries had closed officially and only days before the season began, the league assented to admitting a team from Burton's, the menswear shop.[106] We've already seen above what a range of teams from the various commercial houses of the city such a competition drew.

Although one club dropped out of the minor league during the 1933/34 season, rivalries that emerged in these competitive leagues captured the public imagination in a way that the floundering, inconsistent Free State clubs couldn't hope to match, with the exception of Cork FC when they won the Free State Cup in 1934, and reached the final in 1936, but even this was not sufficient to save the club. Senior league football in the city was in dire straits by 1936, with the MFA even appealing to junior clubs to attempt to step up to the mark as many senior clubs felt a drop in gates and interest with two Free State League sides to compete for people's attention.[107] This troubling development was compounded when in 1937 a new Waterford and North Munster Football Association saw thirty teams across four divisions establish themselves, with Waterford FC's 'B' team abandoning the Munster Senior League for the newer body.[108]

Local clubs in Cork also had the advantage of lesser expenses, not being professional outfits and not having to undertake long journeys for many of their games. Their unwillingness to travel in fact was to be to the detriment of Munster Senior League side Tramore Rookies, as we shall see later on. Rivalries that developed like those between Glasheen and Grattan United caught the imagination of the public in a way that the emerging rivalry between Cork FC and Cork

151

Bohemians doesn't appear to have; perhaps if the two Free State League clubs had survived longer and achieved more, then an exciting rivalry might have had time to develop, but this was not the case.

The sheer localism of a rivalry between the likes of Glasheen and Grattan United meant that the frisson was near instantaneous by comparison. The success and interest in the game at the minor and junior level continued, as did the Inter-house League. Indeed to look at the newspapers towards the end of the 1937 season and see, as well as the Free State sides, the Munster Senior League, the junior and minor leagues, competitions like the Elvery Cup and the Burkley Cup, the Inter-house League and Schoolboys' Challenge Cup, it would be difficult to argue against the participatory aspect of the game being in rude health even if the heyday of the game as a spectator sport may appear to have passed even by then.[109] Despite Cork FC undergoing a name change to become Cork City FC, the club would over the next few seasons – in another name change to Cork United – become a dominating team in what was now styled the League of Ireland, winning the league three times in a row during the 1940s. In this chapter we have seen something of the raised profile soccer achieved in Cork as both a participatory activity and a commercial venture following the foundation of the Irish Free State in 1922. Buoyed by an expanding manufacturing base thanks to companies like Ford, and the city's major retail shops, providing employment and expendable income, the workplace played a key role in providing the impetus for both the participatory and the spectatorial aspects of the game. Of course, the economic downturn of the late 1920s and the increasing unemployment and poverty of the 1930s almost put paid to these developments, yet never quite killed off the spectatorial aspect of the game and may in fact have had a positive influence on the grass-roots game, giving those with endless enforced leisure time something constructive towards which they could put their energies. The grass-roots game in Cork by 1937 was in a very healthy position thanks to the dedication of its mostly working-class adherents on the pitch, the sideline and in the committee rooms through the thick and thin of a sometimes desperate economic situation.

6

SOCCER IN WATERFORD, 1918–1937

. . . well done, Waterford! Keep going ahead like this and next season the clubs in Cork will have more than they can do to hold their own.

Football Sports Weekly, 22 May 1926

The founding of a soccer league was a response to the revived interest in soccer in Waterford which saw ten teams take up the game by 1924. Where prior to the First World War, schools had been keen players of the game in Waterford as we saw with those who made up Waterpark Celtic and Tramore in 1909, the game was now played by a much wider mixture of people in the city and by some in the county. Waterford, following the First World War, was a different place. It had a proportionately high number of men who joined up to fight in the First World War. With many fatalities, and many more casualties, Waterford in the 1920s was haunted by the war's human cost. Unsurprisingly then, the tradition of marking Armistice Day took on important significance in Waterford, in both city and county.

This memorialising began almost immediately, with Armistice Day being marked in the city and county in 1918. Given the domestic upheavals, the divided loyalties and the varying political traditions of the period, the act of remembering was an often complicated business. In Dungarvan in 1920 for instance, there was some concern about whether or not shops would close as a mark of respect during the procession in the town and it appears that the local British forces stationed in the town ensured that businesses did indeed close by marching, fixed bayonets in hand, through the main street just after 11 o'clock in the morning, which prompted most businesses to shut their doors. In Dan Fraher's shop both Fraher and an apprentice carpenter were compelled to leave the shop and marched to remove a Sinn Féin (that's to say the Irish tricolour) flag from a position on the castle in the town and were both then brought to the barracks followed by a group of waggish young lads who whistled *Wrap the Green Flag Around Me*. The tricolour was replaced with a Union Jack, and although a lorry load of Black and Tans apparently arrived on the scene, the tense incident ended without any physical harm coming to anyone.[1]

Meanwhile in 1922, Waterford saw its biggest such gathering yet. The memorials which had been taking place each November in Waterford city were organised by the local Legion of Ex-Service Men's Club. On this, the fourth such marking of Armistice Day, the crowds attending were said to be very large, the largest yet seen for the occasion. The procession, headed by the Legion Club's banner, included both the Barrack Street Brass and Reed Band and the Erin's Hope Band. These bands, who had previously had the job of bringing joy and entertainment to sporting crowds in the city and county, were now engaged in an altogether more painful act of providing fitting music for remembrance. Although the Barrack Street Band led the procession and the Erin's Hope Band were the back marker, interspersed between the various Legion members, including the Portlaw branch, widows and other family members, was the Thomas Francis Meagher Band and the Legion's own band. When the procession along Barrack Street and the Mayor's Walk ended at Ballybricken, all four bands played the 'Dead March' from *Saul*, each in turn.[2] The role of music, and the juxtaposition of musical strains with the two-minute silence that accompanied the marking of the Armistice, was a crucial part of memorialising the First World War generally and the impact it had in Waterford is palpable from the newspaper reports.[3]

Capt Willie Redmond gave a rousing speech to the people assembled on Ballybricken saying that he hoped Irish ex-servicemen would see the benefits that were sure to accrue to Ireland in the future. He finished his speech by saying that he hoped that the Legion 'in each succeeding year, as has been the case in the past . . . will find a still greater manifestation of devotion and reverence for the memories of our comrades of the days gone by'.[4]

The following years the numbers attending the memorial in Waterford apparently increased further. On this fifth anniversary it was noted that the Flanders poppy was 'worn by many' throughout the day. The report also noted that memorial services were held across religious denominations, but Christ Church was noted especially for the tolling of its bells in memory of the dead. The assembly of the marchers began at 2.30, with the procession again headed by the Legion Club's banner and the Barrack Street Band beginning at 3pm. The report in the *Munster Express* noted that one of the most splendid banners was that of the Waterford branch of the Sailors and Firemen's Union. The circuit of the procession, which began in Ballybricken, went from Morgan Street, through Thomas Street, The Quay, The Mall, Parnell Street, Johnstown, Ballytruckle and back to Ballybricken via Bunker's Hill, Barrack Street and the Mayor's Walk. The solemnity of the occasion at the end of the march was remarkable, the banners of the Legion and the Unions were placed in the centre of a circle, when four lone buglers played *The Last Post*, led by Trumpeter Fox, bringing the procession to an end.[5]

The same procession took place the following year, with the circle being formed and all banners and placards with the names of the dead placed in the centre as music was played. It was estimated that 11,000 turned out in 1924 for the Armistice celebration in Waterford.[6] The 1926 procession saw special notice given to eighty-plus Waterford men who perished with SS *Formby* and SS *Coningbeg*, two ships owned by the Clyde Shipping Company, with a specific memorialisation taking place at 11.40am that day on the Waterford Bridge. That year the usual four city bands were joined by a band from New Ross, County Wexford and the Welsh Miner's Band from Maesteg, a part of Wales with deep Irish connections.[7] The favour was returned by the Waterford Legion band the following year, with a large crowd travelling for Remembrance Sunday celebrations by train to New Ross.[8]

On the tenth anniversary of the Armistice, the crowds were not what they had been, though apparently inclement weather had militated against the commemoration on that occasion. The procession was much the same as in previous years, and there were commemorations in both Waterford and Tramore separately.[9] The eleventh anniversary was well marked again but after this, there seems to be a drop off in the scale and coverage of the Armistice Day memorials in Waterford. The reports of 1930 in the local press recognise as much though notice again the sale and wearing of poppies in the city on the Saturday and Sunday around the Armistice, with the *Munster*

Express reporting sales amounting to £91 the previous year, raising an almost identical sum of £90 in 1930.[10]

During the same years that saw such public displays of grief among the people of Waterford for their war dead, there was a return to and resurgence in the playing of soccer, on a scale that the *Cork Sportsman* had dreamed of over a decade earlier. In such an atmosphere of loss, soccer played a role for many in Waterford, helping people to enjoy life again and take pleasure in organised leisure, as it had for those suffering the effects of unemployment in Cork.

Beginnings: the founding of the Waterford and District Football League

Portlaw, who had a team playing the game before the First World War, were once more involved, as were a team from Curraghmore, the seat of the Marquis of Waterford, along with teams from the local CYMS and YMCA, the post office, the employees of Henry Denny's pork factory, the Legion of Ex-Servicemen, the Young Favourites from the Yellow Road in the city, and the customs office in the city.[11] This mixture of gentry, civil servants, workers and youths, Catholics and Protestants, formed the Waterford and District Football League in the Waterford CYMS Hall in late 1924, following a decision made at a meeting of the Young Favourites FC.[12] The first chairman was Frank Phillips. Previously a captain in the army, he was a member of the pals battalion from Dublin rugby circles in the First World War. Phillips was no doubt one of those who thronged each November to Ballybricken to commemorate those who had died in the war. Born in Kinsale, County Cork, Phillips suffered from gunshot wounds and dysentery during the campaign at Suvla Bay before he rejoined his battalion at Salonika, yet afterwards returned to Waterford and ran his photography studio.[13]

Frank Phillips' involvement in sport was not limited to soccer. He was a keen cyclist in the period prior to the First World War and his exploits on WGD Goff's cycling track in The People's Park was often referred to in newspaper articles about him. Phillips was also a keen rugby and cricket player.[14] His contribution to soccer in Waterford was significant. As we shall see, he was involved in Waterford Celtic AFC, the first city team to succeed in becoming a Free State League member. Phillips, a photographer by trade, took many photographs of the various soccer teams in Waterford, and is probably the reason we still have so many today from that period.[15]

The first secretary to be elected was Jim Skelton of Morrison's Road, Waterford. The committee comprised of J. Barry, Isaac Woolfson, J.J. Murray, Jack Mitchell, D. Browne, J. Kennedy and Kiely.[16] The league was established just as soccer teams began forming in the city centre. The Marquis Cup started in the early 1920s as an invitational competition where the Marquis, Hugh Beresford, would assemble a team to play against a local side of his choosing. The first non-military side honoured in this way was Young Favourites. However, it would not be until 1929 that the cup was contested solely among the junior sides, when Parnell Celtic were its first winners, beating St Joseph's AFC in the final. Later knock-out competitions included the George French Shield (originally contested in Belfast) and the Infirmary Cup. The latter was sponsored by Hearne & Cahill & Co. The Infirmary Cup was not competed for until 1929 so the Waterford & District League, set up in 1924, was of vital importance in maintaining the growing interest in the sport between the end of the First World War and 1930. These knock-out competitions buttressed the sport's fledgling revival, allowing it to prosper thereafter.

The George French Shield came to the people of Waterford by way of one of their favourite entertainers. George French was a Scottish singer and comedian who frequently toured in both Dublin and Waterford. French was a popular entertainer at the time, playing the Lyric, Tivoli, Gaiety and Theatre Royal, Dublin and the Theatre Royal in Waterford. One of his most popular acts was a 'madcap Geordie footballer'.[17] He was a supporter not just of soccer, but the Civic Guard Sports and the newly formed Waterford Athletic Club, giving them ten guineas for a cup.[18] The shield is a very impressive prize indeed and continues to be played for annually to the present day. It stands at around four feet high and has a large silver relief depicting a soccer match. Having a patron from the music hall says something about the social makeup of those who made up the bulk of Waterford's soccer-playing public. French loved Waterford so much he retired there, passing away in 1938. In utter contrast to this working-class patron of the game in Waterford stands the Marquis of Waterford, Hugh Beresford. Beresford had been a longtime supporter of soccer in Waterford, as well as rugby. Indeed, he probably was the only significant upper-class patron of the game in the city or county. Judging by one account of a game from 1929, he was a decent player. In this particular match, played by a team of his choosing against a Waterford League Selected XI, his side were soundly beaten 6–2, with the Marquis himself scoring one of the two goals. The day was a success, the gate amounting to £11 10/–, which was donated to the Portlaw Football Club.[19]

The Infirmary Cup was not just a way of promoting the game of soccer, but also of promoting and helping the Infirmary itself. When the hospital required a lift to help its more immobile patients, a flag day was proposed. These were to be held on 21 and 22 June, with the 22nd coinciding with the final of the Infirmary Cup.[20] As well as the chairman Frank Phillips, another military man was among the ranks of that first committee: Jack Mitchell was a member of the armed forces in the First World War. A member of the Flying Corps, and stationed for much of his time in Cairo, he was a noted sportsman. He was 'well known in rugby and association football circles in Waterford'.[21]

Another committee member, Isaac Woolfson, who was Jewish, was born in Latvia and settled in Waterford, where he ran a scrap yard. Isaac became heavily involved in local soccer from the moment of his arrival; as well as being a committee member of the Waterford Junior League, he served on the committee of St Joseph's AFC, becoming their chairman in 1931.[22] He sought a way to increase the popularity and the numbers who played the game, and set up an employers' league, to be contested among the employees of local businesses and factories.[23] Woolfson and his family were one of a number of Jewish families then living in Waterford, including the Sherowitz family, the Osiakowskis, the Smullens, the Morris family, the Rosenthals, Robinsons, Amsdews and Levis. According to the 1911 census, there were sixty-two Jews in Waterford. The Woolfsons were a highly regarded family in Waterford soccer circles, with Isaac's nephews, Duffy, Solly and Maurice all going on to distinguished involvement in the game in the city. As Ray Rivlin notes, 'despite the traditional tendency of Orthodox Jewry to regard sporting pursuits as a waste of learning time, Irish Jewish interest in sport goes back to 1895;[24] though ultimately 'most Jewish communities in Ireland were too small to be self-sustaining in recreational pursuits'.[25] Cormac Ó Gráda notes that 'sport fostered communal pride but it also undoubtedly narrowed the cultural divide between native and immigrant, and in time many Jews joined and supported non-Jewish rugby and football clubs'.[26] The Woolfsons are undoubtedly a great example of this very phenomenon. The contribution of both Woolfson and Phillips was recognised early on, with an article appearing in the *Football Sports Weekly* entitled 'Willing Workers in Waterford' which praised the efforts of both men in fostering the game of soccer in the city.[27]

Rugby saw an upswing in its fortunes during this period, and Frank Phillips was involved here, too. The first report of a game of rugby in the city found in the local newspapers was in 1884. It was played in early December by two teams representing other sports clubs: the Waterford Bicycle Club and the Waterford Boat Club.[28] The next game to make the local newspaper was not played until November 1888 when a Waterford selection played Garryowen.[29] The gap of years between the two matches is telling – if attempts to establish clubs were made, then they went unnoticed. In reality there were only ever two substantial rugby clubs in the city – Waterford City RFC, founded in 1893, and Waterpark RFC. Aside from these two clubs, the mainstays of the game in Waterford, only a handful of other teams playing rugby in Waterford have been encountered: a McMahon's XV and Waterford Rangers in 1900. Aside from a single newspaper report, nothing encountered suggests that either of these teams played again. In 1909, Bohemians were founded. This team does not appear to have ever played any matches after it was formed. If it did, the games were never reported. This seems unlikely, since the *Waterford News*, which reported the meetings to organise the club, never contained any match reports – had there been matches to report, they certainly would have. Either way the club never really got off the ground. A group of Waterford bankers played a game in 1910, according to a report of the *Cork Examiner*.[30] In 1922, a game was played at Grantstown between 'The Town' and local bankers.[31] Waterford City used the same pitch for rugby games against Kilkenny and Enniscorthy around the same period.[32] Enniscorthy were frequent visitors to the City side in those years. In 1926, the CYMS in the city took up the playing of rugby.[33] The same year saw considerable flirtation with the game, with Mount Sion, the Christian Brothers school, Newtown school, Bishop Foy's High School and a team from the Clyde Shipping Company based on the quays in the city all taking part in the game. A team from Tycor also played a match, as did a group from Woodstown.[34]

The establishment of a club in the town of Dungarvan was another positive for the game in the same era, this club forming in 1927.[35] CYMS were able to run two XVs in the 1929/30 season.[36] The City club made an attempt at bringing some big names to Waterford to encourage interest in the game, playing matches against both Dublin University and Dolphin of Cork. Waterford City Rugby Club had, for its secretary, the very capable Frank Phillips, so instrumental in the development of soccer in Waterford.

The Waterford City club managed to get some sponsorship for the 1929/30 season from Beamish & Crawford of Cork.[37] Waterford City Rugby Club's committee also included Martin S. Breen, proprietor of Breen's Hotel on the quays in the city. Breen was president of the club in the period 1928–30 at the same time serving as vice-president of the Waterford Chamber of Commerce.[38] It was in this period that the club won the Munster Junior Cup, beating UCC in the semi-final and Dolphin in the final. It was also their second season entering teams at the Senior Cup level. The club played twenty-two friendly matches that season, which was the bulk of their play – the net result being that the club could not progress to a level that would see them impacting on the game in Munster in a significant way. In 1925, the Leinster branch of the IRFU reorganised its junior competitions, and the Junior Challenge Cup, run since 1888, became the Provincial Towns Cup, played for by clubs outside of Dublin in the province. Waterford CYMS boasted in 1930 that the only defeat they suffered that season had been one against the eventual winners of the Leinster Provincial Towns Cup.[39] It might be the case that Waterford rugby would have been better served by affiliation, not to the Munster branch of the IRFU but to the Leinster branch. That way a season of twenty-two friendly matches could have been avoided, and the chance of some silverware in the form of the Provincial Towns Cup could have been on offer to Waterford's rugby-playing clubs; in addition, the opportunity for the public to watch more regular and less one-sided competitive rugby. A similar competition did exist in Waterford in the period 1926–28, the Waterford City Cup, but failed to have the desired effect, being nowhere near as important as the Provincial

Towns Cup, or similar initiatives in west Cork, or north Munster, like the Cork County Cup or the Garryowen Cup, in providing competition outside the already established clubs in Waterford.[40] Waterford City would win the Munster Junior Cup a second time in 1930; all the same, success at senior level evaded them. The underdog status of Waterford City Rugby Club at this time is summed up in the 'rugby jottings' of the *Limerick Leader*, where Limerick had been described as the 'urbs antiqua' in rugby terms, even if in recent years Waterford was the 'urbs intacta' where the Munster Junior Cup was concerned.[41]

Despite the best efforts of Waterford City, Waterpark and the CYMS, the game seemed to have a limited appeal with the population of Waterford, though undoubtedly the state of the game was much healthier by the end of the 1920s than it had been previously in the city and county. The improved state of the game was even recognised by *The Irish Times*, where a rugby correspondent wrote in 1928 that 'with the revival a few years back, five healthy clubs sprang up'.[42] The Waterpark club, which had begun again in the 1925/26 season, were very active in the city's social life, with dances and dinners that helped to promote the game as well as providing a stall at the Sisters of Charity bazaar which helped to raise £13.[43] The club also donated money to the City and County Infirmary to the tune of £33 on one occasion.[44] The two main Waterford teams relied heavily on competition from Cork and Tipperary to maintain them, also playing a handful of games against teams from Kilkenny and even Carlow. Despite this flowering of the game in city and county in the middle of the 1920s, it did not gain the kind of foothold it had in Cork, Limerick or Tipperary.

The rugby clubs worked together for each other's benefit, securing for the game permanent grounds at Ballinaneeshagh, the Bully Acre, where as we shall see, soccer was also played.[45] Rugby suffered something of a nomadic existence in Waterford, with games played there, at Grantstown, and elsewhere. A move to Ozier Park, the home of soccer in the city, had even been mooted. Although it merely constituted a small fraternity in the city, rugby was a part of Waterford's social life and its place was not entirely negligible in the history of Munster rugby. It is worth considering the factors that saw rugby control such a small part in the sporting landscape in Waterford in this period, despite the considerable and visible activities of the clubs. Even though Waterford would, along with other parts of the south-east province, establish themselves briefly at the end of the 1920s, as O'Callaghan notes, 'little had changed in the fashion in which the Munster committee conducted its business . . . administrative power was shared among a hardcore of seven senior clubs . . .'⁴⁶ Neither the Cork nor Limerick teams were likely to want to give much of a voice to new clubs emerging in the region, having enjoyed a monopoly of power for so long. At the end of 1929, Waterford was given some representation on the committee of the Munster branch, but the other seven committee members were from Cork and Limerick, with another four separate officers elected, meaning the Waterford representative was one in a group of thirteen.⁴⁷ Without much of a say in the affairs of the game, perhaps many were put off by the peripheral role they would be offered.

Martin S. Breen served as president of the Waterford City Rugby Club during its most successful period on the field of play. Breen, a hotel proprietor, was a member of the Waterford Industrial Association, a significant presence in the city's Chamber of Commerce; he was also given to philanthropic interests – subscribing £10 to a fund for a new convent for the Franciscans in the city and encouraging other Chamber members to help send the city's poor children on a holiday excursion.⁴⁸ Breen, though, was foremost commercially minded and when Waterford Celtic AFC were elected to the Free State League in 1930, his hotel was the venue for discussions about raising finances for the club's entry and he was involved in figuring out how such a thing could be achieved. He was to be an important force in the club throughout the 1930s.⁴⁹

An important emerging businessman in Waterford, Breen's patronage alone was not enough to help propel rugby in Waterford and capitalise on its new-found popularity. Equally his business eye alerted him to the trend that saw soccer emerge as a potential money-maker in the world of the new commercial leisure. Another noteworthy feature of Waterford and its rugby was that only some of the schools in Waterford run by a Catholic order took up the game. The biggest, and most influential, schools of the De La Salle brothers and the original Christian Brothers' School of Mount Sion played the game only briefly; it is likely the refusal to allow Sunday rugby was off-putting to them especially. The significance of this absence cannot be overstated. In the end though, it might be argued that what happened to rugby in Waterford, was soccer.

Progress and Expansion in Waterford

In 1924, Young Favourites, the team discussed above, played a team from the Legion of Ex-Service Men at the Sportsfield. Already we've seen in Chapter Two the long battle between those who ran the Waterford Sportsfield Company and a number of people who wished to see the Sportsfield used only for the promotion of Gaelic games. This game may well have been a special dispensation, though it is difficult to know. Either way, the symbolic nature of a team of young men playing war veterans on the pitch that, as we saw in Chapter Two, was the cause of such rancour in the pre-independence era is striking.

Young Favourites were formed sometime in late 1923 or early 1924, since in February of 1924 they played Cahir Park of Tipperary in the first round of the Munster Senior Cup at the Sportsfield in Waterford city.[50] Presumably they did not get far since no mention of them again appears until almost six months later. This time, however, the club was not in the papers for sporting reasons. The dressing rooms of the Sportsfield were broken into and football togs, jerseys, boots and shin guards were stolen, as were the boots of the proprietor, P. Jackman.[51]

Ultimately in the first quarter of the twentieth century at least, the company in charge of the Sportsfield got their way and the Sportsfield was used for general sporting purposes and not just by the GAA. In the 1920s, the Sportsfield was occasionally used by the soccer and rugby teams in the city and in the summer of 1926 there had even been a boxing tournament held there. It seems pragmatism prevailed over principle when it came to sharing pitches.[52] A month after the robbery, Young Favourites found themselves up against Cahir Park once more – this time in the Free State Cup. Cahir Park beat Young Favourites three goals to nil on that occasion. On the same weekend the YMCA played a works team from the bacon curers H. Denny and Sons. The latter team was the club of the pork processors in the centre of the city.

During their brief time as a club, Young Favourites played a great many of the clubs that emerged in Waterford in the wake of the founding of the Waterford and District League. In the period 1924–30 many junior clubs sprang up around the city and county. Among these were CYMS, Mayor's Walk, Temperance Hall, Civil Service, St John's, St Joseph's, Ramblers, O'Connell Celtic and City Rangers. This last side made it all the way to the semi-final of the Munster Senior Cup in 1926; the Dublin paper *Football Sports Weekly* reported that 'the second semi-final of the Munster senior cup was played at Waterford last Sunday, the opposing teams being Victoria Celtic, Cork and City Rangers, Waterford'. It was, the reporter felt, an opportunity for the MFA 'to see for themselves how the game was progressing in that portion of their command . . . any inconvenience [in travelling] was more than compensated by the enthusiasm prevailing amongst the Soccer public in the City of Urbs Intacta'. The report insisted that 'the local governing body are to be congratulated on the strides which have been made with the game . . . well done, Waterford! Keep going ahead like this and next season the clubs in Cork will have more than they can do to hold their own.'[53] Throughout 1927, this same publication was especially positive towards the development of the game in Waterford. In February of that year one article suggests that the Munster FA should endeavour to have some of the bigger Dublin sides such as Shelbourne, Bohemians, Shamrock Rovers and Drumcondra play in Waterford and Limerick in order to promote the game and to give better opposition and bigger gates.[54]

St Joseph's FC, similarly founded in late 1923, came out of their community and its needs, especially the needs of young boys, directly. As discussed in the Introduction, the St Joseph's Boys Club was set up at the same time on Hennessy's Road in the city by the clergy and the St Vincent de Paul Society to provide a place for young boys to attend lectures, engage in physical culture through gymnastics, athletics and soccer, as well as have their 'spiritual health' catered for. This boys' club operated similarly to a CYMS. Its running was overseen by the Rev Dr Bernard Hackett, then Bishop of Waterford and Lismore. Clubs like St Joseph's were vital, given the cramped living conditions and poverty then experienced by many in the centre of Waterford city.

Despite the strongly Catholic influence to be found in the boys' club, the conflation of this ethos with a culturally nationalist one did not necessarily follow and the boys' own choice of soccer did not seem to be problematic to anyone involved in the club. The bishop, who was president of the club and instrumental in its establishment, had no qualms about the prospect of the boys playing soccer, despite its unfavourable association with the recently deposed administration of the country. Concerned more for their physical and spiritual well-being, it's unlikely he cared what they played as long as they did so through the club, where their mortal souls could be guided in the correct fashion and not causing trouble on the streets of the city. However, one commentator in the *Munster Express*, Moltóir,[55] seemed to find the choice of soccer particularly abhorrent to Gaelic sensibilities. In his column 'In the Gaelic Arena' he wrote that 'the only field games being encouraged there [at St Joseph's Boys Club], as far as I know, is soccer and this can hardly be classified as one of Ireland's games, seeing that it owes its introduction to this country to England's army of occupation'.[56] Moltóir then suggests that the playing of Gaelic games would be of more benefit to the boys, stating that if you have never witnessed a hurling final 'you do not know what real enthusiasm is, neither can you form an idea of the mighty deeds that can be performed by the unison of muscle, brain and brawn in a contest of speed, science and skill unrivalled by any team game in the world'.[57] Despite the divided views on the subject, sufficient sympathy ensured soccer witnessed growth rather than decline. Generally speaking, this reflects the dwindling fires of cultural nationalism post-independence, when much of the impetus for the vast majority had disappeared.

St Joseph's Boys Club hosted sports days, and was itself the beneficiary of rugby matches, and frequently held lectures on subjects that were in keeping with the traditions of boys learning 'useful' skills from this period, and which was also a feature of both Catholic and Protestant young mens' associations at this time. Moltóir's was one more of those voices whose charges against soccer we examined in Chapter Four. And like with so many of the commentators and critics examined in that chapter, whatever the protestations of Moltóir, the popularity of the game of soccer amongst Waterford's young in the 1920s can be in no doubt. Nor does it seem likely that Bishop Hackett would castigate the boys for playing the game if it meant their continued involvement with the club as well as the soccer club. Certainly Hackett was not keen on all sporting endeavour and took a dim view in particular of horse and greyhound racing; his views on attending race meetings and greyhound races on religious holidays was even picked up by the English press. Hackett's own patronage extended to the GAA, giving a cup to the East Waterford GAA for the establishment of a schools competition.[58] Of course, it would be wrong to suggest that there was a merely benign influence on the membership – the business of building good, moral, Catholic young men was the primary objective of the club, if not in the finish its ultimate achievement. Again, like industrial paternalism, the sport played was secondary to the ideology of its role in helping to maintain industrial discipline, encourage fitness and accord and asserting social hierarchy.

The remarkable pace of growth for soccer in the city centre during these years can be at least partially explained by the absence of any great competition from other team sports. In the 1920s, Gaelic games was not as well-established in the city centre as it was in parts of the county. This, coupled with the only modest interest in rugby, meant that soccer as a game was well placed to fill a vacuum for competitive team sport. It was significant of course that both Erin's Own and Mount Sion hurling clubs emerged in this period, but the impact of that emergence wouldn't be felt until much later in the 1930s, when Waterford won a first Minor title in hurling in 1938. Thus it was the case, in the meantime, that soccer was best placed to emerge as *the* team sport in the city.

Many of the matches played by the various soccer clubs established in the city took place on the Bully Acre in Ballinaneeshagh to the west of the city, near an area that was appropriately named Pastimeknock. The name of the Bully Acre is itself historic. The Royal Hospital Kilmainham also had near it an unmarked site which acquired the name of 'The Bully's Acre'.[59] There are suggestions that the practice of naming fields in this fashion was popular in the west. In Waterford, the location of the Bully Acre is given as Ballinaneeshagh. Ballinaneeshagh is an area which contains a cemetery: St Otteran's. Opposite this cemetery, a site is currently in use as a sports ground and in the hands of Waterford Crystal Ltd. Since there is ordinarily a continuity to be found in the use of greenfield sites for sport, this seemed a likely candidate for the Bully Acre but the pitch was actually on a greenfield site, adjacent to the current pitches, now a housing estate. One of the earliest direct references to the Bully Acre was in 1926. A game was to be played there between selected Waterford and Tipperary soccer teams.[60] Two years later, an indirect reference to the pitch can be found:

> My earliest recollection of a Mooncoin team brings me away
> back to my early boyhood days, when one fine Sunday, instead

of attending at a catechism class, I hied me to the 'Bully Acre'
where Mooncoin and Tubberadora were listed for a hurling
exhibition it was my first acquaintance of the game and the
speed and skill of the camán wielders made a deep impression
on my young mind.[61]

This piece, written by Moltóir, is significant, since the game it refers
to is not soccer, but hurling. Unfortunately there is no date for us to
place this use of the field. Undoubtedly though, Moltóir would have
been scandalised by the use of this same field now for both soccer
and rugby. A number of years later, further reminiscences of the use
of the field for hurling help us to date this use more accurately, when
we are told how 'hurling came on very slowly in Waterford, though
several good matches were played by Kilkenny and Tipperary teams
at tournaments held at Ballinaneeshagh ('The Bully Acre') during the
revival days of nearly a half a century ago, but little headway was
made locally in hurling'.[62] This notice from 1937 suggests that the
Bully Acre was used for hurling purposes as far back as the 1890s. In
the period after the 1920s, the use of the pitch changed once again
from soccer to another football code, rugby, informing us that
'younger readers may be interested to learn that the Rugby Grounds,
Ballinaneeshagh, generally known as 'The Bully Acre', was the original grounds of the Waterford Football League, and was the scene of
many stirring soccer games in the early 1920s'.[63]

Those teams who used the pitch as a soccer grounds include
O'Connell Celtic, Temperance Hall and St Joseph's, Young Favourites and Red Rovers among others.[64] The switch to rugby took place
relatively early, since 'the work of laying out the new Rugby grounds
at the Bully Acre are advancing rapidly, and the first match – between
Waterford City and Garryowen (Limerick) will take place there on
27 September [1928]'.[65]

The Bully Acre was also the site of at least one Free State League
game, between Waterford and Shelbourne.[66] Such a game could have
only taken place in the period after 1930, suggesting that the pitch's
use as a rugby ground was not exclusive in the period. What is clear
from these newspaper reports is that the Bully Acre was centrally
important to the development of not only soccer, but a wide variety
of sports in a period when grounds were few and far between, much
like the Sportsfield, and were organised at a grass-roots level. Its pre-
eminence as a soccer ground was soon overtaken, however.

The difficulties experienced in developing the Sportsfield or the Bully Acre never seemed to beset Ozier Park. The grounds, on private land owned by the White family, were sold to the Waterford and District Football League for use as the main playing pitch for cup finals in the district and the ground would also serve as the home of Waterford Celtic, the Munster Senior League side that would later become Waterford FC in 1930 when it joined the top division of Irish football, the Free State League. Not only that, but there was another pitch in the area belonging to Erin's Own GAA club, a club that was founded in 1924, the same year that the Waterford and District Football League was formed and moved in to Ozier Park next door.

But the advancement of the game cannot simply be viewed from the perspective of the available infrastructure for the more organised clubs. While social conditions in the heart of the city were often quite poor, football was immensely popular. Such was the popularity of the game among Waterford's young at that time that even with clubs like St Joseph's, the playing of the game in the street had become a considerable nuisance. Between 1927 and 1930, a good number of cases appeared before the district court relating to young boys who had been apprehended for playing football in the street, often with broken windows becoming a problem from stray footballs. On one occasion a total of more than thirty young boys were summoned by the court to pay one shilling for the 'nuisance' they had caused with their ball-playing. The judge said that it was a pity there were not more playing pitches in the city, and thought it a good thing that the boys should be playing football, calling it a 'natural' thing. The previous day he had fined two boys five shillings and warned those in front of him that future fines would be two shillings six pence.[67] So, although it was thought good that boys engaged in vigorous and healthy activity, it was not acceptable to do so on their own terms with their limited resources. This, even though the city corporation, who were evidently aware of the lack of facilities and must have known that street football was causing a nuisance, failed in any appreciable way to alleviate the difficulty. They preferred instead for the courts and civil society to deal with the issue, it seems. In an era when schoolboy football had not yet become organised, incidents like these highlight further the positive role of a club like St Joseph's or the CYMS in catering to Waterford's young men. Not alone that, but given the cramped housing conditions in that area of the city, the necessity of a greater number of green spaces to be provided for local boys and girls.

In 1926, following on from the success of the league established in 1924, a juvenile league was formed by that body to provide an organised setting for adolescent boys to play the game. The following clubs affiliated for the inaugural season: Southward United, Celtic Rovers, St Luke's, Young Favourites, Parnell Celtic, Longcourse Rangers, Civil Service, Éire Óg, Red Rovers and Shamrock Rovers. The last of these took their name from the Dublin club, probably as a result of that recent victory in the Free State League for the 1924/25 season. Another team that is mentioned in this period is Riffs. Some of the other team names stand out too – Parnell Celtic is an interesting name to pick forty years after the height of his powers, as is Éire Óg, with its Fenian connotations. The former though may well refer to Parnell Street rather than the political figure. Another team whose name provides a distinct link is that of Longcourse Rangers. *Cúrsa fada* is the Irish name for Barrack Street in Waterford, previously home to the British Army in the city, which translated, literally means, a long course. As well as this, most of the housing in that area was built in a number of projects from 1897, 1900 and 1901.

Living in small terraced houses, many people from the area would have worked in the pork processing industry run by the Denny family, much like those who lived on the lower Yellow Road and formed Young Favourites. At that time the Yellow Road was mostly occupied by people employed in the pork industry or as general labourers. In 1911, out of a total of seventy-five houses examined in the area, with a total of 104 occupants, twenty-five people were involved in the pork industry and the same number listed as general labourers. Eight of the twenty involved in the pork business were butchers, with the majority of them listed as 'pig dealers/buyers'. Aside from this, there were six shopkeepers, six employed by Great Southern Railway and another six boot makers. Although the houses in the area were not so bad, as was the case in many of the lanes that would be demolished in the 1930s, still they were far from palatial and it is no wonder that in such small houses with so many children, most of them found their way onto the streets to play games, including soccer.

Among the residents in the area were the Hale family. Two of the boys listed in the 1911 census were John and Alfred. John was one year old in 1911 and Alfred was five. By the time Young Favourites came into being in 1924, they were the perfect age for joining the club – fourteen and eighteen respectively. Both would play for the club for many years. Alfie, as he was known, would have a distinguished playing career in England as well as Ireland, along with Tommy Arrigan from the same area. Arrigan, who like Alfie played for a period in Bristol, was the first Waterford man to earn an Irish international cap in 1937. Arrigan's one and only cap was in a 3–3 draw played at Dalymount Park against Norway as part of World Cup qualification.[68]

By 1927, the makeup of soccer in Waterford had again changed with yet more new clubs in existence. Erin's Hope was a new club established that February in the band room of Erin's Hope Prize Fife and Drum Band on Newgate Street.[69] At a meeting prior to the start of the new season, the Waterford teams met with the Munster Football Association, which was chaired by G. Gilligan. Present at the meeting from Waterford were: Waterford Celtic (senior and junior), Hibernian, City Rangers, St Joseph's, Longcourse Celtic, McCrackens, Riffs, Tramore Celtic, Young Favourites, Red Rovers and Mayor's Walk. This meeting was important as two new grounds in the Poleberry area of the city were given over for use for association football. As well as this, a loan of £20 was given to Waterford council for the promotion of the game.[70]

Young Favourites were among the clubs in 1928 to field teams in both the first and second divisions of the Waterford League. The First Division comprised Young Favourites, Tramore Celtic, Longcourse, St Thomas' and Hibernians as well as Waterford Celtic. The teams listed as being Second Division sides were Tramore Rovers, Mayor's Walk and Young Favourites. McCrackens, Riffs and City Rangers were also expected to return, presumably to the Second Division. By this point, a consolidated number of clubs playing the game has emerged since the immediate post-independence period in the city and county. This is similar to what happened with rugby in Cork after 1900, where a strong and well-organised group of clubs maintained the sport. The significant difference in this case is that Waterford was a much smaller area, but was still able to maintain twelve clubs. As the end of the decade approached, yet more teams sprang up in Waterford; we know this thanks to the north Munster section of the draw for the Munster Junior Cup. Bohemians and Tramore Rookies were clubs who had previously gone unmentioned in the papers regarding junior soccer in Waterford.[71]

Despite rising unemployment in Waterford in the 1920s, with around 2,000 men and women idle in the city, and the active labour force falling from 8,017 in 1926 to 7,625 in 1936, work-based soccer developed in the interim. In 1931, a mid-summer league was established, made up of teams from some of the city's major employers, including Graves & Co., Hearne's, Great Southern Railway and the Clyde Shipping Company.[72] Throughout the period, so many teams sprang up in the city, with all age groups playing, although one among them all soon established itself as the premier club. Waterford Celtic rose quickly through the ranks from the local district league to the Munster Senior League before transforming themselves into Waterford FC in 1930 when they joined the Free State League. The work of transforming themselves from Celtic, one of dozens of local sides, to a club representing the aspirations of a soccer-mad city was considerable and required enormous effort from many quarters. As we will see, it was a community effort to ensure the club's first foray into the top level of Irish soccer was a successful one.

From Celtic to City-wide Representation: the making of Waterford FC

By the mid-1930s, the landscape of Waterford soccer had changed greatly from the moribund state in which the game found itself in 1921, with Waterford FC now in the Free State League, a strong local league not just at junior level, but for juveniles and minors too, as well as a factory league. In spite of these developments, unemployment was rampant in the city, reaching such a pitch that the unemployed, as part of a general national movement, organised themselves, like their Cork counterparts discussed in the last chapter, into the Waterford Able-Bodied Unemployed Association. It has been argued that Waterford in the 1930s was unusually productive, driven by the increased industrialisation the city was undergoing as a result of protectionist policy, just as commercial sport like greyhound racing and Free State League soccer was beginning to make its impact in what was increasingly a factory town. One remarkable

171

sign of this industrialisation was the sale, in 1936, of land earmarked by the Waterford Corporation's Public Health Committee for a playground in 1924, for the establishment of a jute factory on the same site, which subsequently opened in 1937.[73]

While still Waterford Celtic, the club made an early attempt at entering the Free State League, with a great deal of support from some in the sporting media, though it would prove unsuccessful. In early 1927, before they first made a bid, an article about the game in the city felt sufficiently confident to say that 'Waterford your hour has arrived. The time is now opportune for you to get together and a launch a club in the Free State League.' Encouragement is offered from the wider soccer community, with the writer insisting that 'Dublin is with you, Cork is with you, all soccer Ireland is with you'. Particular emphasis is laid on the success of Fordsons in Cork, who 'Cork sent . . . into the Free State League, since when they have never looked back. It gave such a fillip to the game down Corkonia that surpassed their wildest dreams of imagination, and now Cork is sending another team into the premier League next season. Corkmen are assured that nothing succeeds like success . . . the game [in Waterford] would spread in a fashion that would take your breath away.'[74]

A year later, the *Football Sports Weekly* was once again eagerly anticipating a Waterford entry to the Free State League, when one of their correspondents wrote 'I am informed from a reliable source, [Waterford] intend to make an application to the Free State League next season. The admission of Waterford to the league would do a great deal of good for the game in that part of the country. At present they have a very good side that includes Hale, Jack Doran and Arrigan. They will have the full financial backing of the townspeople. Their present gates, I am informed, reach close on £100 [per game].'[75]

The club had parallels with Fordsons since its rise was equally rapid. In 1928, the Waterford side, along with Bohemians of Cork and the Leinster League, were part of talks for the development of a Second Division of top-level Irish soccer. *The Irish Times* stated that such a league, including these teams, 'would form the nucleus of an alliance that would be a valuable asset to the game'.[76] Waterford Celtic and Cork Bohemians seemed to be the premier sides in Munster senior soccer circles at this point, excluding Fordsons. This is reiterated by this unusual notice regarding both teams coming joint-second in the Munster Senior League in the 1928/29 season:

Reminiscent of King Solomon's judgment is the proposal of the
Munster Football Council to cut in half the medals offered to
runners-up in the Munster Championship and League Cup for
the year 1928–29. Fordsons, Cork won the championship, and
Waterford Celtic and Cork Bohemians tied for second place. As a
re-play between the latter two teams is doubtful, it is probable, as
already proposed, that the medals will be cut in halves and
divided between the teams.[77]

The club was a significant member of the Waterford and District
League and, in the Munster Senior League, the club's first match
announced them as serious contenders, with a resounding 6–0
victory against an overwhelmed Fermoy. In the summer of 1929, a
year before they became a Free State League side, they discovered
they could no longer rent out Ozier Park for matches and would
have to look elsewhere instead. At this meeting, Frank Phillips
presided, and oversaw the election of T. Long as team manager. On
the same night they also lost Isaac Woolfson, who resigned his position in the club.[78] Interestingly, a report in March of 1928 in the
Football Sports Weekly does not point to any of this, except the wran-
gling over Ozier Park:

> Followers of the soccer code in Waterford are grateful to the
> worthy president of the club [Waterford Celtic] J Wolfson [sic],
> a gentleman of real sporting instinct whose love of the game is
> beyond all else, so much so indeed that it is anything but a prof-
> itable past time. But he doesn't mind in the least. Money with
> him is no object when it comes to popularising the game in his
> native town and district, and football in the Free States owes him
> much. It is no exaggeration to state that only for him football in
> Waterford might be a dead letter. We take our hat off to Mr.
> Woolfson, gentleman and sportsman.[79]

In the same issue, they also tell us that 'the secretary of the local club
assures us that the outlook is very bright down that way. We are
mighty pleased to hear that, but from what we ourselves noticed
there seems no doubt whatsoever that association football in
Waterford has not only caught on, but that it has come to stay.'[80] Not
only that, but it also considers what Ozier would be like were
Waterford Celtic to be in the Free State League, noting that the team
'have a good playing pitch, but the possibilities of increasing the
holding capacity of the ground are somewhat limited by the proximity of the houses'.[81]

Nineteen twenty-nine had been a difficult year for the club. Earlier in July the club had been informed that their application for entry into the Free State League had been turned down, and that Jacob's and Bray Unknowns had been re-elected to the league instead.[82] Despite such a setback, the club was approaching the oncoming season very seriously. They saw it as their duty, not only to do their best in both the Munster Senior League and the Free State Cup, but also to act as custodians of the game in Waterford. We are told that 'Waterford Celtic . . . intend to educate the local material to an extent that will ensure a much higher standard of football than formerly'.[83]

The report tells us they secured a player-manager who had considerable experience in both the English and Scottish Football Leagues. This was a professional outfit. The club also took over the league's grounds at Poleberry, and switched their jerseys to blue and white, traditional colours of Waterford. Their new chairman was Frank Phillips, who had previously been chairman of the Waterford Football League.[84] Their place as the premier club in the city cannot be in doubt in this period. This was not just on an organisational level, but on the pitch also, where we are told 'Waterford Celtic completed on Sunday a record that will hardly ever be equalled in Munster football. They have finished their home fixtures for 1929–29 [sic] and at the completion it is found that they have not once sustained defeat in the two seasons they have competed in the provincial competitions.' At that point it seemed like a certainty that the club should gain admission to the Free State League, especially considering such a track record. The article goes on to say that the record '. . . is a promising prelude to their entry to the Free State League next season'.[85]

Despite such a professional outlook from those who ran the club and those who played for it, the club's relationship with the powers-that-be in Munster soccer was not always easy. An article in *The Irish Times* in 1930 informs us that 'Waterford Celtic wrote complaining [to the Council of the Free State FA] that they had not received a game in the Munster League for eleven weeks. It was agreed that the letter should be sent to the Munster FA for investigation, and to report to the Council.'[86] Evidently, the organisational skills present in Waterford Celtic were not to be found among those who now ran the Munster Senior League. The letter does not appear to have had the desired effect upon the Munster League, as another *Irish Times* article informed us that 'Waterford Celtic are dissatisfied with their treatment from the Munster League authorities. They have not had a league game for weeks, and are arranging friendly games to keep them in tune. Dundalk will visit them on St Patrick's Day, and in the mean-time, the Free State FA will make an effort to straighten matters out for them.'[87] Doubtless the club was glad when they were eventually admitted into the Free State League. Waterford Celtic was no different from any other club in the city at the time, despite their success. They too were reliant upon patronage, voluntary work and voluntary funding. This is also recognised in their own decision to play a benefit match for St Joseph's Boys Club.[88] St Joseph's would no doubt prove a fruitful source of talent in time to come so it was surely in the interests of Waterford Celtic to support the club. A sup-porters' club was established by Waterford Celtic which bought the Foresters Hall for use by members; membership was open to all those affiliated with soccer teams in Waterford.[89] A meeting was held in July to organise support for the club among local businessmen – including as mentioned previously Martin Breen, one of rugby's keenest supporters in the city – and the plans agreed upon were put into action the following month.[90]

A collection was made among the various businesses of the city, which secured £500 before the club began its first season. Support for the club was encouraged too, since it was expected that it would provide a considerable boost to the local economy, with the spending power of individuals attending away games estimated to be 10/– per head, thus a crowd between 1,500 and 5,000 could have a major impact on the pecuniary well-being of local traders.[91] This support is further illustrated by a notice in 1930 of a benefit night for the club held in the Broad Street Cinema in the city. A pro-gramme of singing and music-playing was put on as well as 'the usual picture programme'.[92]

The club's preparations stepped up a gear towards the end of the summer and as they entered their first season in the Free State League: 'the Committee of Management of Waterford Celtic AFC have issued several hundred circulars to football supporters in the city and district to secure debenture shares to the extent of at least £500. The special sub-committee appointed recently is in communication with a number of English and Scottish players, to whom they have offered terms.'[93] In a city with economic problems in the 1920s, the prospect of Free State soccer offered up the potential of both direct and indirect monetary reward. Given this, it is no wonder the new club was so heavily backed by the city's business people.[94] The club seems to be most excited about the prospects of the various Dublin teams coming to Waterford for away matches, since 'St James' Gate have intimated their intention of running an excursion here on 31 August in connection with their league game, and are guaranteeing at least fifteen hundred followers'.[95] A big gate of this kind was ultimately what membership of the Free State League was all about.

Waterford Celtic were no strangers to either St James' Gate or indeed clubs such as Shelbourne. In March of 1930 Waterford Celtic had played St James' Gate in a friendly match in Ozier Park. A similar friendly had been played by Waterford Celtic and Shelbourne a couple of years previously in 1928, when the Dublin side beat the Waterford side 5–2.[96] A couple of weeks after the meeting regarding debenture shares we learn that the club was in talks to take a number of players from Bournemouth, Liverpool and Tottenham Hotspur.[97] The club introduced a large number of non-natives to the side – George Wilson of Bournemouth, Dick Forshaw formerly of Everton and Liverpool, a winger by the name of Lindsay from Tottenham Hotspur who had a spell with Llanelli, and Jack Doran, former international and Celtic player, was appointed to the position of player manager.[98] Doran had played for a large number of teams: Brighton and Hove Albion, Crewe Alexandra and Manchester City in the Football League; in the Southern League he played for Pontypridd, Coventry City, Norwich City and Mid Rhondda United – the last of these clubs folded in 1928. In Ireland he played for both Shelbourne and Fordsons before finishing his playing career with Boston Town in the Midland League.[99]

The considerable influx of foreign talent into the Waterford side is an excellent example of the 'open door' which developed as a result of the founding of the FAIFS and the Free State League. Unlike the Irish League in Northern Ireland, no inter-league board between the FAIFS and the Football League in England had been established to recognise the registration of players with clubs, thus players were able to move freely from England to the new Free State, making relations between the two leagues incredibly strained in the coming years and decades.[100] For Waterford FC though, this brought much-needed experience into the side; it was also a means to draw locals into the ground to see men who'd made it at the very top level of the English game. Despite such high levels of organisation and buying power, the club would finish out the season in ninth place, winning just eight games. The club in this guise would not last long, failing to seek readmission to the league for the 1932/33 season before returning a number of years later to win the Free State Cup in 1937, after which there was never the same trouble.

In some respects Waterford FC came late to the party of the 1920s soccer boom. It is also striking that the club should fail to seek readmission after 1932, a year when the window for exemption of soccer from the entertainments duty imposed by the government was closed.[101] Unlike Fordsons/Cork FC or the other clubs, Waterford FC only benefited from this exemption for half the time of the other clubs; their exit from the league also coincided with the organised unemployed of the city attempting to elect a representative to the Waterford Corporation: Thomas Purdue. Purdue, in one speech given in the People's Park in the city, said that 'if unemployment is not dealt with as a national question, it will become a living cancer on the life of the state. We exceed in number, by far, any other party in the country, and our demands are the largest. It is up to you to concentrate on the goal you set before yourselves . . . work for every unemployed man.'[102] Becoming increasingly incendiary, Purdue exclaimed that 'if we are not going to get what we want, we will have the city like the Temple of Jerusalem. We won't leave a stone upon a stone.' A meeting of the unemployed in November saw the chair of the meeting denounce communism openly and strongly, saying that 'they saw no reason why they should follow in the path of Trotsky, Lenin or Stalin'.[103] This was not uncommon. As Máirtín Ó Catháin has noted of the Derry Unemployed Workers' Movement from the same era, although they were allied with a communist front, they were not themselves communist and in fact disavowed communism.[104] This was not to say however that the organised unemployed of Waterford wouldn't threaten violent tactics, as there was a threat to loot in Dungarvan if the demands for increased assistance weren't met only days later in the pages of *The Irish Times*.[105] Their demands were met, though little seemed to improve in terms of opportunities for many. Small victories were to be won here and there, and while an organised unemployed was stronger in voice than an unorganised one, unemployment continued to plague the south-east right to the end of the 1930s. Things had got to such a state in Waterford that an

Unemployed Men's Club was founded in 1940, taking up residence in the unused Airmount House, including a large farm.

With such pressing issues in the city, that Waterford FC, despite finishing third at the end of the 1931/32 season, opted out and folded as a going concern is perhaps unsurprising, even if it was described by 'Socaro' in the *Irish Press* as 'almost a tragedy' for the sport.[106] In the final analysis it seems likely that the unemployment crisis coupled with the reintroduction of the entertainment tax for soccer caused the club's gates to fall, necessitating their exit from the Free State League much like we have already seen in the case of the Cork sides in that league. This major early setback did not prevent a more successful revival in the mid-1930s, culminating with the victory in the Free State Cup in 1937. It is also worth noting that these issues confronted not alone Waterford FC and the Cork Free State clubs, but the depression of the 1930s affected soccer deeply in Wales and England in the same period. Martin Johnes notes of the game in south Wales that 'the press was sure that, in the larger towns at least, success could overcome the wider economic troubles. However, falling revenue meant that no Welsh club had the financial resources to build a winning team to test the theory.'[107] Similarly, Matt Taylor notes of England's Football League in the interwar period, 'the financial position of clubs during the Depression was also regionally differentiated'. This is important since Taylor himself notes that 'historians themselves are guilty . . . of being too easily dazzled by the big games and the record attendances of the top clubs to see the wider and more complicated picture'.[108]

In the summer of 1932, with Waterford having exited the Free State League, thoughts turned to rebuilding the club for the future. As the *Cork Examiner* reported, 'the desire of the public for a continuance of football has created a new situation, and some prominent supporters of the late club have already taken steps towards organising a team'.[109] The report intimated that this crack team of prominent supporters had informed the Free State League of their plans, which was to begin the season with amateurs and eventually buttress their efforts with professionals as the season progressed. The *Cork Examiner* stuck with the story, later reporting that 'a gathering of about three hundred supporters' at Kilcohan Park, the club's home ground, heard T. Long state that 'in taking over the club from the late directors, it was not the desire of the committee to usurp the position'. Rather the new committee, with the backing of the Waterford Sports Co. Ltd., 'would strive with all its might to merit the loyalty of the public, and in perhaps a small way to repay its faith'.[110] But there was to be no last-minute reprieve where re-entry to the Free State League was concerned, the club having to content itself with football in the Munster Senior League.

'Rookies' No More: the rise and fall of Tramore Rookies FC

Tramore, as we saw in Chapter Two, was an early site of soccer in Waterford in 1910, thanks to the efforts of Belfastman Brother McGurk in the local national school. His influence on his young charges remained even after he departed, with many of the same boys taking the moniker of Tramore Celts around 1917, though this team faded away with no lasting legacy. In 1926, however, a new Tramore Celtic emerged when a Gaelic football team in the seaside town lost a match on an objection that was upheld by the local county board, and exiting the GAA, took up the game of soccer instead. Thus, soccer returned to the seaside town just as the game was blooming in the city, just a short train ride away. Not long after this revival, in August 1932, as the new season was about to commence, the *Munster Express* sent itself into raptures, anticipating the exploits of the seaside club for the coming season. Calling them the 'Stormy Petrels', the paper noted that their 'meteoric rise to fame ... has long been a household topic in Soccer circles'. The club, formed in 1929 where it began competing in the Waterford Juvenile League, quickly made their way up the divisions of the Waterford Junior League, and after a hiatus with many of their players being taken on by Waterford FC in the Free State League, the Rookies returned in 1932 as an outfit playing in the Munster Senior League. The club were anticipating the visit of senior teams and as such were ensuring that their pitch, at Graun Park which overlooked the bay, was in the best possible condition.[111] Where in the past two seasons Rookies had been subordinate to the demands of the Free State side in Waterford, both clubs were now, nominally at least, on equal footing in the Munster Senior League.

However, the election of Tramore Rookies would prove, in the end, a less than auspicious development for the long-term existence of the club. As a purely amateur outfit, with no apparent designs on becoming a professional one, the club was not as financially able as

Waterford FC to undertake the many trips to Cork for their Munster Senior League fixtures, or the trips to Dublin for their frequent cup games.

The club's own success in cup competition thus militated against their long-term survival. Trips like those undertaken in January 1934 to play Bohemians in Dalymount Park, where they were beaten 9–0 for their troubles, where the expenses for the trips came out of the players' own pockets, caused financial hardship for the club. This was compounded by the apparent unwillingness of many Cork clubs in the Munster Senior League to undertake away trips to the seaside town, thus robbing Tramore Rookies, and the players, of gate receipts that would counteract their own expenses. Bad luck had its role to play too, as in February 1934 the clubhouse was razed to the ground by fire. The team used an old railway carriage as dressing rooms and this caught fire, and despite the efforts of local boys who discovered the blaze, along with Gardaí, all but a single football and referee's whistle survived the blaze.[112] The resilience of Tramore Rookies in the face of not only bad luck but also an apparent disinterest in their ability to compete at senior level was summed up best by a reporter in the *Munster Express*. The reporter wrote that 'it would require great penmanship to pay a fitting tribute in hard print to the gallant boys who compose the personnel of the Tramore Rookies'. This was written for a column on their 4–0 victory over Waterford FC in the final of the George French Shield in 1935.[113]

Such resilience as was shown had its limits and in January 1935, signs began to show that the financial cost of keeping the team going was to prove too much, with the players having spent £90 of their own money already that season in travelling expenses, as well as competing with Waterford FC for gates since their games invariably clashed with games taking place in Kilcohan, robbing them of a potential audience from Waterford. Indeed, had they not won the Intermediate Cup in the 1935 season, they probably would have seen little point to carrying on. Though it gave them the impetus, in truth, they were only hobbling along by then, and in September 1936 it was announced that the club was being wound up, considering that the previous season they had racked up £190 in travelling expenses but could only bring in £63 in gate receipts. This was the sad end to the club which had 'started with a tennis ball on the strand' back in 1928.[114]

Figure 6.1: *Tramore Rookies with the George French Shield and their train carriage dressing room*
Reproduced with kind permission of Andy Taylor.

The club's star burned brightly, but only briefly. The story of the Tramore Rookies club, placed in the context of Waterford FC and their return to the fold of the Free State League, further shows that few cities in Ireland, let alone in Munster, could sustain two clubs playing at senior level, whether that was provincially or nationally.

Waterford FC, 1934–1937: the road to cup glory

The loss of Waterford FC from the Free State League was acutely felt in Munster soccer circles, and the progress of the club's attempts to re-enter the league was watched closely not alone in Waterford but especially in Cork too. The meeting of 100 Waterford FC supporters, headed by Isaac Woolfson, by then Waterford's man in the MFA, to establish a ways and means committee to secure Kilcohan Park for the club was noted in Cork's *Evening Echo* in December 1933.[115] The process of re-entry was an arduous one, and to judge by some of the reports in the local press, the club's directors found their stewardship of Kilcohan Park a millstone around their necks.[116] The committee, which was making efforts to see senior Free State soccer return to Waterford, in a meeting chaired by Isaac Woolfson, were asked to pay £300 cash to the directors for the use of Kilcohan Park, or failing that, £200 cash and to issue debenture shares of £300 at 6 per cent – neither of these options seemed reasonable to the committee reviving Waterford FC, and so they were instructed to look for suitable grounds elsewhere.[117] During 1934, Waterford FC played some friendlies against Free State sides, one game against Dundalk, the other against Shamrock Rovers, most likely as a means of reviving interest in the game and the club, as they stepped up their efforts to re-enter the Free State League, something which must have looked increasingly likely given the trouble in which Cork Bohemians had found themselves by then, discussed in the previous chapter. Waterford were duly re-elected into the league in the summer of 1934 and plans could be underway to ensure a more stable, and more successful stint in the Free State League.[118]

When the club finally did re-enter the league in time for the 1934/35 season, it was their cup and shield exploits that gained the revived club its lasting fame, in particular their shield and cup double of the 1936/37 season. Waterford were set to meet St James's Gate of Dublin in the final, and a fortnight before, they played each other in a thrilling game in the league which the Dublin side won 4–2. The *Irish Independent* report of that match asked in its headline, 'Are Waterford Waiting for Cup Final?' The correspondent covering the game certainly thought so, and his hunch was proven right. The final of the cup saw them defeat St James' Gate 2–1 in front of a huge crowd in Dalymount Park in Dublin, estimated to range anywhere from 24,000 to 35,000. It was estimated that around 3,000 made the trip up from Waterford, with the majority, around 2,400, going by special train while the rest went by car or bus.

While supporters from Waterford only made up a fraction of the game's attendees, the crowds that greeted the victorious Waterford side on their return from the capital on the Monday following the game appears from the reports to have been far greater in number. Upon disembarking from their carriage at the back of the train, the players, including Tommy Arrigan holding the cup, were all chaired by the crowd to their open-top vehicle on which they made the short trip across the bridge to Breen's Hotel, where only thanks to a Garda escort did they manage to make their way into the hotel, from which they one by one emerged on a balcony to great cheering. In a remark similar to that made when Fordsons returned following their Free State Cup victory in 1926, the reporter from the *Munster Express* noted that such crowds had not been seen in Waterford since the great political rallies of earlier years. The scorer of the winning goal, Tim O'Keeffe, who had scored Cork FC's opening goal in their 1934 cup triumph, reckoned that the crowd for this victory was equal to if not better than the one in Cork in 1934. O'Keeffe also claimed in the vox pop taken by the *Munster Express* that he would play his football in Waterford so long as there was a Free State side in the city.[119]

O'Keeffe would stay true to that statement for the most part, although his appearance as a guest for Northern Irish side Belfast Celtic saw him suspended from availability for international selection by the FAI following the season's end. Tim's involvement with Waterford FC ended in acrimony when, as the 1940/41 season came to a head, O'Keeffe and others, playing well past the usual point in the season, demanded a £2 bonus for a game and ended up at logger-heads with management, who refused to pay out. This resulted in Waterford forfeiting the league championship, which had gone to a playoff against Cork United, and exiting the league for a second time until 1945, while O'Keeffe and others were cast out of league foot-ball for a year. Returning to Cork, he played for Cork United, winning a league medal with them, although O'Keeffe died of cancer not long after, at the age of thirty-three. His obituary in *The Irish Times* noted that 'a striking tribute was paid to O'Keefe [sic]. St James' Gate and Cork United lined up before the start, and the huge crowd stood in silence as the buglers of the Transport Workers' Band played "The Last Post". It was the most impressive scene ever wit-nessed at an Association Football ground in this country. At Tolka Park, where Drumcondra and Shamrock Rovers met, a two minutes' silence was observed.'[120]

Such sad days were a number of years away yet for Waterford soccer though, and as the 1937 season came to an end, things looked bright for the Free State club, and for soccer in Waterford. When Waterford lifted the cup at Dalymount Park, 'Socaro', writing for the *Irish Press*, had noted that all three of the honours in Free State soccer had gone to the provinces for the first time, while the Waterford victory was seen as 'a final blow to the prestige of Metropolitan clubs this season'.[121] It was a sweet moment of success, shared by all who had built soccer in Waterford in the previous fifteen years. But this was only one form of success in the game. As had been the case in Cork, it was the state of soccer at the junior level which was the true barometer of how far the game had come in the years since the end of the First World War. Though the city was, like the rest of Munster, scarred by the various upheavals of war, civil strife, economic deprivation and the spectre of thousands of unemployed, still sport, and soccer especially, was able to not alone re-emerge amid these sea-changes, but become a permanent fixture of the sporting and social lives of urban and – even in some parts – rural Waterford. In the decades that followed, only hurling challenged soccer for sheer popularity in Waterford life and the foundations of Waterford's great post-war successes in soccer were laid between the period of that first meeting in the CYMS hall in 1924 and the victory at Dalymount in 1937.

7

SOCCER IN LIMERICK, 1918–1937

Limerick, like the rest of Munster, was touched deeply by the upheavals in the period 1914–1923. And like in Waterford, these upheavals were not just of a nationalist hue, but also of a distinctly class-based kind. Limerick was the centre of one of the most famous soviets to occur in the period 1919–23. As well as taking part in the general strike against conscription in April 1918, the same few weeks saw over 10,000 workers in Limerick celebrate May Day. This was a precursor of the show of strength that working-class Limerick displayed when striking against the insistence of the British military in 1919 that all people crossing the bridge in the city required a permit, leading to the short-lived but significant event best known as the Limerick Soviet.[1] The treasurer of the soviet was Jim Casey, whose signature guaranteed the money the soviet printed in 1/–, 5/– and 10/– denominations. Casey was a regular player with Garryowen Rugby Club and later president of the Irish Amateur Boxing Union. His combined interests of politics and sport were shared by others in Limerick, something explored below.[2]

It was following such a remarkable political upheaval that soccer began again to emerge in Limerick, running parallel to the game's re-emergence in Waterford and Cork. Much like Waterford, the game emerged as one that belonged to the city's working-class inhabitants, despite its pre-First World War appeal to Limerick's middle-class inhabitants. If in Waterford, soccer saw off the challenge of rugby, in Limerick, where rugby was a deeply popular game, soccer triumphed in its ability to establish the network it did in the period 1918–37, and to enter the 1937 season with its own Free State League side.

One of the earliest mentions of the game in the city in this period comes from the *Limerick Leader*, in September 1924, when

Prospect FC held their AGM in St Michael's Temperance Hall; whether Prospect had any links to the team we saw previously attached to St Michael's Temperance Hall is difficult to ascertain.[3] This meeting was quickly followed by another meeting held in the city's Drapers' Club by a group calling themselves Dalcassians AFC.[4] These otherwise innocuous notices in the pages of the *Limerick Leader* pointed towards an emerging trend in the city, and soon the game would spread beyond these clubs. The game blossomed from the middle of the 1920s, roughly congruent with the game's development in Waterford in 1924. Among the earliest teams to play were the Protestant Young Men's Association (PYMA), Dalcassians, Prospect, Great Southern Railway, British Petroleum, and a team of Shannon Scheme Workers.[5] Not unlike Waterford in the same period, this mixture of works teams, and those bound together by locality, reflected the widening appeal of soccer in Munster's urban centres.

A crucial development for soccer in Limerick was the decision by locals to play games on Sunday, even then still the main day off for working people in Ireland.[6] This was similar to the GAA nationwide, but importantly, it was also a part of Limerick's rugby culture, where the spread of the junior game and the creation of the particular social tenor of Limerick rugby was so reliant on the ability to play on Sundays, as Liam O'Callaghan's work argues convincingly.[7] Indeed, a short notice on the game in the *Irish Independent* from 1937 noted that 'the popularity of Association Football is growing considerably . . . these games are proving a serious rival to other sports played on a Sunday afternoon, from the point of view of "gates"'.[8] Gates were a good indicator of the growing interest in soccer in Limerick, but something more than just spectating had emerged in the years before that *Irish Independent* notice. Not content with merely watching other men play the game, from the beginning of the 1920s to the foundation of Limerick AFC in 1937, hundreds of boys and young men also played soccer.

This was aided by the work of dedicated volunteers who wished to see the game established on a firm footing with organised structures in the form of leagues and cups across age groups; the fraught business of negotiating ground usage; and a will to see a game which they enjoyed flourish in a city with an already crowded sporting culture. These developments mirrored those elsewhere in Munster at the time and, like in Cork and Waterford, at the heart of these developments were the people who made the game what it was. The enthusiasm and interest that they cultivated among themselves and encouraged in others ensured that in this period, unlike in the era before the First World War, the game bedded down.

As early as the 1924/25 season, Prospect in particular made their mark by winning that season's Munster Junior Cup competition in a game against Freebooters, returning two seasons later to the final only to be beaten by Blackrock Rovers. A decade later, just as Limerick FC finished their first season in the Free State League, Prospect brought a team to the Munster Youths Cup final at the end of the 1937/38 season. Another Limerick club, Trojans, also had an impressive set of cup runs in the latter half of the 1930s. Trojans were beaten in the Munster Junior Cup final in 1935/36 by St Joseph's of Waterford. However, they returned the following season and, making the final again, made no mistake in despatching Cork side Fair Hill. Even in Clare, a team from Ennis emerged: Ennis United.[9] They were champions of the North Munster League in 1928, but fielded no team in the 1928/29 season, before returning for one more season in 1932.[10] Though a club with only a brief history in Munster soccer, the reach of the game into the heart of Clare, and the club's brief glimpse of success, goes some way to showing just how pervasive the soccer bug had become in Munster, and throughout Ireland, by the late 1920s. The game would have to wait a very long time before making any serious inroads in Kerry, where Gaelic football dominated over all other sports by the end of the 1930s.[11]

Tipperary, thanks to clubs like Cahir Park AFC, saw considerable enthusiasm for the game developing. Yet, for much of the 1920s and 1930s, Tipperary's soccer story was tied up with Limerick; their teams competed as part of the Limerick-based North Munster League. A major achievement for Cahir Park in the 1926/27 season was reaching the Munster Senior Cup final against Cork Bohemians. It was a rare occasion on which the club came to the notice of Ireland's sporting press with the Munster correspondent for *Sport* writing that 'the competition for the Munster Senior Cup is rapidly nearing completion, and Cahir Park, one of the "dark horses", by their defeat of Crosshaven at Victoria Cross on Saturday are now qualified for the final. Playing good robust football they fully deserved their victory by the odd goal in three.' The report goes on to say that 'the game was a "cracker" from start to finish and Cahir may well owe their victory to superior staying powers. Judging by the display given by the Tipperary men I should imagine that Bohemians will have a tough nut to crack in them.'[12]

The final, played again in Cork, was lost 2–1 by Cahir Park in front of 6,000 people at Victoria Cross.[13] The club reached the final of the FAIFS Junior Cup in 1928, after beating Bridewell of Cork 4–3.[14] Cahir were defeated this time by Richmond United 3–0. The team finally had success in national cup competition in 1930 when they beat Glasnevin of Dublin 4–2 at Clonmel in the FAIFS Intermediate Cup, which at that time was the qualifying cup competition to enter the Free State Challenge Cup proper. Unluckily for Cahir, the opponents drawn in their first round of the Senior Cup was Glasnevin, who beat the Tipperary men 2–1 in Ballymun, despite having 'battled gamely to the end'.[15]

Figure 7.1: *Cahir Park FC in 1929*
Reproduced with kind permission of Ger Halley.

Where Tipperary was concerned, the story of the game in these years was not solely that of Cahir Park, with Tipperary Wanderers also emerging in the early 1920s as an important Tipperary side. From the very beginning of the new Free State League, Tipperary Wanderers made their presence felt, beating Dublin side Shamrock Rovers in the qualifying round of the inaugural Free State Cup. The bulk of their play was in the Free State Senior and Junior Cup competitions, as well Munster and North Munster Cups. Tipperary Wanderers played their football in the Limerick-centred North Munster League, which developed in parallel with the game in Waterford.[16] The club probably came to greatest notoriety during the Free State Cup of the 1923/24 season when they played Barrackton United of Cork a total of six times before winning the last of these by a single goal. Given this marathon of replays, it is no surprise they lost in the fourth round to Clifton of Cork.[17] The other team to emerge from the region, Tipperary United, were of less prominence in the 1920s, although they would eventually make their mark on the game in the 1930s.[18]

The game in Tipperary for many years occupied a similar position to that of rugby in Waterford – reliant in the main on outside sources of organised competition, either the Munster Senior League or later in its history, entering the Waterford and North Munster Football League, the County Tipperary League, or the Cork Athletic Union League. Indeed, at only the Free State FA's second annual general meeting in 1923, the Tipperary representative expressed much discontent over the poor treatment that Tipperary soccer was receiving from the Munster FA.[19] It found something of a home in north Munster however, and its attachment to Limerick in these years was vital for its sustenance.

Limerick District Football Council and the re-emergence of Soccer

A perceptible sign that the popularity of soccer was on the rise in Limerick in the 1920s was the increasing coverage the game attracted from the city's leading newspapers, the *Limerick Leader*. We have already seen how a similar growth of interest from the local media was precipitous of a wider trend in both Cork and Waterford in the province. From around 1925 onwards in particular, the level of coverage provided for soccer shifts, from the sporadic notices which characterised coverage of the game up to then, to a more dedicated, weekly set of notices, usually under the headline of 'Soccer Notes' and written by a phalanx of journalists under assumed names that included 'Pivot', 'Ranger', 'Soccerite', 'Socaro', 'The Spy', 'Spectator' and 'Rover'. The notes were just that to begin with: snatches of match reports, minor notes and notices for players, the regularity of appearance pointing towards soccer's growing stature in a city where junior rugby was king. Like the same notes in other local newspapers like the *Munster Express* in Waterford and the *Evening Echo* in Cork, these weekly columns were a vital part of the culture of soccer in Limerick. They were used to cater for the soccer-playing people of the city. These were public notice boards of announcement and debate, as they were in the rest of the province. By the end of the 1920s and on into the 1930s, the 'Soccer Notes' became steadily more detailed, providing fixture lists, tables, match reports, gossip, reports of meetings and even hints and tips for those who were new to the game. They were a vital part of the functioning of the game at a local level. They helped to form Limerick's soccer players into a real community.

A big issue for Limerick soccer during this period was, like in Cork and Waterford before it, the securing of a dedicated ground for playing soccer. Throughout the period from 1925 to 1937, soccer was played in Limerick in a huge range of venues: Corkanree, at the grounds of rugby club Young Munster, at Crescent College's grounds, along the Roxboro Road, Longpavement, the Catholic Institute grounds at Island Field and the Markets Field. The last of these would eventually be secured by the Limerick District Football Association (LDFA) as a home for soccer, after their first agreement for its use on Sundays throughout the season was made in August 1934. Much of the story of Limerick soccer, its increasing popularity and the desire by those who were involved in soccer for the game's wider acceptance, can be told through the struggle to secure a playing pitch of its own.

Like in the rest of Munster, teams came and went in this period, some disbanding, other clubs amalgamating. Some would achieve fame in their day, others ignominy, and yet many more are for-gotten. The strong sense of parish loyalty that Liam O'Callaghan's work on rugby in Munster noted as being crucial to the frisson of the game was as much in evidence in some of the clubs found to be playing soccer in Limerick city too. The relationship between soccer and rugby in Limerick was an important one, and many of those involved in soccer, aware of the other code's pre-eminence, were keen to make allies with those in Limerick's rugby circles. Soccer in Limerick, unlike either Cork or Waterford, was a less self-contained enterprise, with teams from Ennis and many of the teams from Tipperary as vital for the game in Limerick as any of the clubs in the city. The creation of 'North Munster' as a particular region for organising soccer emerged from the expansion of soccer in Limerick during the 1920s and 1930s. As it was in Cork and Waterford, the workplace would also provide Limerick soccer with clubs and, in time, extra competition. The wave of popularity that soccer experienced in Limerick, when added to what we've already seen in the previous chapters, ranging from teams of young boys calling themselves the Pirates to more serious outfits like the equally romantically-named Dalcassians, suggests that soccer's rising popularity was truly a phenomenon in Munster in the 1920s and 1930s, one which led to the province being represented by three teams at the national level by 1937, some sixty years after a group of boys had set out from Lismore to Mallow in 1877.

Within a few short years of the initial games being played by Prospect, Dalcassians, the PYMA and the various works teams, soccer was more firmly bedded down in Limerick, yet even in 1929 there was some anxiety about the permanence of soccer in Limerick's sporting landscape. A fifth-round tie in the Free State Challenge Cup, between Dalcassians and Freebooters from Cork, prompted the reporter to state that 'this tie should provide some thrills, as the Freebooters XI have disposed of many clubs in Cork, where soccer has come to stay'.[20] Yet such trembling seems at odds with the structures then in place for soccer in Limerick: the North Munster League with Dalcassians, O'Brien's Bridge, Deutch's (sic) Sports Club, Limerick United and Ardnacrusha; the Limerick Minor League featuring Prospect, Victoria Celtic, Richmond, Lansdowne, Distillery and Crusaders, as well as a wide variety of cup competitions including minor cups, junior cups and the Cromer Cup.[21] The Shannon electrification scheme, then under way, provided plenty of opportunities for soccer and the Deutch's (sic) Sports Club was made up of the skilled German workers who had a large part to play in the scheme at

Ardnacrusha. When Dalcassians beat the Germans 4–1, the *Limerick Leader* reported that 'the Germans were first to score per Heine-mann. "Dals" soon equalised and towards the end of the game routed the German defence.'[22] How friendly a game this was is difficult to say since a strike during the scheme a few years earlier over the difference in pay between Irish and non-Irish workers had as one of its targets many of the German workers.[23]

The good fortune of soccer in Limerick continued as the 1930/31 season approached, with a report on the upcoming season noting that Castle United had survived a first season and were preparing to begin their second, while a new club calling themselves Brideville were to have teams at the junior, minor and juvenile levels, and Trojans, another new club, had acquired the services of some Victoria Celtic players.[24] Despite such signs of strength, however, shortly after, 'Soccer Notes' insisted that 'organisation is really what is wanted, and any person who is interested and would like to see the game progressing here, as it is in Cork and Waterford, should make it a point to attend the meeting of the Council, where they will be welcome'.[25] Here we can see those who give voice to soccer in Limerick, comparing the developments there to those elsewhere in Munster, just as those in Waterford had done in comparing them-selves to Cork. One key development to emerge in this particular season was the establishment of a Limerick United, competing in the Free State Junior Cup, the team being made up of five players from Crusaders to play against Cahir Park. A bus was to be run from the corner of Glentworth Street Bank of Ireland to Cahir for supporters wishing to travel for the price of 4s.[26]

When the following season began, the call that had been made at the beginning of 1930/31 for organisation still rang true. However, 1931/32 would prove a pivotal season for soccer: it was the season in which that call for organisation was finally beginning to find an answer. The Limerick District Football Council became the Limerick District Football Association (LDFA). The chairman, Liam Simmonds, proved pivotal in this change. In late November 1931, the minor fixtures set for that weekend were put off when an MFA dele-gate was due to come up from Cork, yet in the event they did not make it. The MFA were sending a delegate because trouble at a match involving Prospect FC saw both the MFA and the LDFA clash. A report in the *Limerick Leader* early in December 1931 saw the journalist acknowledge that 'things have been happening recently that are not for the benefit or the progress of the game. A serious dispute has arisen which, if not remedied in the proper way, will have a retrogressive effect on local football.'[27] So what happened?

During a game involving Prospect in which there was some controversy, the newly-named LDFA had suspended two Prospect players. Prospect however appealed the decision to the MFA, an appeal which was upheld, since the MFA saw that the LDFA had no powers of suspension over any players. The deadlock that ensued saw all the city league games being cancelled until some agreement could be reached. The situation was not helped by a Munster FA delegation arranged for the last weekend in November that never showed. In the week between 'Soccer Notes' detailing this and the following set of 'Soccer Notes' appearing in the *Leader*, an MFA delegate, Mr Looney, did indeed meet with the LDFA regarding this matter. From the report we learn that 'in his concluding remarks Mr Looney said he hoped to see Limerick one day enjoy the same status in Free State football as is now held by Waterford and Cork'.[28] As for his initial reason for visiting, the Prospect FC suspension controversy, the two suspensions were lifted and the LDFA agreed that all future suspensions should be handled by the MFA, rather than locally. Another key issue to emerge from the meeting was the need for a ground solely for the playing of soccer in Limerick, as games were at the mercy of other bodies who owned the grounds on which the city's soccer games were played. In the second half of the 1931/32 season, this problem became especially acute.

The Need for a Ground in the City: Limerick soccer's search for a home

Around the St Patrick's Day holiday 1932, a match was due to take place between Dalcassians and Shelbourne (of Limerick), but the game was postponed due to the unavailability of a ground. The game was eventually played over a week later, with Shelbourne beating Dalcassians 4–3.[29] A week following this re-fixed match, 'Soccer Notes' of the *Leader* contained a subheading which ran, 'A Blank Weekend'. In the notes, 'Pivot' writes that the blank weekend was the result of 'inclement weather conditions and other causes'. We are left in no doubt as to what those 'other causes' were, as another sub-heading ran 'The Ground Question Again', and here 'Pivot' argues for the need to flag the issue with the Munster FA in Cork and the FAIFS in Dublin. The exasperation evident in 'Pivot's' notes that week stem no doubt, to some degree, from the feeling that soccer was being moved from pillar to post without any control over its own fixture list. Things had looked a little brighter in January when a big fourth round Munster Junior Cup game between Shelbourne and Cahir Unknowns was played at the Catholic Institute grounds. This successful event saw another game, this time the fifth round Free State Junior Cup match between Shelbourne and Glasheen of Cork take place again at the same grounds. However, this game finished in a 3–3 draw, and saw considerable crowd trouble. According to 'Pivot', when the pitch invasion by the crowd took place, play was delayed fifteen minutes and not alone were 'sticks used freely' but 'a regular "pitched battle" ensued'.[30] Such trouble was in 'Pivot's' view cause for concern: to his mind such trouble could prove to be 'detrimental to the progress of the game in Limerick'. Of special concern to 'Pivot' though was not the violence *per se*, but the fact that the game was played on the Catholic Institute grounds and he did not imagine the organisation would look favourably on the use of their pitch for soccer in the future given what had happened at that game. This seems a particular worry given how the use of those grounds was viewed for the game in January. Back when that game was arranged it was written that:

> Decidedly, they [the LDFA] got a more cordial reception from the Institute folks than from another source approached. Apart from the question of the flying of the tri-colour at the international rugby matches it is quite apparent that there are some people in Limerick determined in so far as they are able, to prevent the flag of soccer flying in the better known and more centrally situated enclosures in the city.[31]

This tantalising quote made reference to a controversy surrounding the failure of the IRFU to fly the tricolour at a match in Dublin against South Africa, and the support Limerick clubs gave to University College Galway when they aired a protest.[32] The dig here then was that the Limerick rugby clubs would rally to defend the flying of the Irish flag at internationals, but would not help those playing soccer to secure good, centrally located grounds for big provincial or national games. Nor indeed would anyone else. Yet by April 1932, there seems to have been something of a thaw in the heated relationship that the above quote indicates. When the local City Junior Cup draw was made, there was some concern about whether Crusaders would be able to field a team against Prospect, and so Prospect were instead drawn against 'Dolphin', a crack team that was largely made up of players from Garryowen RFC. The commentary in the newspaper felt that it was 'good to see this spirit amongst us, and it augurs well for the progress of the game. Soccer is perhaps the finest training for Rugger, especially for the forwards of the handling code.'[33] This overlap of players was in itself nothing new, a report from August 1930 noting the strong links between Prospect itself and those who played rugby, but given recent developments, the reassertion of these links was important.[34]

Despite these more positives noises, soccer in Limerick was still some way off a permanent home despite the increasingly cordial relationship with the rugby clubs. Some indication of this comes from the fact that it was flagged what a bad state the ground at Corkanree was in by April 1932, due to overuse, while the 1932 season ran well into the middle of June, with many games being played midweek during the longer summer nights in order to complete the fixture list.[35] Here was an instance where soccer's increased popularity had yet to be met with increased capacity for those wanting to play the game.

The grounds question wasn't going away either, and it was raised by the Limerick delegate (from the Shelbourne club) to the MFA's AGM that summer. Undaunted by this persistent problem, planning for the season ahead continued, while the summer saw the institution of a summer league for children under sixteen by the LDFA chairman Liam Simmonds. The plans for the coming season included petitioning Carroll's Cigarettes of Dundalk for a trophy, the paying of weekly subs of 6d from each club affiliated to the LDFA to raise money beginning in September and, most importantly from the point of view of the game itself, the new season saw the restructuring of football in Limerick with the re-establishment of a North Munster League, with two divisions. The First Division was made up of four sides from Limerick and four sides from Tipperary while the Second Division comprised six Limerick-based clubs.[36]

Those last two initiatives were decided at the LDFA's own AGM, which that year was attended by Myles Murphy and J. Younger of the FAIFS and by Mr Looney and D.J. Crowley of the MFA. At the AGM, Murphy, speaking for the FAIFS, said that 'not alone in Limerick do we want the game flourishing but in all of Munster'.[37] Despite such positive words, nothing appeared to be forthcoming about securing a ground for soccer in the city. In November 1932, some players from a local city team were found to be trespassing on a local rugby club's ground, something which they were asked to refrain from doing by the new LDFA Management Committee, who presumably wished to keep the rugby clubs onside until such time as a ground was secured. Something did begin to happen as 1932 came to a close, with a visit from Mr Kenny of the FAIFS to discuss further the possibility of securing a ground.[38] It would take another whole season, however, before something like a permanent home for soccer would be found in Limerick. Nonetheless, the growth of soccer in Limerick was beginning to be recognised nationally, as the *Irish Press* briefly commented on the large number of Limerick clubs entering the Free State Junior Cup in the 1932/33 season.[39]

In the *Limerick Leader*'s 'Rugby Notes' in August 1934, the correspondent expressed some dismay and concern about the fact that the LDFA had secured Sunday lettings for the 1934/35 season at the Markets Field. This development proved a steadying and important one for Limerick soccer, and in time was fundamental to the bringing of senior soccer to the city in 1937. At the end of the season it was even remarked that 'senior football would be a success here, as the gates all-round at the Markets Field this season have been indeed very good, even though the football served up is only of the junior standard'.[40] The public appetite for the game had grown, and, as argued elsewhere in this book, soccer in interwar Ireland was not only a sport with the potential to stand as a civic representation, but was also, for those who became directors of the clubs, a viable commercial enterprise.

Other signs were visible of the increased stature of soccer in Limerick: new clubs were still emerging in the city, like Shamrock Villa, based in the city parish of St Munchin's. This new club actually amalgamated with Shelbourne to form Shelbourne Villa as they wanted one good club in the parish rather than spreading the talent too thinly.[41] This decision by both clubs says something about the desire to represent 'the parish' as strongly as possible on the evidently competitive larger stage of city-wide soccer. With the popularity of the game growing, and new adherents joining the ranks, 'Soccer Notes' began to regularly include in the column an analysis of the game at the Free State League level and even offered hints and tips to those who were new to the game, while the Great Southern Railway began running special trains to international matches from Limerick. On the pitch, a former Trojans player, W. Keane, was lining out in the Free State League for Drumcondra. In such an atmosphere of growth and confidence in the game's place in the cultural life of the city, it was only a matter of time before the desire to establish a senior club would become overwhelming.

As the game grew and the number of junior clubs playing the game increased, rivalry between clubs, who were only streets apart in some instances, was strong. In a replication of a similar degree of rivalry in junior rugby, this was an important feature of what made the local soccer leagues so attractive to players and spectators alike. It was also at the heart of the decision to form Shelbourne in the parish of St Munchin's. Pride was very much at stake in these games. A certain working-class male pride in toughness is readily apparent in the desire to win – it was an important hallmark of working-class amateurism, that competitive edge. A match between Dalcassians and Trojans during the 1934 season was highly anticipated in the pages of the local press. In the words of the reporter, Dalcassians 'represent the North City', while Trojans represented the south. Looking forward to the game the reporter asked, 'Will Dals. stumble again? That is the question. I hear that they are confident . . . The Parish boys have prepared well for Sunday's engagement. They have indulged in plenty of training. It's hard to know who will win. Then what must I say. Oh, it's just wait and see!'[42] This game was an early round of the Munster Junior Cup. Cup football, where such rivalries could be aired, was equally important for the popularity of soccer locally. A key local cup competition was the cup put up by local watchmakers, opticians and jewellery shop C. Cromer of 18 O'Connell Street in the city. The company, as well as presenting this cup to the local soccer committee, also presented cups for juvenile sports days and similar events. As the main local cup competition, it unsurprisingly got especially heated in the final rounds. During the semi-finals of the 1934 cup, in the second semi-final between Crusaders United and Dalcassians a spectator was alleged to have rushed the field interfering with a player, causing the rest of the crowd to rush the pitch and there were even reports of people being kicked on the ground. The referee had no option but to abandon the match.[43]

Even the way the incident was reported was up for debate with the secretary of the LDFA, H. O'Brien, in a letter to the *Limerick Leader* suggesting that from the 'strain' of the correspondent's reporting he was 'condoning with the clubs concerned' and had not checked his facts properly regarding the ability of the MFA to suspend players as a result of the incidents.[44] Both teams were suspended from further competition for that season. Crusaders United would have been especially disappointed. They were something of cup specialists having won, against the odds, a local cup double of the juvenile and minor cups in 1929/30.[45] When both of the same sides were drawn against each other in the third round of the Free State Junior Cup, it was noted that they had not met since the game which was abandoned. 'Socaro' however noted, 'I am aware that the Limerick District Association will deal drastically with any teams that commit themselves to any serious offence.'[46] One of the most regular referees of Limerick junior soccer in this period was a Mr. M. Mackey. He refereed the Dalcassians and Crusaders game that was abandoned and, in the following season, he oversaw another game that was abandoned in the Cromer Cup, again a semi-final. This time the game was between Trojans and Ashbourne Rovers. According to the press, 'the game terminated in a most extraordinary manner'. 'Socaro' takes up what happened:

> The match, on a whole, was a very hard robust encounter, which Mr. Mackey (referee) found a bit difficult to control. From what could be seen it was a succession of fouls and frees. An Ashbourne Rover player was ordered off for rough play, then when it came to another player from the same side receiving his 'marching orders' the climax came. Mr. Mackey abandoned the match.

The LDFA decided to pass the referee's report on to the MFA. The MFA cautioned both clubs severely but the match was refixed for early in the following season, on 20 October 1935. The game was further postponed as the Markets Field was being used by Limerick United for an FAIFS Intermediate Cup tie against Barrackton of Cork. Staggeringly, the match was postponed again when no referee showed, the *Limerick Leader* describing it in a headline as 'A Fiasco'.[47] The game was finally played on 17 November 1935 and won by Ashbourne Rovers.[48] The long-delayed final was eventually won by Shamrock Villa; by winning, Shamrock Villa succeeded in bringing the Cromer Cup 'down town' for the first time, again reflecting the deep sense of place felt by the people behind these teams. The Cromer Cup for 1934/35 had hardly been won when in the same report of the final, the new season's cup competitions were looked forward to, with 'Rover' noting of cups that they 'usually tend to stimulate more interest in local activities'.[49] The localism of the Cromer Cup was also reflected in the use of a Cromer Cup double bill in 1936 as a means to raise funds for charity.[50] This strength, and the strength of the other local cup competitions, formed the bedrock of the local game.

The Foundation of Limerick FC, 1937

As we've already seen with Cork and Waterford, the strength of local soccer was considered a litmus test for the potential of each place having a senior team in the Free State League. So it was also the case in Limerick. No doubt, those involved in playing, organising and covering the game looked about them at the inroads made by the various Cork and Waterford senior teams in the Free State League and would have felt they were equally capable of competing at that level as well as having the business and fanfare a Free State League team brought with it.

Early hints of a hoped-for senior side in the city emerged in April 1935, when the possibility that a combination team might start playing in the Munster Senior League was indicated in 'Soccer Notes'. Such a development never transpired; however, a combination side going under the moniker of Limerick United was entered into the Free State's Intermediate Cup and the Munster Senior Cup. The team bowed out of the Munster Senior Cup following defeat by Barrackton of Cork, though the players were described in the match report that followed as being 'fit for a higher grade of football'. While that may have partially been local bias when the push was very much on to bring senior-level soccer to the city, it was nevertheless given some fillip when an exhibition game was arranged between Limerick United and Free State League side Dolphin and encouragement was received from the FAIFS itself in Limerick's attempts to establish a senior club in the city.[51] This was especially important as there had been numerous unsuccessful attempts to bring

Bohemians from Dublin. All of this – the securing of the Markets Field as a regular home for the game, the continued local interest at grass-roots level and the emergence of new clubs, and the coverage afforded the game in the *Limerick Leader* – helped to create a situation where senior-level soccer for Limerick was not a dream, but increasingly looked to be a reality.

A key figure in making this dream a reality was William Shute, who in 1934 became the treasurer of the LDFA, and also acted as a referee in the local game. Shute was born in 1893 in Limerick. Like his father, William senior, who had been a clerk in Mattersons bacon factory, William was also a clerk when he was a young man in the shipping office. Shute clearly caught the sporting bug from his father. On William senior's passing in 1934, it was noted in the *Limerick Leader* that, during a meeting of the city health board, a Mr J. Cronin offered a vote of condolence to the Shute family saying that William senior was 'a well-known sportsman, having an interest in sport in all departments'.[52] William junior was apparently involved in soccer from its earliest days in Limerick; certainly, he was an instrumental figure in the 1930s, and with the help of his brother-in-law, Michael Brouder, an alderman on Limerick City Council, also deeply involved in soccer, helped bring senior soccer to Limerick in 1937 and remained involved in the game until his death in 1953.[53]

Michael Brouder's sporting interests were also varied, having a special interest in coursing. During the 1930s, he was secretary of the Limerick City Coursing Club, having been present at the club's establishment in 1928, and before being elected to the city council, he was also a member of the executive of the Irish Union of Distributive Workers and Clerks. While on the council, he was a member of the public health board. Among other things, he sought tenders for unemployed men when part-time work arose within the council and when an increase in rates was required due to the increased expenditure on home relief for Limerick's urban poor; in a challenge to critics of the increased rates he suggested that they 'come before a meeting of this Board and examine the books, which are open for inspection. If he will then take the responsibility of cutting off any of the people to whom we grant home assistance let him do so . . . some of the critics I refer to do not care about [the] poor as long as they were well off themselves.'[54] Brouder was first elected to his seat in the Dock Ward in the city in 1928 and retained it in 1931 as a Labour candidate, remaining on until 1934. A number of tenement houses collapsed on George's Quay in 1932 and according to Jim Kemmy, those whose houses had collapsed were 'forced to erect tents on the grass margin by the riverside in front of there [sic] site where the houses stood'.[55] The poor housing conditions in Limerick had long been a concern, with workers' newspaper *The Bottom Dog* criticising the housing in the city as far back as 1917. No wonder then, as a Labour councillor, Brouder felt antipathy towards the city's ratepayers. Outside of the realm of local politics, Brouder's involvement in soccer grew in the 1930s and by 1934 he was elected as a committee member of the LDFA, but this was amid a deepening unemployment crisis that was causing serious damage to the local health board's finances.[56]

In 1934, when the city council was to be re-arranged under the Limerick City Management Act, Brouder ran as an Independent Labour candidate but was unsuccessful. The board of health in Limerick was struggling financially, thanks to its obligation under a government directive from the Department of Local Government in 1924 for local authorities to be responsible for the paying of unemployment relief. Such ham-fisted organisation saw many unemployed families in Limerick go a fortnight without any form of relief while waiting for application forms to apply for the relief under the new Act. With the new Unemployment Assistance Act, 1934 slow to begin operating in Limerick, it was suggested the board carry on paying out.[57] With the likes of Brouder no longer on the council – no doubt his views on ratepayers damaged his election hopes – to call for increased rates to alleviate the deficit the health board was amassing, the board applied to the city council for permission to raise a loan of £2,500, already having exceeded their budget due to the crisis to the tune of £1,700. A Mr Gilligan, who requested the loan, felt the new Act was 'a fraud and a humbug', even suggesting that you would need to be 'a Carnero [sic] or a weight thrower to get anything at the Labour Exchange'.[58] It would take until September 1934 before the new act would come fully into effect in the city.

Brouder's honourable turn in local politics proved to be relatively short-lived. Still, in the sporting arena, Brouder would make an equal impact and his role encouraging senior soccer in Limerick was as strong as his almost decade-long involvement in coursing. Brouder was instrumental in arranging visits from Dolphin and Bray Unknowns, the latter seen by between four and five thousand people, games which went some way towards encouraging the potential of senior soccer in the city. It was on the back of these successes that he joined the LDFA as he said goodbye to the city council.[59]

The good done by such visits, as well as the experimental entries of Limerick United sides into a range of competitions, began to bear fruit in the second half of the 1930s. Not until February 1937 did the *Irish Independent* carry a column entitled 'Limerick Sports Letter' and part of this 'letter' informed the readers of the *Irish Independent* of the healthy state of soccer in the city, while the confirmation of the establishment of a senior club elected to the Free State League saw the new club's secretary, William Shute, and Liam Simmonds profiled in the national daily as late as June 1937, just two months before the new league was due to get underway.[60] Things had been slow to develop, however, and even in April 1937 nothing seemed especially definite following an exhibition game to promote senior soccer between Bohemians and Shelbourne at the Markets Field.[61] Not until the end of May 1937 was there any apparent certainty in the newspapers about Limerick joining the Free State League.[62] The club seems to have been set up similarly to Waterford FC with appeals to local business owners to test out the viability of such a venture. Details of the club's share capital were published in the paper that summer, with the club capitalised for £1,000 with 1,000 shares available at £1 each.

The club was established and won its debut game against Shamrock Rovers in Dalymount Park 1–0. Despite a promising start, the club would finish the season in tenth. In one of the early league games that Limerick FC played against Drumcondra, the *Irish Independent* suggested that 'comparatively speaking, the game is a novelty in Limerick, but the size of the crowd on Sunday last demonstrated that given the goods, the crowd will turn up'.[63] This of course ignores the fact that junior and lower levels of soccer had been strong in the city for well over a decade at that point and a word of warning was sounded in the *Irish Independent* by one columnist who felt it would be 'hard lines' on the junior clubs in the city for them to be forgotten now that Limerick had senior soccer. The writer added that 'attendances are small, gates are "nil" and ground arrangements are naturally imperfect, so that unless some special interest is taken in their progress, damage may be done to the junior clubs to whom, after all, we are indebted for putting Limerick on the Soccer map'.[64] This sums up perfectly the antagonism that developed in Irish soccer and that manifested itself in Munster's three major urban centres during the 1920s and 1930s: the antagonism between a desire to, on the one hand, see soccer develop at the grass-roots level, to encourage interest and participation locally and, on the other hand, to allow the flourishing of the game at a senior level to truly make the Free Sate League nationally representative. In the cases of Cork, Waterford and Limerick, these contradictory aspirations were not always easily navigated.

8

CONCLUSION

Over the course of the previous three chapters, we have seen how, by 1937, Cork, Tipperary, Waterford and Limerick had established themselves as places with strong soccer networks on a variety of levels, with the three cities each having a team in the Free State League. Sport was now imprinted onto the landscape of every village, town and city in Munster. From the Mardyke on the banks of the River Lee, the racing track and soccer pitch at Kilcohan Park in Waterford city to Semple Stadium on the edge of Thurles, and the Markets Field in Limerick, the sports ground imposed itself on the public space of the region – a place to meet and play just as the school was a place to learn, or the factory a place to work. It was a renegotiation of space, offering another focal point for community life – increasingly, between the beginning of the 1880s and the end of the 1930s, as well as their church, school and pub, people had their sports field. The shared use of many grounds, from Turner's Cross in Cork, to the Bully Acre or the Sportsfield in Waterford, for a wide variety of sports from rugby, soccer, Gaelic games and athletics and more besides indicates that pragmatism prevailed more frequently over narrow dogma and diktats.

Rather than being an era of triumph for an evermore militant nationalist project that had its roots in Ireland's nineteenth-century political movements of land agitation and home rule politics, the post-independence landscape, which has been the main focus of this book, showed that with independence, the unifying principles of nationalism gave way. Returning to more fractious cultural divisions and the politics of class, haunted often by the shadow of unprecedented levels of unemployment, the divisions between people manifested themselves in a wide variety of cultural practices including through the different sports they played. In some ways, the desire to see all sportsmen and women under the single flag of Gaelic games was an extension of the desire to see a nation united in the project of creating an illusory Irish-Ireland. Importantly, and not a little ironically perhaps, it was so-called 'foreign' sports like soccer and rugby, along with the Olympics, which provided the Irish Free State a means to project the nation onto an international stage. International soccer provided an additional arena for generating and cultivating an alternative current of nationalist sentiment not available to the GAA. Despite calls, as early as 1892, from Douglas Hyde for the de-anglicising of Ireland and the cultural battle between the two parallel civilisations that ensued, much of Irish culture, either through the cinema, the stage, dance hall or sports ground, was comfortable with its post-independence British elements. For most people, their sense of Irishness and the Irishness of their entertainment was not inextricably linked. This was no mutually exclusive relationship. Yet, whether through Aonach Tailteann, the mode of operation of the entertainment tax, or an implicit support for the ban on foreign games within the GAA, the Free State government was clearly intent on the promotion of sport, but it was intent even more clearly on the promotion of one particular sporting culture. This was a sporting culture that fit with particular notions of Irish identity, often far removed from the lived realities of many people's daily lives. It was one that ignored the shared Anglophone culture enjoyed by Ireland from across the Irish Sea and the Atlantic. This lived reality for many urban people in Munster included playing or watching games of soccer with their friends and neighbours. The game's evolution in Munster was a remarkable one that reflected the changed political and cultural landscape of the country.

As I argued in the first chapter of this book, the early role of a middle-class and largely British influence was significant in the game's development in Munster. Their access to resources to build foundations and subsequent developments of soccer was paramount. This is best exemplified by access to land, for free or for rent, time to organise and hold meetings for administrative purposes, and the time to devote to the game. The administrative impulse was a key facet of both formal and informal empire building. The vast army of young male clerks, and the camaraderie sport could offer, in often otherwise lonely years in their early twenties, was a crucial spur for much sporting activity. Yet even then, as we saw, civilian teams were not just happy to take on their military counterparts but were an important part of the game's early history in the province, especially in Cork. The dominance of the military sides, in Cork especially, proved ultimately detrimental since, by playing soccer on Saturday afternoons they prevented many interested in the game from being fully-fledged members of the MFA and the local leagues, though some teams organised soccer for themselves outside of official structures. These were the players, like the young boys who were guided by Brother McGurk in Tramore, County Waterford, or the young men of Limerick who first gave soccer a go, who would ultimately provide the game with its future players and administrators at all levels in the wake of Irish independence and soccer's remarkable revival.

The regional development of the game after 1921 was a result of the split between the IFA and the Leinster FA that preceded political independence and saw the founding of the FAIFS. It was also part of a broader trend of the game's varying fortunes across Ireland and Britain in a time of deep economic crisis. Seen in this larger frame, Munster can be understood as a region where soccer increased participation and interest as part of the broader shifting fortunes of the game on two islands that were linked economically and socially, if no longer entirely politically. Soccer in Munster benefited in this period in having not just dedicated players and administrators who wished (though often didn't succeed) to place the game on a sure footing. It also benefited, and was primed, to succeed in an era of new leisure practices, commercial forms of entertainment, and so the concept of being a follower of soccer without necessarily being a player of the game gained currency.

So it was that in the 1920s and 1930s, soccer in Ireland, in Munster and other provincial outposts especially, became one more option on an ever-growing menu of entertainments on offer, from dancing and betting to buying jazz records and watching movies at the cinema. Soccer, a sport largely enjoyed by those working and living in urban environments, was particularly suited to an emerging modern culture of leisure as consumed product. It might in this way perhaps be seen as a signifier of one's modernity, to have enjoyed watching or playing soccer in the Ireland of the 1920s and 1930s, just as listening to the latest 'jazz' record was. Since much of the game at grass-roots and senior level prior to the First World War was restricted in terms of its social and geographic reach in Ireland, the game's apparent explosion in a province like Munster on a scale unlike anything seen before the war must be seen as part of this modernising drive. Following the violence and trauma of the years 1914–23, soccer in Munster was poised, along with all of the new emerging leisure forms, to grow and expand in a region which was sorely in need of fun and enjoyment. Given the fact that the majority of clubs to emerge at the grass-roots level in Munster did so after the end of the Civil War lends strength to this. With clubs and leagues beginning to surface from the end of 1923 onwards in many places, soccer as a sport was undoubtedly for many as fresh and new a diversion as any radio programme, threepenny matinee or record from the local Woolworths. Soccer's newness – its modernity – was its strength.

During the early days of the Football Association of the Irish Free State, it seems the regional FAs were left very much to their own devices initially. Indeed the FAIFS was not really noticed by the new state until the 1924 Paris Olympics showed it was possible to assert the identity of the new state, as a result of being one of the only sporting bodies to take the state as its founding parameter, even if this was more by accident than design.[1] In terms of legislation, for example, when the Irish Free State came into being in 1922, there was an implied exemption of the GAA from entertainment duties, something naturally felt to be an unfair advantage by those in soccer circles. It was not until the Finance Act of 1925 that anything was set down in legislation to ensure that it was not just the GAA who was exempt from this tax, although this would change twice more, in 1932 and 1934.

There is no denying that the exemption from entertainment duty in 1925 coincided with a period of immense popularity for soccer, although I would argue that the increased popularity in Munster was buttressed and led in the main by the success of the revived Munster FA, and the work of locals involved in playing, in running the game and through their organisation of a whole slew of competitions and cups. From big competitions like the Munster Senior League to local contests like Cork's Burkley Cup, Limerick's Cromer Cup and Waterford's George French Shield, ordinary people gave over huge amounts of their leisure time to attend meetings and carry out other tasks to ensure the smooth running of these contests, in the majority of cases as an end in itself. Similarly, whether it was the Waterford and District League, the Limerick District Football Association, senior clubs like Fordsons, Cork FC, Cork Bohemians, Waterford Celtic and Limerick FC or junior clubs like Tramore Rookies in Waterford, Cahir Park in Tipperary, Dalcassians in Limerick or Grattan United in Cork, throughout the region little or no soccer at all would have been organised and played but for a huge voluntary effort, readily given by people who loved the game.

Financial woes were not restricted to the big clubs who made it to the Free State League, but their success was more open to the vicissitudes of changing tax legislation than the smaller, junior and minor soccer clubs in Munster. Indeed, the repeal of the entertainment tax exemptions for a two-year period from 1932 until 1934, when they were reinstated, coincided with Waterford FC's folding as a going concern and, unluckily, with Cork Bohemians' brief stint as a Free State League team. The failure of both clubs during those particularly hard years had as much to do with an over-reliance on paying non-locals, professional and English players rising unemployment in both cities, and as it had with the repeal of the entertainments exemption. Without these successes, by no means guaranteed, the chances of soccer gaining the critical mass for two teams to compete in the Free State League from the region inside a five-year period were low. Not unlike the development of Northern Union rugby, described by Tony Collins as 'neither simple class expression nor mere passive diffusion, [where] working-class culture contained strong elements of commercialism and sought to utilise existing leisure outlets for its own purposes'.[2] That success is perhaps the ultimate indicator of soccer's strength in the interwar years, despite the huge difficulties the game endured in the early 1900s: a game whose roots in the province had been set down in schools like Fermoy College, Penn's in Mallow, Lismore College and the provincial army barracks and had transformed into a game played in the streets and in front of crowds of tens of thousands. The success of this revival and transformation is thrown into yet sharper relief when placed in the context of the aftermath of the political and social upheavals from 1914 to 1923. In other words, despite the open hostility displayed towards soccer in many quarters of the media and officialdom, the game thrived because people chose to play it – in the street, on fields and playing pitches – and chose to put what little extra money and extra time they had into the hands of clubs, as they made their way to Dublin for cup games, raised funds to give fans a meeting place, clicked through the turnstiles, or more importantly, ran clubs in their spare time, kitted out, refereed, and managed teams.

In Munster, people took soccer and made it their own thing. The three final chapters of this book all show one vital thing that is undeniable: schools, colleges and universities, the military and workplaces had their role to play in encouraging games, but it took people to play the game. Whether it was those who attended elite schools and the region's university, soldiers and ex-soldiers, workers in factories and businesses, young boys in the street, members of the local CYMS or boys' club, they all helped to create the dappled, vibrant and varied sporting landscape of which they were a part. Ultimately, soccer was a popular sport among many of Munster's young men and its appeal was neither homogenous nor was its spread simplistically top-down. As the wise and wise-cracking correspondent of the *Nenagh Guardian* had it, in these things, people go their own way. Like many before them, this perhaps more than any other is the reason why the boys of St Joseph's, and the dozens upon dozens of clubs throughout the province with their disparate and varied origins, were more inclined to kick a ball with their feet more than anything else. They too were going their own way, making their own history. The garrison game, after the garrison was gone, was here to stay.

A NOTE ON SOURCES

Sports history is a sub-discipline of social and cultural history that was born out of, initially, interest from those historians of the working classes who wished to know what it was the working class did when they weren't working. Since then it has been tied, as Mike Cronin noted a number of years ago, to a variety of shifting trends in the historical mainstream – sports history as practised by some bears the hallmarks of the cultural turn, postmodernism, the material turn and much more besides. Yet as Cronin argued in the same article, there is something to be said for 'counting' – for more old-fashioned, and indeed occasionally deeply unfashionable, modes and methods of researching and writing history.[1] However, such demographic material is not always easily available, as this study and others have shown. Nonetheless, we can, through other sources, still say important things about the nature of class in history.

In this spirit I would make the point to the reader that this work is constructed from a wide variety of sources that ranges from print (newspapers) to the handwritten (diaries and minute books), the archival, the official, the ephemeral and the visual (photographs, cinema newsreels). There is counting, but there is much else besides. This veritable mélange of sources and the pluralist methodological approach it necessitated was born of the nature of this book's subject matter: sport. Like much else in the past, sport and the mark it leaves on the historical record – when neither great triumph nor disaster – is more often than not fleeting. Matches, contests, games (call them what you will) last only as long as they are required to for a winner to be declared. Yes, the result may be logged, a newspaper report may appear or a team photograph of those who are victorious might also be printed, but by and large, once a match is over it is gone, so too one more part of human endeavour of which only a fractional account can remain.

As such, to give an account of the history of soccer in Munster from 1877 to 1937, as this book attempts to do, required the author to draw on the wide and varying (but incomplete) sources that he could to tell the story. As has been the case for much other sports history, the newspapers – local, national, sporting, daily or weekly – have, in the place of detailed archival sources, provided this work with its bedrock and foundation. I have also been lucky to gain access to a variety of archives that have helped flesh out and fill in gaps where the newspapers fell silent – in particular the archives of the Football Association of Ireland, the Irish Football Association and the Leinster and Connacht FAs.

The Munster Football Association was founded in 1901, lay dormant following the outbreak of the First World War, before being reformed and rejuvenated in 1922. Yet it is our great misfortune that records for that long-standing organiser of the game in Munster do not have the wealth of archival records that a fellow body, the Leinster Football Association, has. Naturally then, the nature of the history of soccer presented in this book has been tempered in great part by the relative paucity of archival material relating directly to the game of soccer in Munster in the period the book covers. Where it has been useful, I have used records of both national bodies for the sport and fellow provincial associations, including both the Leinster and Connacht FAs, though each only offer shadows of the workings of their Munster counterparts. Without the MFA's own records to check against these other bodies, there are things that we cannot come to know. Thus it has fallen in the main to a close critical reading of the many local newspapers in Munster (chief among them being the *Waterford News, Munster Express, Limerick Leader, Evening Echo, Cork Examiner, Cork Constitution* and *Cork Sportsman*) to recover the story of soccer there. It should be noted too that, given the extensive breadth of geographic space which this book covers, the kind of demographic work produced by, in particular, Tom Hunt and Richard McElligott in their county studies of, respectively, Westmeath and Kerry was simply impractical in the case of this work. Additionally, and echoing Liam O'Callaghan and his work on rugby in the province of Munster, the generic nature of many names of those who played (when players' names were provided) allied to the sheer scale of the area and time covered in this study meant that a particular kind of socio-economic and demographic methodology was unlikely to be a fruitful labour.[2]

As such this study is a social history of the game that does not seek to definitively say that throughout its history, soccer in Munster was the preserve of one socio-economic class or another but rather that soccer, as one of a handful of British sports with a broad popular appeal in Ireland, had a fluid history and was played by a wide range of people whose social (and by extension political and economic) relationships changed over time and as a result, so too did the nature of what soccer as a game looked like, sounded like, even felt like, over a period of sixty years in Munster. At any rate, these things are broadly pointed at by the names of clubs and their origins as workplace, school or even geographic entities.

While this book has taken a largely chronological approach in relating the social history of soccer, an attempt has also been made to weave within that chronology analyses around themes of amateur and professional sporting endeavour and the antagonism between the two, commercialisation, and sport as situated in a broader popular culture and leisure industry.

The themes which are peppered throughout this book – work, unemployment, the availability of playing grounds, club finances, gate receipts, the nature of local rivalry, the daily trials and tribulations of keeping clubs going – have all emerged thanks to the sources, insofar as is possible; many of the thematic issues which arise again and again throughout the book do so because they arose organically from the sources to hand. This approach has been taken as a result of reading a variety of histories of soccer in Britain, but was also influenced by the increasing amount of scholarship on not alone Gaelic games but other sports in the Irish context, each book taking a differing approach – some utilising the thematic, others the chronological, and still others a combination of the two. For it to be another way would be to leave it without a context that it requires. Specifically, the sources indicated that these were the questions that needed to be answered – and which demanded a response. The richness of the newspaper sources, especially those soccer notes in various papers which were a weekly fixture, provided many of the central questions which this book has attempted to answer in a thoroughgoing fashion.

Muddy fields, rain-soaked jerseys, heavy leather balls, crunching tackles, baying crowds – these visceral, tactile elements of matches are all the intangibles of the game's history. How it felt in 1910 to face off against Manchester City at Turners Cross, to stand as a representative of a province in which the game was still so young against a team which, already by then, had gained national and international fame – that was surely a great and dreadful feeling. To have come by train into Glanmire station, gleaming silver cup in hand, or to have crossed Waterford's bridge surrounded by family, friends and well-wishers with the very same cup; what it was like to change clothes in a train carriage on the side of a pitch, are things no source can truly convey. This book nevertheless has a mission to bring to life those fleeting moments – to make known what kinds of days they were when soccer had its place in the lives of all those who played it.

BIBLIOGRAPHY

Primary Sources

NEWSPAPERS AND PERIODICALS:

An Phoblacht
Celtia
Clonmel Chronicle
Cork Weekly News
Cork Examiner
Cork Constitution
Cork Free Press
Cork Sportsman
Derby Daily Telegraph
Dundee Courier
Evening Echo
Evening Telegraph
Football Sports Weekly
Freeman's Journal
Gaelic Athlete
Honesty
Irish Coursing Calendar
Irish Field and Gentleman's Gazette
Irish Independent
Irish Nation
Irish Times
Irish Worker
Kerryman
Limerick Leader
Nenagh Guardian
Munster Express
QCC Magazine
Southern Star
Sport
Sunday Independent

The Harp
The Leader
The Nationalist (Clonmel)
United Irishman
Waterford News
Waterford News & Star
Weekly Irish Times
Western Daily Press
Western Morning News

CONTEMPORARY PUBLICATIONS, C.1877–1937:

Barry, Tadhg, *Hurling and How to Play It*, Dublin: Talbot Press, 1916

Beere, T.J., 'Cinema Statistics in Saorstát Éireann', *JSSISI*, Vol. XV, No. 6, 1935/1936, pp. 83–110

Bulfin, William, *Rambles in Éirinn*, Dublin: M.H. Gill & Son Ltd., 1907

Campbell, Agnes, *Report on Public Baths and Wash-houses in the United Kingdom*, Aberdeen: The Carnegie United Kingdom Trust, 1918

Coey Bigger, E., *Report on the Physical Welfare of Mothers and Children, Vol. IV: Ireland*, Dublin: Falconer, 1917

Eason, J.C.M., 'An Analysis Showing the Objects of Expenditure and the Sources of Revenue during the Financial Years 1924–25 to 1929–30', *JSSISI*, Vol. XV, No. 1, 1930/1931, pp. 1–13

Fitzgerald, Dick, *How to Play Gaelic Football*, Cork: Francis Guy and Co., 1914

Kiernan, T.J., 'The National Expenditure of the Free State in 1926', *JSSISI*, Vol. XV, No. 3, 1932/1933, pp. 91–103

O'Brien, Eoghan, 'The Growth of Electricity Supply and its Relations to Civilisation', *JSSISI*, Vol. XV No. 3, 1932/1933, pp. 69–90

Redmond, Cornelius P., *Beauty Spots of the South-East and How to See Them by Car or Cycle*, Waterford: Redmond Printing Co., 1903

Saunders, J.C., *County Borough of Cork Annual Report of the Medical Officer of Health for the Year 1935*, Cork: Eagle Printing Works, 1936

Saunders, J.C., *County Borough of Cork Annual Report of the Medical Officer of Health for the Year 1936*, Cork: Eagle Printing Works, 1937

Various, *The Collegian: The Christian Brothers' College Annual*, Cork: Francis Guy & Co., 1919

Various, *Irish Greyhound Studbook, Vol. I*, Clonmel: Irish Greyhound and Sporting Press Ltd., 1927

Various, *Cork, a Civic Survey: prepared by the Cork Town Planning Association*, London: Hodder & Stoughton, 1926

STREET AND TRADE DIRECTORIES:

Guy's Cork Directory, Cork: Francis Guy & Co. Ltd., 1883–1924 inclusive
Guy's Munster Directory 1886, Cork: Francis Guy & Co. Ltd., 1886
Thom's Waterford Directory 1910, Dublin: Thom & Co., 1910

OFFICIAL PUBLICATIONS:

Census of Population Report 1926, Vol. II: Occupation, Dublin: Stationery Office, 1928

Census of Population Report 1936, Vol. II: Occupation, Dublin: Stationery Office, 1938

Companies Annual Reports 1928, Dublin: Stationery Office, 1929

Companies Annual Reports 1930, Dublin: Stationery Office, 1931

Finance Accounts of Saorstát Éireann, 1927, Dublin: Stationery Office, 1928

Finance Accounts of Saorstát Éireann, 1928, Dublin: Stationery Office, 1929

Finance Accounts of Saorstát Éireann, 1929, Dublin: Stationery Office, 1930

Finance Accounts of Saorstát Éireann, 1930, Dublin: Stationery Office, 1931

Finance Accounts of Saorstát Éireann, 1931, Dublin: Stationery Office, 1932

Interim Report on Betting Act, 1926, Dublin: Stationery Office, 1929

BOOLE LIBRARY AND UCC SPECIAL COLLECTIONS:

British in Ireland microfilm series: *RIC Monthly Reports*

Various, *UCC RFC Centenary History 1874–1974*, Wexford: John English & Co., 1974

UNIVERSITY COLLEGE CORK ARCHIVES:

UC/ATH/MB/1 *Cork Athletic Grounds Committee Minute Books*

UC/FC/MB/01–11 *UCC Finance Committee Minute Books 1912–1937*

CORK CITY AND COUNTY ARCHIVES:

SP/CC/1/1 *Cork Constitution Rugby Football Club Minutes Book*

SP/CC/3/1 *Cork Constitution Rugby Football Club Accounts*

U/216/1/4 *Cork Council of Trade Unions Minute Books 1929–1934*

U341/7/3 *Cork Catholic Young Men's Society Minute Books 1882–1888*

U344/5 *J.J. Walsh personal papers*

U600/3 *Cork Sick Poor Society (North Parish) Minute Books 1923–1951*

LIMERICK CITY ARCHIVES:

IE LA L/MIN/16 *Limerick City Council Minute Book*, 2 January 1930–14 December 1932

IE LA L/MIN/17 *Limerick City Council Minute Book*, 5 January 1933–31 October 1934

IE LA L/MIN/18 *Limerick City Council Minute Book*, 22 November 1934–12 March 1940

WATERFORD CITY ARCHIVES:

LA1/13/D/1 *Waterford Corporation Public Health Committee Minute Books*

COMPANIES REGISTRATION OFFICE:

Clonmel Golf Club Limited, Particulars of Directors; Particulars of Shareholders

Clonmel Greyhound Racing Company Limited, Particulars of Directors; Particulars of Shareholders

Dublin Greyhound and Sports Association Limited, Particulars of Directors; Particulars of Shareholders

NATIONAL LIBRARY OF IRELAND:

9A/1791 *Elvery's Rugby, Gaelic, Soccer, Handball and Hurling Catalogue*

OP/IE/PP/29/5 *Oireachtas Report into Betting Act, 1926*, Dublin: Stationery Office, 1929

NATIONAL ARCHIVES (IRELAND):

DFA2/34/170 International association football matches between France and Saorstát

DFA/1/GR/888 International association football match between Italy and the Saorstát, April 1927

DFA/1/GR/1489 Franco-Irish international rugby match, Paris 1931

DFA/2/1/38 National flag at international rugby football matches, Lansdowne Road, February 1932

TSCH/3/S2950 National flag: flying at international rugby matches in Dublin, February 1932

NATIONAL ARCHIVES (BRITAIN):

Cork Skating Rink Co. Ltd, Director Particulars

FOOTBALL ASSOCIATION OF IRELAND ARCHIVES (UNIVERSITY COLLEGE, DUBLIN):

P137/1–6 *International Recognition of the Football Association of the Irish Free State, 1922–1956*

P137/7 *Administration of the FAIFS 1934 (Correspondence from J.A. Ryder, January –August 1934)*

P137/11–12 *Minute Book of the Finance Committee, 1921–1937*

P137/14–15 *Minute Book of the Protest and Appeals Committee and Emergency Committee 1921–1932*

P137/21 *Minute Book of the Senior Council 1932–1937*

P137/25–27 *Junior Committee Minutes 1923–1940*

P137/35 *Rules, Ratification and Referees' Committees*

P137/38 *Consultative Committee Minutes 1924–1934*

LEINSTER FOOTBALL ASSOCIATION ARCHIVES (UNIVERSITY COLLEGE, DUBLIN):

P239/21–42, *Committee Minutes Books, 1901–1932*

P239/42 *Finance Committee Minute Books*

CONNACHT FOOTBALL ASSOCIATION ARCHIVES: (UNIVERSITY COLLEGE, DUBLIN):

P243/1 *Committee Minute Book, 1928–1938*

IRISH FOOTBALL ASSOCIATION ARCHIVES (PUBLIC RECORD OFFICE OF NORTHERN IRELAND):

D4196/A/1–3, *Council Minute Books*
D4196/AA/1, *Committee Minute Books*
D4196/G/1, *Junior Committee Minute Books*
D4196/R/1, *Finance Records*

GAELIC ATHLETIC ASSOCIATION ARCHIVES (CROKE PARK, DUBLIN):

MUN/001 *Munster Council Minute Books 1928–1937*

IRISH MILITARY ARCHIVES:

A/0745 *South Tipperary Brigade, No. 3 Brigade Report*, November 1921

OTHER:

Cork City FC Gate Receipts Book 1938 (privately held)
Imperial Tobacco Co. of Britain and Ireland Ltd., *WD&HO Wills' 50 Hurlers*, Cigarette Card Series (privately held)

Secondary Sources

ARTICLES AND BOOK CHAPTERS:

Bielenberg, Andy and O'Mahony, Patrick, 'An Expenditure Estimate of Irish National Income in 1907', *The Economic and Social Review*, Vol. 29, No. 2, April 1998, pp. 107–132

Bielenberg, Andy, 'Late Victorian Elite Formation and Philanthropy: The Making of Edward Guinness', *Studia Hibernica*, No. 32, 2002–2003, pp. 133–154

Bielenberg, Andy and Hearne, John M., 'Malcomsons of Portlaw and Clonmel: Some New Evidence on the Irish Cotton Industry, 1825–1850', *Proceedings of the Royal Irish Academy*, Vol. 106C, pp. 339–366

Bielenberg, Andy, 'Exodus: The Emigration Of Southern Irish Protestants During the Irish War of Independence and the Civil War', *Past & Present*, No. 218 (February 2013), pp. 199–233

Bielenberg, Andy, 'British Competition and the Vicissitudes of the Irish Woolen Industry: 1785–1923', *Textile History*, Vol. 31, No. 2, 2000, pp. 202–221

Bromhead, John, 'George Cadbury's Contribution to Sport', *The Sports Historian*, Vol. 20, No. 1, May 2000, pp. 97–117

Bubb, Alexander, 'The Life of the Irish Soldier in India: Representations and Self-Representations, 1857–1922', *Modern Asian Studies*, Vol. 46, No. 4 (2012), pp. 769–813

Carey, Tadhg, 'Ireland's Footballers at the Paris Olympics, 1924', *History Ireland*, Vol. 20, No. 4, July/August 2012

Collins, Tony, 'From Bondi to Batley: Australian Players in British Rugby League, 1907–1995', *Sporting Traditions*, Vol. 16, No. 2, May 2000, pp. 71–86

Collins, Tony, 'English Rugby Union and the First World War', *The Historical Journal*, Vol. 45, No. 4, 2002, pp. 797–817

Cronin, Mike, 'Blueshirts, Sports and Socials', *History Ireland*, Autumn 1994, pp. 43–47

Cronin, Mike, 'Enshrined in Blood: The Naming of Gaelic Athletic Association Grounds and Clubs', *The Sports Historian*, Vol. 18, No. 1, May 1998, pp. 90–104

Cronin, Mike, 'An Historical Identity: Historians and the Making of Irish Nationalist Identity in the Gaelic Athletic Association', *Football Studies*, Vol. 1, No. 2, August 1998, pp. 89–102

Cronin, Mike, 'Projecting the Nation through Sport and Culture: Ireland, Aonach Tailteann and the Irish Free State, 1924–32', *Journal of Contemporary History*, Vol. 38, No. 3, July 2003, pp. 395–411

Cronin, Mike, 'What Went Wrong with Counting? Thinking about Sport and Class in Britain and Ireland', *Sport in History*, Vol. 29, No. 3, 2009, pp. 392–404

Cronin, Mike, 'Trinity Mysteries: Responding to a Chaotic Reading of Irish History', *The International Journal of the History of Sport*, Vol. 28, No. 18, 2011, pp. 2753–2760

Curran, Conor, 'The Development of Gaelic football and Soccer Zones in Donegal, 1884–1934', *Sport in History*, Vol. 32, No. 3, 2012, pp. 426–452

Curry, Graham, 'The Origins of Football Debate: Comments on Adrian Harvey's Historiography', *The International Journal of the History of Sport*, published online 14 May 2014.

Dann, Jeff, 'The Representation of British Sports in Late Nineteenth and Early Twentieth Century Elite Irish School Publications', *Media History*, Vol. 17, No. 2, 2011, pp. 133–145

Daly, Mary E., 'The Employment Gains From Industrial Protection in the Irish Free State During the 1930s: A Note', *Irish Economic and Social History*, Vol. XV, 1988, pp. 71–75

Daly Mary E., '"Turn on the Tap": The State, Irish Women and Running Water', in Mary O'Dowd, and Maryann Valiulis (eds), *Women & Irish History*, Dublin: Wolfhound Press, 1997

Darby, Paul, 'The Gaelic Athletic Association, Transnational Identities and Irish-America', *Sociology of Sport Journal*, Vol. 27, 2010, pp. 351–370

Dixon, Paula and Garnham, Neal, 'Drink and the Professional Footballer in 1890s England and Ireland', *Sport in History*, Vol. 25, No. 3, 2005, pp. 375–389

Drucker, Nicola, 'Hunting & Shooting – Leisure, Social Networking and Social Complications: Microhistorical Perspectives on Colonial Structures and Individual Practices – the Grehan Family, Clonmeen House, Ireland', in Terrence McDonough (ed.), *Was Ireland a Colony? Economics, Politics and Culture in Nineteenth Century Ireland*, Dublin: Irish Academic Press, 2005, pp. 117–145

Dwyer, Michael, 'Abandoned by God and the Corporation: Health, Housing and the Cork Working Classes, 1914–1924', *Saothar*, No. 38, 2013, pp. 105–118

Finn, Gerry P.T., 'Trinity Mysteries: University, Elite Schooling and Sport in Ireland', *The International Journal of the History of Sport*, Vol. 27, No. 13, 2010, pp. 2255–2287

Garnham, Neal, 'Both Praying and Playing: "Muscular Christianity" and the YMCA in North-East County Durham', *Journal of Social History*, Vol. 35, No. 2, Winter 2001, pp. 397–407

Garnham, Neal, 'Sport History: The Cases of Britain and Ireland Stated', *Journal of Sport History*, Vol. 31, No. 2, Spring 2004, pp. 139–144

Hassan, David, 'A People Apart: Soccer, Identity and Irish Nationalists in Northern Ireland', *Soccer and Society*, Vol. 3, No. 3, Autumn 2002, pp. 65–83

Humphries, M., 'An Issue of Confidence: The Decline of the Irish Whiskey Trade in Independent Ireland, 1922–1992', *Journal of European Economic History*, Vol. 23, 1994, pp. 93–103

Huggins, Mike, 'Projecting the Visual: British Newsreels, Soccer and Popular Culture, 1918–1939', *The International Journal of the History of Sport*, Vol. 24, No. 1, 2007, pp. 80–102

Huggins, Mike, 'Betting, Sport and the British, 1918–1939', *Journal of Social History*, Vol. 41, No. 2, Winter 2007, pp. 283–306

Hyde, Douglas, 'The Necessity for de-Anglicizing Ireland', *The Revival of Irish Literature*, New York: Lemma, 1973

Johnes, Martin, '"Poor Man's Cricket": Baseball, Class and Community in South Wales c.1880–1950', *International Journal of the History of Sport*, Vol. 17, No. 4, December 2000

Kemmy, Jim, 'Housing and Social Conditions, 1830–1940', *Old Limerick Journal*, No. 24, Winter 1988, pp. 69–74

Lane, Fintan, 'Music and Violence in Working-Class Cork: "The Band Nuisance" 1879–1882', *Saothar*, No. 24, 1999, pp. 17–33

Lane, Padraig G., 'Daniel Corkery and the Cork Working Classes', *Saothar*, No. 38, 2013, pp. 43–51

Leeworthy, Daryl, 'The Forgotten Hurlers of South Wales: Sport, Society and the Irish, 1910–1925', *Llafur: Journal of Welsh People's History*, Vol. 11, No. 2, 2012, pp. 33–48.

Mangan, J.A., 'Play Up and Play the Game: Victorian and Edwardian Public School Vocabularies of Motive', *British Journal of Educational Studies*, Vol. 23, No. 3, October 1975, pp. 324–335

Mangan, J.A., 'Grammar Schools and the Games Ethic in the Victorian and Edwardian Eras', *Albion*, Vol. 15, No. 4, Winter 1983, pp. 313–335

Mangan, J.A., 'Missing Men: Schoolmasters and the Early Years of Association Football', *Soccer & Society*, Vol. 9, No. 2, July 2008, pp. 170–188

McCabe, Conor, '*Football Sports Weekly* and Irish Soccer 1925–28', *Media History*, Vol. 17, No. 2, May 2011, pp. 147–158

McElligott, Richard, 'Degenerating from Sterling Irishmen to Contemptible West Brits', *History Ireland*, Vol. 19, No. 4, July/August 2011

McElligott, Richard, '1916 and the Radicalization of the GAA', *Éire-Ireland*, Vol. 48, Nos 1 & 2, Spring/Summer 2013, pp. 95–111

McSharry, Majella, 'Stuck in a Ruck: The Impact of Rugby in Social Belonging', in Mary P. Corcoran and Perry Shoe (eds), *Belongings: Shaping Identity in modern Ireland*, Dublin: Institute of Public Administration 2008

Mosely, Phil, 'Factory Football: Paternalism and Profit', *Sporting Traditions: The Journal of the Australian Society for Sports History*, Vol. 2, No.1, November 1985, pp. 25–37

Nicholsen, Michael D., 'Identity, Nationalism, and Irish Traditional Music in Chicago, 1867–1900', *New Hibernia Review*, Vol. 13, No. 4, Winter 2009, pp. 111–126

O'Callaghan, Liam, 'The Red Thread of History', *Media History*, Vol. 17, No. 2, May 2011, pp. 175–188

O'Callaghan, Liam, 'Rugby Football and Identity Politics in Free State Ireland', *Éire-Ireland*, Vol. 48, Nos 1 & 2, Spring/Summer 2013, pp. 148–167

Ó Catháin, Mairtín, '"Struggle or Starve": Derry Unemployed Workers' Movements, 1926–1935', *Saothar*, No. 28, 2003, pp. 49–60

Rouse, Paul, 'The Politics of Culture and Sport in Ireland: A History of the GAA Ban on Foreign Games 1884–1971, Part One: 1884–1921', *The International Journal of the History of Sport*, Vol. 10, No. 3, December 1993, pp. 333–360

Ryan, Frederick W., 'What the Worker Should Know', *JSSISI*, Vol. XIV, Part 2, 1920–1923, pp. 133–143

Sangster, Joan, 'The Softball Solution: Female Workers, Male Managers and the Operation of Paternalism at Westclox, 1923–60', *Labour/Le Travail*, No. 32, Fall 1993, pp. 167–199

Selenick, Laurence, 'Politics as Entertainment: Victorian Music Hall Songs', *Victorian Studies*, Vol. 19, No. 2, December 1975, pp. 149–180

Stoddart, Brian, 'Sport, Cultural Imperialism, and Colonial Response in the British Empire', *Comparative Studies in Society and History*, Vol. 30, No. 4, October 1988, pp. 649–673

Thompson, E.P., 'Time, Work-Discipline and Industrial Capitalism', *Past & Present*, Vol. 38, No. 1, 1967, pp. 56–97

Toms, David, 'Notwithstanding the Discomfort Involved: Fordsons' Cup Win of 1926 and How "the Old Contemptible" Were Represented in Ireland's Public Sphere in the 1920s', *Sport in History*, Vol. 32, No. 4, December 2012, pp. 504–526

Toms, David, 'The Electric Hare: The Development of Greyhound Racing in Ireland, 1927–58', *Irish Economic and Social History*, Vol. XXXX, 2013, pp. 63–85

BOOKS:

Alford, B.W.E., *WD and HO Wills and the Development of the UK Tobacco Industry, 1786–1965*, London: Metheun, 1973

Andrews, C.S., *Dublin Made Me*, Dublin: Mercier Press, 1979

Bailey, Peter (ed.), *Music Hall: The Business of Pleasure*, Milton Keynes: Open University Press, 1986

Bairner, Alan (ed.), *Sport and the Irish: Histories, Identities, Issues*, Dublin: UCD Press, 2006

Bairner, Alan and Sugden, John, *Sport, Sectarianism and Society in a Divided Ireland*, Leceister: Leceister University Press, 1993

Bale, John, *Landscapes of Modern Sport*, London: Leicester University Press, 1994

Bielenberg, Andrew, *Cork and the Industrial Revolution 1780–1880*, Cork: Cork University Press, 1991

Bielenberg, Andrew, *Ireland and the Industrial Revolution: The impact of the industrial revolution on Irish industry, 1801–1922*, London: Routledge, 2009

Bielenberg, Andrew and Ryan, Raymond, *An Economic History of Ireland since 1922*, London: Routledge, 2013

Borgonovo, John, *The Dynamics of War and Revolution: Cork City, 1916–1918*, Cork: Cork University Press, 2013

Boyce, D. George, *Nationalism in Ireland*, Dublin: Gill & Macmillan, 1982

Buckley, Paul, *Cameos of a Century*, Cahir: Cahir Park FC, 2010

Brailsford, Denis, *British Sport: A Social History*, Cambridge: Lutterworth Press, 1997

Bracken, Patrick, *Foreign and Fantastic Field Sports: Cricket in County Tipperary*, Tipperary: Liskeveen Books, 2004

Brady, Donal (ed.), *Joseph Hansard's History of Waterford*, Dublin: Colour Books Ltd., 1997

Bratton, J.S. (ed.), *Music Hall: Performance & Style*, Milton Keynes: Open University Press, 1986

Breen, Daniel and Spalding, Tom, *The Cork International Exhibition, 1902–1903: A Snapshot of Edwardian Cork*, Dublin: Irish Academic Press, 2014

Brosnan, John Joe and Ó Murchada, Diarmaid, *Cork GAA: A History, 1886–1986*, Cork: GAA, 1986

Byrne, Peter, *Football Association of Ireland: 75 Years*, Dublin: Sportsworld Publications, 1996

Byrne, Peter, *Green is the Colour: The Story of Irish Football*, London: Andre Deutsch, 2012

De Búrca, Marcus, *The GAA: A History 2nd Edition*, Dublin: Gill & Macmillan, 1999

Cadogan, Tim, and Falvey, Jeremiah J., *A Dictionary of Cork Biography*, Dublin: Mercier Press, 2006

Carter, Plunkett, *A Century of Cork Soccer Memories*, Cork: Evening Echo publications, 1996

Chambers, Ciara, *Ireland in the Newsreels*, Dublin: Irish Academic Press, 2012

Clusky, Jim (ed.), *Cork County Cricket Club 1874–1974*, Cork: Cork County Crickey Club, 1975

Coleman, Marie, *The Irish Sweep: A History of the Irish Hospitals Sweepstake 1930–1987*, Dublin: UCD Press, 2009

Collins, Tony, *Rugby's Great Split: Class, Culture and Origins of Rugby League*, London: Routledge, 2006

Collins, Tony, *Sport in Capitalist Society: A Short History*, London: Routledge, 2013

Collins, Tony and Vamplew, Wray, *Mud, Sweat and Beers: A Cultural History of Sport and Alcohol*, Oxford: Berg, 2002

Comyn, John, *Trap to Line: 50 Years of Greyhound Racing in Ireland, 1927–1977*, Dublin: Aherlow Publishers, 1977

Comerford, R.V., *Inventing the Nation: Ireland*, London: Hodder Arnold, 2003

Convery, David (ed.), *Locked Out: A Century of Irish Working-Class Life*, Dublin: Irish Academic Press, 2013

Cooke, Richard T., *Cork's Barrack Street Band: Ireland's Oldest Amateur Musical Institution*, Cork: Seamus Curtin, 1992

Corry, Eoghan, *The History of Gaelic Football*, Dublin: Gill & Macmillan, 2010

Costello Murray and Beaumont, *An Introduction to the Royal Hospital Kilmainham: Its Architecture, History and Restoration*, Criterion: Dublin, 1987

Coughlan, Barry, *Rags to Riches: The Story of Munster Rugby*, Cork: The Collins Press, 2009

Creedon, C., *The Cork and Macroom Direct Railway: A Short History*, Cork: City Printing Works, 1980

Cronin, Jim, *Munster GAA Story*, Ennis: Clare Champion, 1986

Cronin, Mike, *The Blueshirts and Irish Politics*, Dublin: Four Courts Press, 1997

Cronin, Mike, *Sport and Nationalism in Ireland: Gaelic Games, Soccer and Irish Identity Since 1884*, Dublin: Four Courts Press, 1999

Cronin, Mike, Duncan, Mark and Rouse, Paul, *The GAA: A People's History*, Cork: The Collins Press, 2009

Cronin, Mike, Duncan, Mark and Rouse, Paul, *The GAA: County by County*, Cork: The Collins Press, 2011

Cronin, Mike and Higgins, Roisín, *Places We Play: Ireland's Sporting Heritage*, Cork: The Collins Press, 2011

Cronin, Mike, Murphy, Will and Rouse, Paul (eds), *The GAA: 1884–2009*, Dublin: Irish Academic Press, 2009

Cronin, Mike and Mayall, David (eds), *Sporting Nationalisms: Identity, Ethnicity, Immigration and Assimilation*, London: Frank Cass, 2001

Cronin, Sean, *Irish Nationalism: A History of its Roots and Ideology*, Dublin: The Academy Press, 1980

Cullen, Donal, *Freestaters: The Republic of Ireland Soccer Team 1921–39*, Essex: Desert Island Books, 2007

Cunningham, Hugh, *Leisure in the Industrial Revolution c.1780–1880*, London: Croom Helm, 1980

D'Arcy, Fergus A., *Horses, Lords and Racing Men: The Turf Club 1790–1990*, Kildare: The Turf Club, 1991

Daly, Mary E., *County and Town: One Hundred Years of Local Government*, Dublin: Institute of Public Administration, 2001

Daly, Mary E., *Industrial Development and Irish National Identity 1922–39*, Syracuse, NY: Syracuse University Press, 1992

Dennis, Norman, Henriques, Fernando and Slaughter, Clifford, *Coal Is Our Life: An Analysis of a Yorkshire Mining Community*, London: Tavistock, 1969

Dooley, Thomas, *Irishmen or English Soldiers?* Liverpool: Liverpool University Press, 1995

Donnelly, J.S. and Miller, Kerby A. (eds), *Irish Popular Culture, 1650–1850*, Dublin: Irish Academic Press, 1999

Dunning, Eric and Sheard, Kenneth, *Barbarians, Gentlemen & Players: A Sociological Study of the Development of Rugby Football*, Oxford: Robertson, 1979

Ferriter, Diarmaid, *A Nation of Extremes: The Pioneers in Twentieth Century Ireland*, Dublin: Irish Academic Press, 1999

Ferriter, Diarmaid, *The Transformation of Ireland, 1900–2000*, London: Profile Books, 2005

Fleitz, David L., *The Irish in Baseball: An Early History*, Jefferson NC: McFarland & Co., 2009

Fogarty, Philip, *Tipperary's GAA Story*, Thurles: The Tipperary Star, 1960

Gallimore, Andrew, *A Bloody Canvas: The Mike McTigue Story*, Cork: Mercier Press, 2007

Garnham, Neal, *Association Football and Society in Pre-Partition Ireland*, Belfast: Ulster Historical Foundation, 2004

Garnham, Neal, *The Origins and Development of Football in Ireland, being a reprint of R.M. Peter's Football Annual 1880*, Belfast: Ulster Historical Foundation, 2008

Garvin, Tom, *The Evolution of Irish Nationalist Politics*, Dublin: Gill & macmillan, 1981

Garvin, Tom, *1922: The Birth of Irish Democracy*, Dublin: Gill & Macmillan, 2005

Glennon, Chris and Wynne, Tom, *90 Years of the Irish Hockey Union*, Kildare: Leinster Leader, 1985

Goldberg, David and Solomos, John (eds), *A Companion to Racial and Ethnic Studies*, Oxford: Blackwell, 2002

Goldblatt, David, *The Ball is Round: A Global History of the Game*, London: Penguin, 2006

Greer, Desmond and Nicolson, James W., *The Factory Acts in Ireland 1802–1914*, Dublin: Four Courts Press, 2003

Griffin, Brian, *Cycling in Victorian Ireland*, Dublin: Nonsuch Publishing, 2005

Guttmann, Allen, *Games and Empires: Modern Sports and Cultural Imperialism*, New York: Columbia University Press, 1994

Guttmann, Allen, *From Ritual to Record: The Nature of Modern Sports*, New York: Columbia University Press [1978], 2004 edn.

Hachey, Thomas E., and McCaffrey, Lawrence J., *Perspectives on Irish Nationalism*, Lexington: University Press of Kentucky, 1989

Hanna, Henry, *The Pals at Suvla Bay*, Uckfield: Naval & Military Press, 2009

Hartmann, Doug, *Race, Culture and the Revolt of the Black Athlete: The 1968 Olympics Protests and Their Aftermath*, Chicago: University of Chicago Press, 2003

Harvey, Adrian, *Football: The First Hundred Years*, London: Routledge, 2004

Hassan, David, McAnallen, Donal and Roddy Hegarty, *The Evolution of the GAA*, Belfast: Ulster Historical Foundation, 2009

Healy, James N. and O'Donovan, Con, *Comic Songs of Cork and Kerry*, Cork: Mercier Press, 1978

Hearne, John M., *Waterford Central Technical Institute 1906–2006: A History*, Waterford: CTI, 2006

Herlihy, Jim, *Royal Irish Constabulary Officers: A Biographical Dictionary and Geneaological Guide 1816–1922*, Dublin: Four Courts Press, 2005

Herr, Cheryl, *Joyce's Anatomy of Culture*, Urbana: University of Illinois Press, 1986

Hinds, Ross (ed.), *Stanford: Memoirs of William Bedell Stanford, Regius Professor of Greek 1940–80, Trinity College Dublin*, Dublin: Hinds, 2001

Hobsbawm, Eric, *Nations and Nationalism since 1780: Programme, Myth, Reality*, Cambridge: Cambridge University Press, 1991

Hobsbawm, Eric, *Uncommon People: Rebellion, Resistance and Jazz*, London: Abacus, 1998

Hobsbawm, Eric and Ranger, Terence (eds), *The Invention of Tradition*, Oxford: Oxford University Press, 1983

Hodkinson, Ger, *In the Beginning: A Celebration of One Hundred Years of Dolphin RFC*, Cork: Dolphin Rugby Club, 2002

Holt, Richard, *Sport and the British: A Modern History*, Oxford: Clarendon Press, 1989

Hunt, Tom, *Sport and Society in Victorian Ireland: The Case of Westmeath*, Cork: Cork University Press, 2006

Hutchinson, John, *The Dynamics of Cultural Nationalism*, London: Allen & Unwin, 1987

Hutchinson, John and Smith, Anthony D. (eds), *Nationalism*, Oxford: Oxford University Press, 1994

Hyde, Douglas, *The Revival of Irish Literature*, New York: Lemma, 1973

Inglis, Simon, *Football Grounds of Britain, 3rd Edition*, London: Harper Collins, 1996

Jacobs, Jane M., *Edge of Empire: Postcolonialism and the City*, New York: Routledge, 1996

Jenkins, S.C., *The Cork, Blackrock and Passage Railway*, Oxford: Oakwood Press, 1993

Jerram, Leif, *Streetlife: The Untold History of Europe's Twentieth Century*, Oxford: Oxford University Press, 2011

Johnston, Michael, *The Big Pot: The Story of the Irish Senior Rowing Championship 1912–1991*, Dublin: Shandon Books, 1992

Johnes, Martin, *Soccer and Society in South Wales, 1900–1939: That Other Game*, Cardiff: University of Wales Press, 2002

Jones, Stephen G., *Workers at Play: A Social and Economic History of Leisure 1918–1939*, London: Routledge Keegan Paul, 1986

Jones, Stephen G., *Sport, Politics and the Working Class: Organised Labour and Sport in Interwar Britain*, Manchester: Manchester University Press, 1988 [1992 paperback edn.]

Joyce, Patrick, *Work, Society and Politics*, London: Methuen, 1982

Kearney, Hugh F., *Ireland: Contested Ideas of Nationalism and History*, Cork: Cork University Press, 2007

Kearns, Kevin C., *Dublin Tenement Life*, Dublin: Gill & Macmillan, 1994

Kemmy, Jim, *The Limerick Anthology*, Dublin: Gill & Macmillan, 1996

Kennedy, Brian, *Blow It Up Ref!*, Waterford: Zesty Thorndyke Publishing, 2011

Kennedy, Brian, *Just Follow the Floodlights! The Complete Guide to the League of Ireland*, Dublin: Liffey Press, 2012

Kenny, Jennifer and Comerford, R.V. (eds), *Associational Culture in Ireland and Abroad*, Dublin: Irish Academic Press, 2010

Kiberd, Declan, *Inventing Ireland*, London: Jonathan Cape, 1995

King, Seamus J., *A History of Hurling: Second Edition*, Dublin: Gill & Macmillan, 2005

Lee, David (ed.), *Remembering Limerick: 800 Years*, Limerick: Limerick Civic Trust, 1997

Lee, David and Jacobs, Debbie (eds), *Made in Limerick: History of Industries, Trade and Commerce, Volume One*, Limerick: Limerick Civic Trust, 2003

Lee, J.J., *Ireland: 1912–1985*, Cambridge: Cambridge University Press, 1989

Leeworthy, Daryl, *Fields of Play: The Sporting Heritage of Wales*, Aberystwyth: Royal Commission on Ancient and Historical Monuments of Wales, 2012

Legg, Marie-Louise, *Newspapers and Nationalism: The Irish Provincial Press 1850–1892*, Dublin: Four Courts Press, 1999

Levitas, Ben, *The Theatre of Nation: Irish Drama and Cultural Nationalism, 1890–1916*, Oxford: Oxford University Press, 2002

Lloyd, David, *Irish Culture and Colonial Modernity, 1800–2000*, Cambridge: Cambridge University Press, 2011

Maloney, Paul, *Scotland and the Music Hall, 1850–1914*, Manchester: Manchester University Press, 2003

Mangan, J.A., *Athleticism in the Victorian and Edwardian Public Schools*, Cambridge: Cambridge University Press, 1981

Mangan, J.A., *The Games Ethic and Imperialism: Aspects of the Diffusion of an Ideal*, London: Frank Cass, 1986

Martin, John, *Tales of the Dogs: A Celebration of the Irish and Their Greyhounds*, Belfast: Blackstaff Press, 2009

Martin, Micheál, *Freedom to Choose: Cork and Party Politics in Ireland, 1918–1932*, Cork: The Collins Press, 2009

Mason, Tony, *Association Football and Society 1863–1915*, Brighton: Harvester Press, 1980

Mason, Tony and Riedi, Elizabeth, *Sport and the Military: The British Armed Forces 1880–1960*, Cambridge: Cambridge University Press, 2010

Mathews, P.J., *Revival: The Abbey Theatre, Sinn Féin, the Gaelic League and the Co-Operative Movement*, Cork: Cork University Press and Field Day, 2003

MacRaild, Donald M., *Irish Migrants in Modern Britain, 1750–1922*, London: Palgrave Macmillan, 1999

McAnallen, Donal, *The Cups That Cheered: A History of the Fitzgibbon, Sigerson and Higher Education Gaelic Games*, Cork: The Collins Press, 2013

McCarthy, Kevin, *Green, Silver and Gold: The Irish Olympic Journey 1896–1924*, Cork: Cork University Press, 2009

McDevitt, P.F. *'May The Best Man Win': Sport, Masculinity, and Nationalism in Great Britain and the Empire, 1880–1935*, London: Palgrave Macmillan, 2008

McDonagh, Oliver, Mandle, W.F. and Travers, Pauric, *Irish Culture and Nationalism 1750–1950*, London: Macmillan, 1983

McDowell, Jim, *Beyond the Footlights: A History of Belfast Music Halls and Early Theatre*, Dublin: The History Press Ireland, 2007

McDowell, R.B., *Crisis and Decline: The Fate of Southern Unionists*, Dublin: Lilliput Press, 1997

McElligott, Richard, *Forging a Kingdom: The GAA in Kerry, 1884–1934*, Cork: The Collins Press, 2013

McMahon, Timothy G., *Grand Opportunity: The Gaelic Revival and Irish Society, 1893–1910*, Syracuse: Syracuse University Press, 2008

Menton, William A., *The Golfing Union of Ireland 1891–1991*, Dublin: Gill & Macmillan, 1992

Metcalfe, Alan, *Leisure and Recreation in a Victorian Mining Community: The Social Economy of Leisure in North-East England, 1820–1914*, London: Routledge, 2008

Moloney, Bernie, *Times to Cherish: Cashel and Rosegreen Parish History 1795–1995*, Kildare: Leinster Leader, 1994

Moore, Cormac, *Douglas Hyde v the GAA: The Removal of Ireland's First President as GAA Patron*, Cork: The Collins Press, 2012

228

BIBLIOGRAPHY

Moran, D.P., *The Philosophy of Irish Ireland*, Dublin: UCD Press, 2006

Morris, Ewan, *Our Own Devices: National Symbols and Political Conflict in Twentieth-Century Ireland*, Dublin: Irish Academic Press, 2003

Murray, McNeill, *The Great Southern & Western Railway*, Wicklow: Irish Railway Record Society, 1976

Murphy, Donal A., *Nenagh Ormond's Century: A Rugby History*, Nenagh: Relay, 1984

Murphy, John A., *The College: The History of Queen's/University College Cork 1845–1995*, Cork: University College Cork, 1995

Murphy, John A., *Where Finbarr Played: A Concise History of Sport in UCC 1911–2011*, Cork: University College Cork, 2011

Myler, Patrick, *The Fighting Irish: Ireland's Role in World Boxing History*, Dingle: Brandon Books, 1987

Nye, Joseph S., *Soft Power: The Means to Success in World Politics*, New York: Public Affairs, 2004

Nyhan, Miriam, *'Are You Still Below?' The Ford Marina Plant, Cork 1917–1984*, Cork: The Collins Press, 2007

Ó Canainn, Tomás, *Songs of Cork*, Dublin: Dalton, 1978

O'Callaghan, Liam, *Rugby in Munster: A Social and Cultural History*, Cork: Cork University Press, 2011

O'Connor, Emmet, *A Labour History of Waterford*, Waterford Trade Union Council, 1987

O'Connor, Emmet, *A Labour History of Ireland, 1848–1960*, Dublin: Gill & Macmillan, 1992

O'Connor, Frank, *My Oedipus Complex and Other Stories*, London: Penguin, 2005

O'Connor, Peter, *Soldier of Liberty: Recollections of a Socialist and Anti-fascist Fighter*, MSF: Dublin, 1996

O'Connor-Lysaght, D.R., *The Story of the Limerick Soviet: The 1919 General Stroke against British Militarism* (3rd Edition), Limerick: Limerick Soviety Commemoration Committee, 2003

O'Donoghue, Tony, *Irish Championship Athletics 1873–1914*, Kilkenny: Kilkenny People Printing, 2005

O'Dwyer, Michael, *The History of Cricket in Kilkenny: The Forgotten Game*, Kilkenny: O'Dwyer Books, 2007

O'Flanagan, P. and Buttimer, C.G., *Cork: History and Society*, Dublin: Geography Publications, 1993

Ó Gráda, Cormac, *Jewish Ireland in the Age of Joyce: A Socioeconomic History*, Princeton: Princeton University Press, 2006

O'Kelly, Eoin, *Old Private Banks of Munster*, Cork: Cork University Press, 1959

O'Leary, Don, *Vocationalism & Social Catholicism in Twentieth-Century Ireland*, Dublin: Irish Academic Press, 2000

O'Mahony, Bertie, *Munster Football Association: 75 Years of Service to the Beautiful Game, 1922–1997*, Cork: Munster Football Association, 1998

Ó Maitiú, Séamus, *The Humours of Donnybrook: Dublin's Famous Fair and Its Suppression*, Dublin: Irish Academic Press, 1995

O'Neill, Ciaran (ed.), *Irish Elites in the Nineteenth Century*, Dublin: Four Courts Press, 2013

Oram, Hugh, *The Newspaper Book*, Dublin: MO Books, 1983

Pine, Richard, *2RN and the Origins of Irish Radio*, Dublin: Four Courts Press, 2005

Pine, Richard, *Music and Broadcasting in Ireland*, Dublin: Four Courts Press, 2005

Pope, S.W. and Nauright, John (eds), *Routledge Companion to Sports History*, New York: Routledge, 2010

Power, Dermot, *Ballads and Songs of Waterford: From 1487 with Musical Notation*, Waterford: 1992

Power, Patrick C., *Carrick-on-Suir and Its People*, The Carrick Society/Anna Livia Books, 1976

Power, Patrick C., *History of South Tipperary*, Cork and Dublin: Mercier Press, 1989

Reid, Colin and Nic Dháibhead, Caoimhe (eds), *From Parnell to Paisley: Constitutional and Revolutionary Politics in Modern Ireland*, Dublin: Irish Academic Press, 2010

Rivlin, Ray, *Shalom Ireland: A Social History of Jews in Modern Ireland*, Dublin: Gill & Macmillan, 2003

Rockett, Kevin and Rockett, Emer, *Film Exhibition and Distribution in Ireland, 1909–2010*, Dublin: Four Courts Press, 2011

Rockett, Kevin and Rockett, Emer, *Magic Lantern, Panorama and Moving Picture Shows in Ireland, 1786–1909*, Dublin: Four Courts Press, 2011

Russell, Dave, *Football and the English: A Social History of Association Football in England, 1863–1915*, Lancaster: Carnegie, 1997

Ryan, Gregg, *The Works: Celebrating 150 Years of Inchicore Works*, Dublin: ColourBooks, 1996

Shiel, Michael J., *The Quiet Revolution: The Electrification of Rural Ireland*, Dublin: O'Brien Press, 1984

Sisson, Elaine, *Pearse's Patriots: St. Enda's and the Cult of Boyhood*, Cork: Cork University Press, 2005

Somervillle-Large, Peter, Daly, Mary E. and Murphy, Colin (eds), *The Mount Street Club: Dublin's Unique Response to Unemployment 1934–Present*, Bray: Foxrock Media Limited, 2014

Stradling, Robert, *The Irish and the Spanish Civil War, 1936–39: Crusades in Conflict*, Manchester: Manchester University Press, 1999

Taylor, Andy, *Echoes from a Seashell*, Tramore: GK Print, 1990

Taylor, Matthew, *The Leaguers: The Making of Professional Football in England, 1900–1939*, Liverpool: Liverpool University Press, 2005

Taylor, Matthew, *The Association Game: A History of British Football, 1863–2000*, Harlow: Pearson, 2008

Taylor FitzSimon, E.A. and Murphy, James H. (eds), *The Irish Revival Reappraised*, Dublin: Four Courts Press, 2002

Tomlinson, Alan and Woodham, Jonathan (eds), *Image, Power and Space: Studies in Consumption and Identity*, Maidenhead: Meyer & Meyer Sport, 2007

Tosh, John, *A Man's Place*, New Haven: Yale University Press, 1999

Tranter, Neil, *Sport, Economy and Society in Britain 1750–1914*, Cambridge: Cambridge University Press, 1998

Vamplew, Wray, *Pay Up and Play the Game: Professional Sport in Britain 1875–1914*, Cambridge: Cambridge University Press, 1988

Van Esbeck, Edmund, *One Hundred Years of Irish Rugby*, Dublin: Gill & Macmillan, 1974

Walsh, Barbara, *When the Shopping Was Good: Woolworths and the Irish Main Street*, Dublin: Irish Academic Press, 2011

Walsh, Joseph J., *Waterford's Yesterdays and Tomorrows and an Outline of Waterford History*, Waterford: Munster Express, 1968

Walsh, J.J., *Recollections of a Rebel*, Tralee: The Kerryman Press, 1943

Watters, Eugene and Murtagh, Matthew, *Infinite Variety: Dan Lowrey's Music Hall, 1879–97*, Dublin: Gill & Macmillan, 1975

White, Gerry, *The Barracks*, Cork: Mercier Press, 2004

White, Gerry and O'Shea, Brendan, *A Great Sacrifice: Cork Servicemen Who Died in the Great War*, Cork: Echo Publications, 2010

West, Trevor, *The Bold Collegians: The Development of Sport in Trinity College, Dublin*, Dublin: Lilliput Press/Dublin University Central Athletic Club, 1991

West, Trevor, *Dublin University Football Club, 1854–2004: 150 Years of Trinity Rugby*, Dublin: Wordwell, 2004

THESES:

Cogan, Paula, 'The Effects of Industrialisation on the Development of a Town, Ballincollig and the Royal Gunpowder Mills: A Case History 1794–1994', unpublished MA thesis, School of History, UCC, 1995

Falvey, Jeremiah J., 'The Cork Career of Sir John Arnott 1837–1898', unpublished PhD thesis, School of History, UCC, 2007

O'Donovan, Diarmaid, 'How They Sported and Played: The Growth and Development of Two Clubs on the North-side of Cork City from Their Foundation to the Present Day', unpublished MA thesis, School of History, UCC, 2010

Pincombe, Ian, 'Out of Rexville: G.F. Lovell and the South Wales Confectionery Industry, c.1830–c.1940', unpublished PhD thesis, University College of North Wales, Bangor, 2000

Tynan, Mark, 'Association Football and Irish Society during the Interwar Period, 1918–1939', unpublished PhD thesis, NUI Maynooth, 2013

AUDIO-VISUAL AND ONLINE MATERIAL:

1901 and 1911 Census Return Forms: http://www.census.national archives.ie

British Pathé Film Archive: http://www.britishpathe.com

British Universities Film and Video Council, News on Screen: http://bufvc.ac.uk/newsonscreen

Clonmel Workman's Boat Club Archives:

http://www.cruiskeen.ie/the_Cruiskeen%2C_a_River_Suir_racing_boat/p ublications_2.html

Dáil Debates: http://debates.oireachtas.ie

Dictionary of Irish Biography: http://dib.cambridge.org

Hoban, Gerry and Walpole, Robert (dirs.), *Green is the Colour: The History of Irish Soccer* (DVD), Treasure Entertainment, 2012

Mitchell and Kenyon, *The Lost World of Mitchell and Kenyon*, BFI Publishing (DVD), 2004

Mitchell and Kenyon, *Mitchell and Kenyon Edwardian Sports*, BFI Publishing (DVD), 2004

Mitchell and Kenyon, *Mitchell and Kenyon in Ireland*, BFI Publishing (DVD), 2005

NOTES AND REFERENCES

INTRODUCTION

1 There remains considerable debate around the origins of the various football codes. Recent offerings include Harvey, Adrian, *Football: The First Hundred Years*, London and New York: Routledge, 2004. A good survey of the debate can also be found in Taylor, Matthew, *The Association Game: A History of British Football*, London and New York: Routledge, 2008. Among the most recent contributions to the debate, which continues to rage on, is Curry, Graham, 'The Origins of Football Debate: Comments on Adrian Harvey's Historiography', *The International Journal of the History of Sport*, published online 14 May 2014.

2 Dann, Jeff, 'The Representation of British Sports in Late Nineteenth and Early Twentieth Century Elite Irish School Publications', *Media History*, Vol. 17, No. 2, 2011, pp. 133–145.

3 Hassan, David and O'Kane, 'Ireland', *Routledge Companion to Sports History*, London and New York: Routledge, 2010, p. 462.

4 *Munster Express*, 23 December 1927; 27 December 1929; 24 December 1930.

5 *Munster Express*, 17 December 1926; *Munster Express*, 24 December 1930.

CHAPTER TWO

1 The key text for understanding the game in Britain remains Mason, Tony, *Association Football and English Society, 1863–1915*, Brighton: Harvester Press, 1980. It also remains a model for analysing the sport. Other important works include Russell, Dave, *Football and the English: A Social History of Association Football in England, 1863–1915*, Lancaster: Carnegie, 1997. Recent work by Matt Taylor, including *The Leaguers: The Making of Professional Football in England, 1900–1939*, Liverpool: Liverpool University Press, 1995 and his more recent work *The Association Game: A History of British Football, 1863–2000*, London and New York: Routledge, 2008 offers a good general history of the game and its various aspects from the professional to the international in Britain and Ireland.

2 Garnham, Neal, *Association Football and Society in Pre-partition Ireland*, Belfast: Ulster Historical Foundation, 2004, passim; Hunt, Tom, *Sport and Society in Victorian Ireland: The Case of Westmeath*, Cork: Cork University Press, 2006, pp. 170–190; Curran, Conor, *Sport in Donegal: A History*, Dublin: The Irish History Press, 2009, passim. See also Curran, Conor, 'The Development of Gaelic Football and Soccer Zones in Donegal, 1884–1934', *Sport in History*, Vol. 32, No. 3, 2012, pp. 426–452.

3 O'Sullivan's work, published in 2010, doesn't engage with the small secondary literature for Ireland, the absence in particular of Neal Garnham's work a glaring omission. See O'Sullivan, Donal, *Sport in Cork: A History*, Dublin: The Irish History Press, 2011, pp. 99–134.

4 Carter, Plunkett, *A Century of Cork Soccer Memories*, Cork: Evening Echo Publications, 1996; O'Mahony, Bertie, *Munster Football Association: 75 Years of Service to the Beautiful Game, 1922–1997*, Cork: Munster Football Association, 1998.

5 Byrne, Peter, *Green Is the Colour: The Story of Irish Football*, London: Andre Deutsch, 2012.

6 Cronin, Mike, *Sport and Nationalism in Ireland: Gaelic Games, Soccer and Irish Identity since 1884*, Dublin: Four Courts Press, 1999.

7 Curran, *Sport in Donegal: A History*, pp. 44–75.

8 Mastriani, Margaret, 'Down on the Docks: Histories and Memories of the Limerick Docks', in Lee, David and Jacobs, Debbie (eds), *Made in Limerick: History of Industries, Trade and Commerce, Volume One*, Limerick: Limerick Civic Trust, 2003, p. 107.

9 Mastriani, 'Down on the Docks', p. 116.

10 Johnes, Martin, *Soccer and Society: South Wales, 1900–1939*, Cardiff: University of Wales Press, 2002, p. 3.

11 Holt, Richard, *Sport and the British: A Modern History*, Oxford: Clarendon, 1989, pp. 253–254.

12 McDowell, Matthew L., 'Football, Migration and Industrial Patronage in the West of Scotland, c.1870–1900', *Sport in History*, Vol. 32, No. 3, 2012, pp. 405–425.

13 Holt, *Sport and the British*, p. 237.

14 Holt, *Sport and the British*, pp. 236–245.

15 Garnham, *Association Football*, p. 19.

16 Hunt, *Sport and Society*, pp. 180–181; Garnham, *Association Football*, p. 19.

17 Hunt, *Sport and Society*, p. 188.

18 Curran, *Sport in Donegal*

19 A game between the 14th Hussars and a local side *Sport*, 2 January 1897; Garnham, *Association Football*, p. 19.

20 Mason, Tony and Riedi, Elizabeth, *Sport and the Military: The British Armed Forces 1880–1960*, Cambridge: Cambridge University Press, 2010, pp. 20–25.

21 Taylor, Matthew, *The Association Game: A History of British Football*, London and New York: Routledge, 2008, pp. 90–98.

22 Garnham, *Association Football*, p. 96. Taylor, *The Association Game*, p. 91.

23 *Cork Examiner*, 18 December 1896.

24 Garnham, *Association Football*, p. 17.

25 *Cork Examiner*, 12 March 1901.

26 *Cork Examiner*, 19 March 1904.

27 *Cork Examiner*, 28 March 1904.

28 UCD Archives (hereafter UCDA): P239/21, *Leinster Football Association Senior Committee Minute Books*, 4 November 1901; 8 January 1901.

29 UCDA: P239/22, *Leinster Football Association Senior Committee Minute Books*, 7 January 1903; 24 February 1904.

30 *Cork Examiner*, 24 February 1904.

31 UCDA: P239/42 *Leinster Football Association Finance Committee Minute Books*, 4 May 1903.

32 Public Record Office of Northern Ireland (hereafter PRONI): D4196/A/1, *IFA Committee Minute Books*, 8 October 1901.

33 PRONI: D41196/A/2, *IFA Committee Minute Books*, 27 September 1904.

34 *Sunday Independent*, 21 October 1906.

35 PRONI: D41196/A/2, *IFA Committee Minute Books*, 28 March 1907.

36 PRONI: D41196/A/2, *IFA Committee Minute Books*, 2 June 1908.

37 PRONI: D41196/A/2, *IFA Committee Minute Books*, 9 May 1908.

38 PRONI: D4196/A/3, *IFA Committee Minute Books*, 10 January 1911; 7 March 1911.

39 PRONI: D4196/A/3, *IFA Committee Minute Books*, 9 January 1912.

40 PRONI: D4196/R/1, *IFA Finance Committee Minute Books*, 15 April 1913; PRONI: D4196/A/3, *IFA Committee Minute Books*, 22 April 1913.

41 PRONI: D4196/A/3, *IFA Committee Minute Books*, 2 September 1913.

42 PRONI: D4196/R/1, *IFA Finance Committee Minute Books*, 14 October 1913.

43 PRONI: D4196/R/1, *IFA Finance Committee Minute Books*, 9 December 1913.

44 PRONI: D4196/A/2, *IFA Committee Minute Books*, 12 May 1906.

45 UCCA: UC/Council/25/75, *List of Officers for UCC Association Football Club*; *Irish Independent*, 5 February 1914; As John A. Murphy has wryly noted too, for a long time after a club was finally founded in UCC, they were shy of success, a fact encapsulated best in the name of a booklet published on their history, *At Least We Won the Toss*; see Murphy, *Where Finbarr Played*, p. 104; the handful of match reports and round-ups can be found in *QCC*, Vol. II, No. 1; Vol. II, No. 2, and Vol. II, No. 3.

46 *Cork Sportsman*, 24 April 1909; 1 May 1909; 8 May 1909.

47 *Cork Sportsman*, 22 May 1909.

48 *Cork Sportsman*, 30 April 1910; 28 May 1910.

49 *Cork Sportsman*, 29 October 1910.

50 *Cork Sportsman*, 18 September 1909.

51 *Cork Examiner*, 28 January 1911.

52 PRONI: D4196/A/3, *IFA Committee Minute Books*, 3 May 1910.

53 *Cork Sportsman*, 7 January 1911.

54 Ibid., 7 January 1911.

55 *Cork Sportsman*, 24 December 1910.

56 *Cork Examiner*, 24 April 1912.

57 *Cork Sportsman*, 12 March 1910; 19 March 1910.

58 *Cork Sportsman*, 17 October 1908; 22 May 1909; 17 December 1910.

59 PRONI: D/4196/A/1, *IFA Senior Council Minute Books*, 5 November 1901.

60 PRONI: D/4196/A/1, *IFA Senior Council Minute Books*, 11 May 1907.

61 Byrne, Peter, *Green is the Colour: The Story of Irish Football*, London: Andre Deutsch, 2012, p. 34.

62 *Cork Sportsman*, 5 June 1909.

63 *Cork Sportsman*, 2 January 1909.

64 *Waterford News*, 8 January 1898.

65 *Waterford News*, 12 March 1898.

66 *Waterford News*, 5 March 1899.

67 *Waterford News*, 12 December 1902; 10 November 1905; 25 September 1908; 16 April 1909.

68 *Cork Sportsman*, 23 January 1909; 13 March 1909.

69 *Cork Sportsman*, 27 March 1909.

70 *Cork Sportsman*, 22 May 1909.

71 PRONI: D4196/A/3, *IFA Senior Council Minute Books*, 2 February 1909.

72 A shoneen is an Irish person who affects English mannerisms and customs, rejecting traditional Irish manners, customs and culture; *Football Sports Weekly*, (*FSW*), 25 February 1928.

73 Taylor, Andy, *Echoes from a Seashell*, Waterford: GK Print, 1990, p. 146.

74 *Cork Sportsman*, 28 May 1910.

75 Buckley, Paul, *Cameos of a Century*, Cahir: Cahir Park FC, 2010, p. 9.

76 Buckley, Paul, *Cameos of a Century*, Cahir: Cahir Park FC, 2010, pp. 4–28.

77 Military Archives, Dublin, A/0745 *South Tipperary Brigade No. 3 Brigade Report*, November 1921; Other institutions listed as enemies in the same document included the golf clubs of Tipperary, Clonmel, and Cahir; interestingly, one of the players for Cahir Park, James McNamara, as well as playing for Cahir Park before the First World War was also a senior All-Ireland medal winner with Tipperary in 1920, playing in the famous 'Bloody Sunday' match in Croke Park; see Buckley, *Cameos of a Century*, p. 9.

78 Buckley, *Cameos of a Century*, p. 9.

79 McElligott, Richard, *Forging a Kingdom: The GAA in Kerry, 1884–1934*, Cork: The Collins Press, 2013, pp. 100–101.

80 *Limerick Leader*, 1 May 1918.

81 *Cork Sportsman*, 14 November 1908.

82 *Limerick Leader*, 16 December 1908.

83 *Cork Sportsman*, 2 January 1909.

84 *Limerick Leader*, 30 October 1908; 11 November 1908; 15 February 1909.

85 *Cork Sportsman*, 15 January 1910.

86 *Cork Sportsman*, 21 March 1911.

87 *Limerick Leader*, 4 September 1912; 7 October 1912.

88 Ibid., 4 September 1912.

89 *Cork Constitution*, 22 February 1913.

90 Garnham, *Association Football*, pp. 67–77.

91 White, Gerry and O'Shea, Brendan, *A Great Sacrifice: Cork Servicemen Who Died in the Great War*, Cork: Echo Publications, 2010, p. 36.

92 Dooley, Thomas P., *Irishmen or English Soldiers?* Liverpool: Liverpool University Press, 1994.

93 *Southern Star*, 20 March 1915; 13 January 1917.

94 *Freeman's Journal*, 11 January 1918.

CHAPTER THREE

1 To get some grasp of these events at a local level, the interested reader could do worse than seek out the following: O'Connor, Emmet, *A Labour History of Waterford*, Waterford: Waterford Trades Council, 1989; Borgonovo, John, *The Battle for Cork*, Cork: Mercier Press, 2012; Borgonovo, John, *The Dynamics of War and Revolution: Cork, 1916–1918*, Cork: Cork University Press, 2013.

2 *Cork Constitution*, 11 April 1877; *Munster Express*, 28 September 1877; *Munster Express*, 20 September 1878; *Nenagh Guardian*, 23 October 1880.

3 Rockett, Kevin and Rockett, Emer, *Magic Lantern, Panorama and Moving Picture Shows in Ireland, 1786–1909*, Dublin: Four Courts Press, 2011, p. 205. The authors also note this same circuit provided a round of theatres for early film exhibitors.

4 *Munster Express*, 15 September 1877; 21 September 1877. In Cork forty years later, the relationship between local women and American sailors would cause

similar consternation: Borgonovo, John, 'Exercising a Close Vigilance over Their Daughters': Cork Women, American Sailors, and Catholic Vigilantes 1917–1918', *Irish Historical Studies*, Vol. 38, No. 149, May 2012, pp. 89–107.

5 *Munster Express*, 2 June 1877; this linking of sport and temperance was common, though not, as we shall see below, a necessarily straight-forward relationship.

6 Rockett and Rockett, *Magic Lantern, Panorama and Moving Picture Shows*, p. 205.

7 *Munster Express*, 21 July 1877; *Cork Constitution*, 10 January 1878. Here we are still a long way though from the star or superstar of English football treated by Joyce Woolridge, 'Mapping the Stars: Stardom in English Professional Football 1890–1946', *Soccer & Society*, Vol. 3, No. 2 (2002), pp. 51–69.

8 Murphy, John A., 'Quill, Timothy (Thady)', *Dictionary of Irish Biography*, *http://dib.cambridge.org/* accessed online 25/5/2013; generally there are quite a lot of sports-related ballads from the late nineteenth century and early twentieth century. See for instance Power, Dermot, *Ballads and Songs of Waterford: From 1487 with Musical Notation*, Waterford: 1992 or in Cork see Ó Canainn, Tomás, *Songs of Cork*, Dublin: Dalton, 1978 and Healy, James N. and O'Donovan, Con, *Comic Songs of Cork and Kerry*, Cork: Mercier Press, 1978.

9 Rockett and Rockett, *Magic Lantern, Panorama and Moving Picture Shows*, pp. 169–216. Of course, the music halls and similar venues frequented by working-class people often used the forms to poke fun at their social superiors; see for instance Selenick, Laurence, 'Politics as Entertainment: Victorian Music Hall Songs', *Victorian Studies*, Vol. 19, No. 2, December 1975, pp. 149–180. See also Bratton, J.S. (ed.), *Music Hall: Performance & Style*, Milton Keynes: Open University Press, 1986 and Bailey, Peter (ed.), *Music Hall: The Business of Pleasure*, Milton Keynes: Open University Press, 1986. Little is written on music halls in Ireland except for Watters, Eugene and Murtagh, Matthew, *Infinite Variety: Dan Lowrey's Music Hall, 1879–97*, Dublin: Gill & Macmillan, 1975 and McDowell, Jim, *Beyond the Footlights: A History of Belfast Music Halls and Early Theatre*, Dublin: The History Press Ireland, 2007; on the suppression of Ireland's most famous fair, Donnybrook, see Ó Maitiú, Séamus, *The Humours of Donnybrook: Dublin's Famous Fair and Its Suppression*, Dublin: Irish Academic Press, 1995.

10 *Munster Express*, 29 September 1877.

11 *Nenagh Guardian*, 16 January 1869.

12 *Nenagh Guardian*, 16 September 1871.

13 *Nenagh Guardian*, 10 June 1876.

14 *Nenagh Guardian*, 28 January 1865; 10 February 1877.

15 Hunt, *Sport and Society*, p. 254.

16 Vamplew, Wray, 'The Economics of a Sports Industry: Scottish Gate-money Football, 1890–1914', *Economic History Review*, Vol. 35, No. 4, November 1982, pp. 549–567.

17 Tranter, *Sport, Economy and Society*, p. 74.

18 Tranter, *Sport, Economy and Society*, p. 77.

19 Thomas, W.A., *The Stock Exchanges of Ireland*, Liverpool: Francis Cairns 1986, pp. 153–157. A similar crash occurred in the skating rink business just before the First World War.

20 British Parliamentary Papers (BPP) LXXX.39 1897 Annual Joint Stock Listings; BPP LXXXVII.895 1904 Annual Joint Stock Listings. Other such companies

include Fermoy Race Co. Ltd. and Fermoy Athletic Ground Co., Waterford Gaelic Sportsfield Co. Ltd. which was capitalised for £1,000, and New Cork Park Race Course Ltd., capitalised for some £5,000.

21 Bielenberg, Andy and O'Mahony, Patrick, 'An Expenditure Esitmate of Irish National Income in 1907', *The Economic and Social Review*, Vol. 29, No. 2, April 1998, pp. 107–132; Kiernan, T.J., 'The National Expenditure of the Free State in 1926', *Journal of Social and Statistical Inquiry Society of Ireland (JSSISI)*, Vol. XV, No. 3, 1932/1933, pp. 91–103.

22 Census Enumerator Return Forms *http://census.nationalarchives.ie*, accessed 4/3/2013.

23 UCC Archives (UCCA): *UCC Finance Committee Minute Books*, 1926, Cheque no. 6523.

24 Cork City and County Archive (CCCA): SP/CC/1/1 *Cork Constitution Minute Books.*

25 *Cork Sportsman*, 21 November 1908.

26 Ibid.

27 *Limerick Leader*, 21 December 1914.

28 *Football Sports Weekly* (*FSW*), 24 April 1926.

29 Collins, Tony and Vamplew, Wray, *Mud, Sweat and Beers: A Cultural History of Sport and Alcohol*, Oxford: Berg, 2002, p. 11; See also Dixon, Paula and Garnham Neal, 'Drink and the Professional Footballer in 1890s England and Ireland', *Sport in History*, Vol. 25, No. 3, 2005, pp. 375–389; Malcolm, Elizabeth, 'The Rise of the Pub: A Study in the Disciplining of Popular Culture', in Donnelly, J.S. and Miller, Kerby A. (eds), *Irish Popular Culture, 1650–1850*, Dublin: Irish Academic Press, 1999, pp. 50–78.

30 *Cork Sportsman*, 17 September 1910; See Ferriter, Diarmaid, *A Nation of Extremes: The Pioneers in Twentieth Century Ireland*, Dublin: Irish Academic Press, 1999, p. 47.

31 McGrath, John, 'An Urban Community: St Mary's Parish, Limerick and the social role of Sporting and Musical Clubs, 1885–1905', in Kelly, Jennifer and Comerford R.V. (eds), *Associational Culture in Ireland and Abroad*, Dublin: Irish Academic Press, 2010, p. 129.

32 It is evident from the history of this band that their involvement in providing entertainment at sport was extensive, from Gaelic games, athletics events, to water polo. See Cooke, Richard T., *Cork's Barrack Street Band: Ireland's Oldest Amateur Musical Institution*, Cork: Seamus Curtin, 1992.

33 Lane, Fintan, 'Music and Violence in Working-Class Cork: "The Band Nuisance" 1879–1882,' *Saothar*, No. 24, 1999, pp. 17–33.

34 *Munster Express*, 14 September 1928.

35 *Munster Express*, 12 July 1890.

36 *Munster Express*, 28 July 1894.

37 *Munster Express*, 14 July 1895.

38 *Sport*, 20 July 1895, reprinted in *Munster Express*, 27 July 1895.

39 *Munster Express*, 26 August 1927.

40 *Nenagh Guardian*, 27 March 1880.

41 *Nenagh Guardian*, 21 August 1880.

42 *Nenagh Guardian*, 23 April 1910.

43 CCCA: SP/CC/1/1 *Cork Constitution Minute Books.*

44 Hunt, *Sport and Society*, pp. 204–205.

45 Hunt, *Sport and Society*, p. 235.

46 Much remains to be written about the development of band culture in Ireland from the middle of the nineteenth century on. A cursory glance at local newspapers reveals that as well as the brass and reed bands, fife and drum as well as pipers' bands were part of this movement, and that it was intimately tied up with the temperance as well as sporting movement of the same period. For instance, *Munster Express*, 2 December 1911: 'On Sunday evening last, the Carrick-on-Suir Workingmen's Temperance Club fife and drum band, accompanied by a very large crowd walking in processional order marched through the streets in celebration of the anniversary of the [Manchester Martyrs].'

47 *Southern Star*, 19 February 1898.

48 *Nenagh Guardian*, 7 April 1917.

49 It's worth noting that the football schedule was bigger than the hurling, in keeping with the relative strength of football over hurling in the Waterford and south-east area at that time.

50 *Munster Express*, 6 July 1895; similarly when funds were being raised for the National Monument in Cork, a hurling and football tournament was arranged for that May in Turner's Cross: *Southern Star*, 5 April 1902.

51 *Cork Sportsman*, 24 October 1908.

52 Jerram, Leif, *Streetlife: The Untold History of Europe's Twentieth Century*, Oxford: Oxford University Press, 2011, p. 1.

53 Bale, John, *Landscapes of Modern Sport*, London: Leicester University Press, 1994, pp. 10–13 and pp. 120–147; Inglis, Simon, *Football Grounds of Britain 3rd Edition*, London: Harper Collins, 1996. See also Cronin, Mike, 'Enshrined in Blood: The Naming of Gaelic Athletic Association Grounds and Clubs', *The Sports Historian*, Vol. 18, No. 1, May 1998, pp. 90–104.

54 The latter of these was especially popular for early motor racing in Waterford. Where horse racing had begun in the previous century, in the early twentieth century, Tramore strand was being used to race motor cycles just before the First World War: *Munster Express*, 26 July 1913. The practice was revived again in 1929, with the meeting in the summer of 1930 on one weekend attracting over 20,000 to the seaside town according to the *Munster Express*, 20 June 1930.

55 Leeworthy, Daryl, *Fields of Play: The Sporting Heritage of Wales*, Aberystwyth: Royal Commission on Ancient and Historical Monuments, 2012, p. 1.

56 Cronin, Mike and Higgins, Roisín, *Places We Play: Ireland's Sporting Heritage*, Cork: The Collins Press, 2012, p. 15.

57 Jerram, *Streetlife*, p. 192.

58 Leeworthy, *Fields of Play*, p. 1.

59 See UCCA: UC/ATH/MB/1, *Cork Athletic Grounds Committee Minute Books*, 16 July 1927 and 28 February 1928. Mr Donal O'Sullivan paid rent of £7.10.0 to set up two stalls at the grounds.

60 CCCA: U341/1, *Cork CYMS Minute Books* of 29 March 1886 and 16 May 1888 give two examples of the many fights in the billiard rooms of the Cork CYMS.

61 Hinds, Ross (ed.), *Stanford: Memoirs of William Bedell Stanford, Regius Professor of Greek 1940–80, Trinity College Dublin*, Dublin: Hinds, 2001, p. 42.

62 Rockett, Kevin and Rockett, Emer, *Film Exhibition and Distribution in Ireland, 1909–2010*, Dublin: Four Courts Press, 2011, p. 22.

63 O'Sullivan, *Sport in Cork: A History*, p. 102; see *Freeman's Journal*, 30 May 1898, 15 January 1901, 6 April 1901; *Irish Independent*, 26 September 1906, 5 September 1923, 17 September 1923. Despite the extensive use the grounds

were put to, a notice of closing the grounds from Nemo Rangers appeared in the *Irish Independent*, 20 June 1929.

64 Collins, Tony, *Sport in Capitalist Society: A Short History*, London: Routledge, 2013, p. 56.

65 Tranter, *Sport, Economy and Society*, p. 76.

66 Rouse, Paul, 'Sport and the Irish in 1881', in Bairner, Alan (ed.), *Sport and the Irish*, Dublin: UCD Press, 2005, p. 9.

67 Rouse, 'Sport and the Irish in 1881', pp. 9–10.

68 Ibid.

69 Corry, Eoghan,'The Mass Media and the Popularisation of Gaelic Games, 1884–1934', in Hassan, David, McAnallen, Donal and Hegarty, Roddy (eds), *The Evolution of the GAA: Ulaidh, Éire agus Eile*, Belfast: Stair Ulaidh, 2009, pp. 100–112.

70 *Report of the Advisory Committee on the Greyhound Industry 1952*, p. 44.

71 *Cork Sportsman*, 20 May 1911.

72 *Cork Sportsman*, 30 May 1908.

73 *Cork Sportsman*, 6 June 1908.

74 *Cork Sportsman*, 14 May 1909.

75 *Cork Sportsman*, 22 May 1909.

76 *Cork Sportsman*, 20 May 1911.

77 *Cork Sportsman*, 30 May 1908.

78 *Guy's Cork Directory* 1912, Cork: Francis Guy & Co. Ltd., 1912.

79 Legg, Marie-Louise, *Newspapers and Nationalism: The Irish Provincial Press, 1850–1892*, Dublin: Four Courts Press, 1999.

80 Vamplew, Wray, *Pay Up and Play the Game: Professional Sport in Britain 1875–1914*, Cambridge: Cambridge University Press, 1988, p. 282.

81 McCabe, Conor, '*Football Sports Weekly* and Irish Soccer 1925–28', *Media History*, Vol. 17, No. 2, May 2011.

82 Walsh, Barbara, *When the Shopping Was Good: Woolworths and the Irish Main Street*, Dublin: Irish Academic Press, 2011, p. 70.

83 Walsh, Barbara, *When the Shopping Was Good*, Appendix I, Tables 1–3, pp. 247–248.

84 Rockett and Rockett, *Film Exhibition and Distribution*, Appendix, Table 1, pp. 456–457; See *Companies Annual Reports*, Dublin: Stationery Office, 1929–32.

85 For a history of the newsreel in Ireland see Chambers, Ciara, *Ireland in the Newsreels*, Dublin: Irish Academic Press, 2012.

86 See Mitchell and Kenyon, *Mitchell and Kenyon in Ireland*, BFI Publishing (DVD), 2005; Mitchell and Kenyon, *The Lost World of Mitchell and Kenyon*, BFI Publishing (DVD), 2004; Mitchell and Kenyon, *Mitchell and Kenyon Edwardian Sports*, BFI Publishing (DVD), 2004.

87 Little enough of sporting items on newsreels is extant, although a full idea of the amount filmed can be gleaned from the British Universities Film and Video Council's News on Screen searchable online archive (http://bufvc.ac.uk/newsonscreen); As well as Pathé, Gaumont Graphic, Movietone, British Paramount News and Topical Budget who all filmed in Ireland, and between 1910–30 and further, sport was an ever present part of their productions. See Chambers, *Ireland in the Newsreels*, Filmography, for a comprehensive list of Ireland-related newsreels, pp. 256–301.

88 Chambers, *Ireland in the Newsreels*, p. 48; She writes that 'garrulous cinema audiences were often heard shouting out the names of friends or family as they appeared on screen'.

89 British Pathé: Canister: G825 Film ID: 248.06 http://www.british
    pathe.com/search/query/Bective/playlist/2; British Pathé: Canister: G807
    Film ID: 242.32 http://www.britishpathe.com/video/city-of-waterford-races;
    British Pathé: Canister: G1245 Film ID: 434.17 http://beta.
    britishpathe.com/video/football-5/query/01325300; British Pathé: Canister:
    G1455 Film ID: 708.10http://www.britishpathe.com/video/rugby-inter-
    provincial; British Pathé: Canister: G1170 Film ID: 380.05 http://
    www.britishpathe.com/video/irish-coursing, all accessed 30/4/2013.

90 Rouse, Paul, '*Sport* and the Irish in 1881', in Bairner, Alan (ed.), *Sport and the
    Irish: Histories, Identities, Issues*, Dublin: UCD Press, 2005.

91 Duncan, Mark, 'The Early Photography of the GAA, 1884–1914', in Cronin,
    Mike, Murphy, Will and Rouse, Paul (eds), *The Gaelic Athletic Association
    1884–2009*, Dublin: Irish Academic Press, 2009, p. 109.

92 CCCA: SP/CC/3/1 *Cork Constitution Minute Books*, 22 March 1922.

93 Huggins, Mike, 'Projecting the Visual: British Newsreels, Soccer and Popular
    Culture, 1918–1939', *The International Journal of the History of Sport*, Vol.
    24, No. 1, 2007, 80–102.

94 Beere, T.J., 'Cinema Statistics in Saorstát Éireann', *JSSISI*, Vol. XV, No. 6,
    1935/1936, pp. 83–110. A comprehensive history of Irish cinema, Kevin and
    Emer Rockett's *Film Exhibition and Distribution in Ireland, 1909–2010*, p. 65
    notes of cinema audiences in the 1920s that they were made up predominantly
    of 'the working and lower middle classes', precisely the same people for whom
    sport was such an integral part of their lives, especially where leisure time was
    concerned.

95 *Census of Population Report 1926, Vol. II: Occupations*, Dublin: Stationery
    Office, 1928.

96 Eason, J.C.M., 'An Analysis Showing the Objects of Expenditure and the
    Sources of Revenue during the Financial Years 1924–25 to 1929–30', *JSSISI*,
    Vol. XV, No. 1, 1930/1931, pp. 1–13.

97 O'Brien, Eoghan 'The Growth of Electricity Supply and its Relations to
    Civilisation', *JSSISI*, Vol. XV, No. 3, 1932/1933, pp. 69–90.

98 Brown, *Ireland: A Social and Cultural History*, p. 141.

99 Gorham, Maurice, *Forty Years of Broadcasting*, Dublin 1967 pp. 17–54,
    quoted in Ferriter, *The Transformation of Ireland*, p. 396.

100 *FSW*, 19 February 1928.

101 *The Irish Times*, 26 February 1927. A match against Wales was broadcast a little
    later, *Irish Independent*, 11 March 1929.

102 Ferriter, Diarmaid, *The Transformation of Ireland: 1900–2000*, London: Profile
    Books, 2005, p. 429.

103 Daly, Mary E. '"Turn on the Tap": The State, Irish Women and Running
    Water', in O'Dowd, Mary and Valiulis, Maryann (eds), *Women & Irish History*,
    Dublin: Wolfhound Press, 1997, p. 208; See also Shiel, Michael J., *The Quiet
    Revolution: The Electrification of Rural Ireland*, Dublin: O'Brien Press, 1984.

104 Pine, Richard, *2RN and the Origins of Irish Radio*, Dublin: Four Courts Press,
    2002, p. 172.

105 The 1907 figure comes from Bielenberg and O'Mahony, 'An Expenditure
    Estimate of Irish National Income in 1907', *The Economic and Social Review*,
    Vol. 29, No. 2, April 1998, pp. 107–132; Kiernan, T.J., 'The National Expen-
    diture of the Free State in 1926', *JSSISI*, Vol. XV, No. 3, 1932/1933, pp.
    91–103.

241

106 Coleman, Marie, *The Irish Sweep: A History of the Irish Hospitals Sweepstake 1930–1987*, Dublin: UCD Press, 2009, p. 13.

107 *Companies Annual Reports 1928*, Dublin: Stationery Office, 1929; *Companies Annual Reports 1930*, Dublin: Stationery Office, 1931.

108 *Census of Population 1926 Report, Vol. II: Occupations*, pp. 86–87 and *Census of Population 1936 Report, Vol. II: Occupations*, pp. 88–89.

109 Tranter, *Sport, Economy and Society*, p. 53.

110 *Irish Field and Gentleman's Gazette*, 24 April 1926.

111 Ibid.

112 Ibid.

113 Ibid.

114 *Irish Field*, 1 May 1926.

115 Ibid.

116 Ibid.

117 *Football Sports Weekly* (*FSW*), 15 May 1926.

118 *FSW*, 12 June 1926.

119 *Evening Echo*, 5 June 1926.

120 IFS 1926/38 Betting Act, 1926 16.1.

121 NLI: OPIE/PP/29/5 *Oireachtas Report into Betting Act, 1926*, Dublin: Stationery Office 1929.

122 NLI: OPIE/PP/29/5 *Oireachtas Report into Betting Act, 1926*, p. ix.

123 Ibid.

124 Ibid.

125 NLI: OPIE/PP/29/5 *Oireachtas Report into Betting Act, 1926*, pp. 3–4.

126 For all of these figures see *Census of Population, 1936 Report, Vol. II: Occupations*, Dublin: Stationery Office 1940, pp. 88–89.

127 NLI: OPIE/PP/29/5 *Oireachtas Report into Betting Act, 1926*, p. 3.

128 NLI: OPIE/PP/29/5 *Oireachtas Report into Betting Act, 1926*, pp. 98–104.

129 NLI: OPIE/PP/29/5 *Oireachtas Report into Betting Act, 1926*, pp. 104–109.

130 Coleman, *The Irish Sweep*, p. 17; Coleman also notes it would take until 1960 before financial necessity overrode moral qualms for the Adelaide to take part in the Sweepstakes.

131 NLI: OPIE/PP/29/5 *Oireachtas Report into Betting Act, 1926*, p. 90.

132 This is similar to the taxation on spirits in Ireland, especially whiskey. See Humphries, M., 'An Issue of Confidence: The Decline of the Irish Whiskey Trade in Independent Ireland, 1922–1992', *Journal of European Economic History*, 23, 1994, pp. 93–103.

133 Vol. 16, Cols. 1559–1560, 22/06/1926, Dáil Debates online: www.debates.oireachtas.ie, accessed 25/9/2012.

134 Holt, Richard, *Sport and the British: A Modern History*, Oxford: Clarendon Press 1989, p. 182.

135 NLI: OPIE/PP/29/5 *Oireachtas Report into Betting Act, 1926*.

136 The Entertainment tax, first introduced by the British, was openly defied by the GAA. The tax was repealed and then reintroduced by the first Free State government. It was a tax levy on the sale of tickets to sporting and other entertainment events.

137 For early attempts to establish a track in Cork see UCCA: UC/ATH/MB/1, *UCC Athletics Ground Committee Minute Book*, 18 October 1927. For a general, popular history of greyhound racing in Ireland see Martin, John, *Tales of the Dogs: A Celebration of the Irish and their Greyhounds*, Belfast: Blackstaff Press 2009.

138 Huggins, Mike, 'Betting, Sport and the British, 1918–1939', *Journal of Social History*, Winter 2007, p. 301.

139 *FSW*, 26 June 1926.

140 *Finance Accounts of Saorstát Éireann*, Dublin: Stationery Office, 1927–1932 inclusive.

141 Eason, J.C.M., 'Sources of Revenue 1924–25 to 1929–30', *JSSISI*, 1931, p. 12.

142 *The Irish Times*, 20 April 1927.

143 *The Irish Times*, 16 May 1927.

144 UCCA, UC/ATH/MB/1: *UCC Athletics Ground Committee Minute Book*, 8 October 1927.

145 *The Irish Times*, 28 November 1927.

146 Huggins, 'Betting, Sport and the British', pp. 283–306.

147 *Limerick Leader*, 3 February 1934.

148 Ayto, John and Simpson, John, *Oxford Dictionary of Modern Slang*, Oxford: Oxford University Press, 2008.

149 See *Clonmel Workman's Boat Club Minutes*, 23 October 1910, 26 October 1910.

150 *Clonmel Workman's Boat Club Expenses Book 1927/1928*.

151 Erskine Childers (1870–1922) was a London-born British civil servant and Sinn Féin propagandist.

152 *Munster Express*, 24 May 1929; 22 April 1927; 21 June 1929; 25 February 1927; 29 March 1929.

153 *Nenagh Guardian*, 26 January 1929; 9 March 1929; 31 August 1929; 25 January 1930.

154 *Southern Star*, 28 December 1928; 1 March 1930; 19 July 1930; 30 August 1930; 4 October 1930; 27 December 1930.

155 Leeworthy, Daryl, 'The Forgotten Hurlers of South Wales: Sport, Society and the Irish, 1910–1925', *Llafur: Journal of Welsh People's History*, Vol. 11, No. 2, 2012, pp. 33–48.

156 *Limerick Leader*, 8 January 1927.

157 See Tosh, John, *A Man's Place*, New Haven: Yale University Press, 1999.

158 *Cork Examiner*, 30 November 1931; 4 February 1936.

159 For all of these see: *Munster Express*, 20 December 1924; 8 January 1926; 10 February 1928; 5 February 1926; 11 May 1928; 29 April 1927; 26 November 1926; 17 September 1926; 27 December 1924; 22 March 1929.

160 Walsh, *When the Shopping Was Good*, p. 78.

161 *Dáil Debates*, 1 July 1932, Vol. 43, Col. 2040.

162 *Dáil Debates*, 1 July 1932, Vol. 43, Cols. 2047–2048.

163 *Dáil Debates*, 1 July 1932, Vol. 43, Col. 2049.

164 Ibid.

165 Valerie A. Austin, 'The Céilí and the Public Dance Halls Act, 1935', *Éire-Ireland*, Vol. 28, No. 3, Fall, 1993. See also Gearoid Ó hAllmhurain, 'Rural Communities in Clare and the Dance Halls Act of 1935', *New Hibernia Review*, Vol. 9, No. 4, Winter 2005, pp. 9–18.

166 Jones, Stephen G., *Workers At Play: A Social and Economic History of Leisure 1918–1939*, London: Routledge Keegan Paul, 1986, p. 6.

167 Jones, *Workers At Play*, p. 9.

CHAPTER FOUR

1 Hobsbawm, Eric, *Nations and Nationalism since 1780: Programme, Myth, Reality*, Cambridge: Cambridge University Press, 1991. The literature on

243

nationalism is extraordinarily vast, but you will still be well served by Hutchinson, John and Smith, Anthony D. (eds), *Nationalism*, Oxford: Oxford University Press, 1994 for a general primer on the topic.

2 Irish nationalism can prove tricky terrain to traverse, although some key writing and perspectives on the development of the historiography surrounding it can be gained by reading Cronin, Sean, *Irish Nationalism: A History of its Roots and Ideology*, Dublin: The Academy Press, 1980; Garvin, Tom, *The Evolution of Irish Nationalist Politics*, Dublin: Gill & Macmillan, 1981; Boyce, D. George, *Nationalism in Ireland*, Dublin: Gill & Macmillan, 1982; Hachey, Thomas E. and McCaffrey, Lawrence J., *Perspectives on Irish Nationalism*, Lexington: University Press of Kentucky, 1989. More recent work includes Kearney, Hugh F., *Ireland: Contested Ideas of Nationalism and History*, Cork: Cork University Press, 2007.

3 Again here see Hutchinson, John, *The Dynamics of Cultural Nationalism: The Gaelic Revival and the Creation of the Irish Nation State*, London: Allen & Unwin, 1987; with regard to sport and nationalism the standout work on the topic in an Irish context remains Cronin, *Sport and Nationalism in Ireland*. On the cultural revival and high culture in Ireland see for instance Levitas, Ben, *The Theatre of Nation: Irish Drama and Cultural Nationalism, 1890–1916*, Oxford: Oxford University Press, 2002; Taylor FitzSimon, E.A., and Murphy, James H. (eds), *The Irish Revival Reappraised*, Dublin: Four Courts Press, 2002; Mathews, P.J., *Revival: The Abbey Theatre, Sinn Féin, the Gaelic League and the Co-operative Movement*, Cork: Cork University Press/Field Day, 2003; McMahon, Timothy G., *Grand Opportunity: The Gaelic Revival and Irish Society, 1893–1910*, Syracuse: Syracuse University Press, 2008.

4 Hutchinson, *The Dynamics of Cultural Nationalism*, pp. 310–312.

5 Hyde, Douglas, 'The Necessity for de-Anglicizing Ireland', *The Revival of Irish Literature*, New York: Lemma, 1973, pp. 156–157.

6 Comerford, R.V., *Inventing the Nation: Ireland*, London: Hodder Arnold, 2003, p. 220.

7 Sugden and Bairner, *Sport, Sectarianism and Society in a Divided Ireland*.

8 Cronin, *Sport and Nationalism in Ireland*, p. 124.

9 Hanley, Brian, 'Irish Republican Attitudes to Sport since 1921', in McAnallen, Hassan and Hegarty (eds), *The Evolution of the GAA*, p. 175.

10 Hobsbawm, *Nations and Nationalism*, p. 143.

11 Cronin, Mike, 'Projecting the Nation through Sport and Culture: Ireland, Aonach Tailteann and the Irish Free State, 1924–32', *Journal of Contemporary History*, Vol. 38, 2003, pp. 395–411.

12 Ryan, Louise, 'Aonach Tailteann, the Irish Press and Gendered Symbols of National Identity in the 1920s and 1930s', in Bairner (ed.), *Sport and the Irish*, pp. 69–84.

13 CCCA: U355/4, *J.J. Walsh Personal Papers*, Correspondence with P.D. Mehigan.

14 Brown, Terence, *Ireland: A Social and Cultural History 1922–2002*, London: Harper Perennial, 2004, p. 123.

15 Ibid.

16 Rouse, Paul, 'The Politics of Culture and Sport in Ireland: A History of the GAA Ban on Foreign Games 1884–1971, Part One: 1884–1921', *The International Journal of the History of Sport*, Vol. 10, No. 3, December 1993, pp. 333–360.

17 McElligott, Richard, '1916 and the Radicalization of the GAA', *Éire-Ireland*, Vol. 48, Nos 1 & 2, Spring/Summer 2013, pp. 95–111.

18 See also O'Callaghan, *Rugby in Munster*, pp. 142–169.

19 McAnallen, *The Cups That Cheered*, p. 266; hence the change of heart that occurred in later years for players like Moss Keane, from Gaelic footballers, to rugby international.

20 GAA Archives: MUN/001, *Munster Council Minute Book*, 1928 Annual Convention Report.

21 *Nenagh Guardian*, 27 July 1918.

22 *Nenagh Guardian*, 31 May 1919.

23 *Nenagh Guardian*, 3 March 1923.

24 *Nenagh Guardian*, 16 February 1924.

25 Ibid.

26 *Sport*, 15 March 1924.

27 *Sport*, 26 April 1924.

28 *Southern Star*, 13 August 1910.

29 *Southern Star*, 4 October 1913.

30 *Nenagh Guardian*, 26 April 1924.

31 Ibid.

32 *Limerick Leader*, 14 March 1924.

33 *Munster Express*, 26 February 1926.

34 *Nenagh Guardian*, 13 February 1926.

35 *Southern Star*, 7 April 1923.

36 *Southern Star*, 21 February 1925, reprint from *Gaelic Athlete* undated.

37 *Gaelic Athlete*, 21 March 1925.

38 *Gaelic Athlete*, 11 April 1925.

39 *Nenagh Guardian*, 21 August 1926.

40 *Evening Echo*, 4 June 1926.

41 *Munster Express*, 8 March 1929.

42 *Munster Express*, 15 March 1929.

43 *Nenagh Guardian*, 14 January 1928.

44 *Nenagh Guardian*, 8 September 1928.

45 *Nenagh Guardian*, 14 July 1928.

46 *Nenagh Guardian*, 5 October 1929.

47 *Munster Express*, 8 February 1929.

48 *Nenagh Guardian*, 16 November 1929.

49 *Nenagh Guardian*, 16 November 1929.

50 Dáil Debates, Volume 35, 5 June 1930, Finance Bill, 1930-Committee Stage. Accessed online at www.oireachtas-debates.gov.ie 11/7/2011.

51 Ibid.

52 Ibid.

53 Ibid.

54 *Nenagh Guardian*, 17 March 1928.

55 Dáil Debates, Volume 35, 5 June 1930, Finance Bill, 1930-Committee Stage. Accessed online at www.oireachtas-debates.gov.ie 11/7/2011.

56 Ryan, 'Aonach Tailteann, the Irish press and gendered symbols of national identity in the 1920s and 1930s', in Bairner (ed.), *Sport and the Irish*, pp. 79–80.

57 *An Phoblacht*, 19 June 1925.

58 Brennan, Cathal, 'The Tailteann Games 1924–1936', *The Irish Story* http://www.theirishstory.com/2011/02/23/the-tailteann-games-1924-1936/, accessed 16/4/2012.

59 *An Phoblacht*, 26 June 1925.

60 *Munster Express*, 1 February 1935
61 *An Phoblacht*, 21 August 1925.
62 O'Callaghan, *Rugby in Munster*, pp. 115–140.
63 *An Phoblacht*, 25 December 1925.
64 *An Phoblacht*, 1 January 1926.
65 *An Phoblacht*, 8 January 1926.
66 *An Phoblacht*, 5 February 1926.
67 *Irish Worker*, 15 September 1923.
68 *Irish Independent*, 21 March 1930.
69 *The Star*, 5 January 1929.
70 Ibid.
71 Ibid.
72 *The Star*, 19 October 1929.
73 *Nengah Guardian*, 26 January 1929.
74 *Nenagh Guardian*, 2 March 1918.
75 Dick Fitzgerald, *How to Play Gaelic Football*, Cork: Francis Guy & Co., 1914, p. 14. Throughout Fitzgerald's introduction there is the latent language that would be employed, especially after independence, to suggest that Gaelic games alone are most suited to the Irish temperament.
76 Dick Fitzgerald, *How to Play Gaelic Football*, p. 15.
77 *Nenagh Guardian*, 10 February 1923.
78 *Southern Star*, 6 September 1924.
79 *Southern Star*, 27 October 1928.
80 *Nenagh Guardian*, 16 August 1924.
81 *Southern Star*, 7 November 1925.
82 *FSW*, 25 February 1928.
83 Ibid.
84 *Cork Examiner*, 11 December 1931.
85 *Munster Express*, 28 November 1930.
86 *Limerick Leader*, 27 August 1932.
87 GAA Archive: MUN/001, *Munster Council Minute Book*, 21 February 1932.
88 *Nenagh Guardian*, 16 September 1927.
89 *Munster Express*, 8 November 1929.
90 Cronin, Mike, 'An Historical Identity: Historians and the Making of Irish Nationalist Identity in the Gaelic Athletic Association', *Football Studies*, Vol. 1, No. 2, August 1998, pp. 89–102.
91 See King, *A History of Hurling*, pp. 266–337.
92 GAA Archive: MUN/001, *Munster Council Minute Book*, 28 September 1928; 12 December 1928; 2 March 1930; 21 February 1932.
93 P.J. Mathews, *Revival: The Abbey Theatre, Sinn Féin, The Gaelic League and the Co-Operative Movement*, Cork: Cork University Press and Field Day, 2003, p. 35.
94 P.J. Mathews, *Revival*, p. 65.
95 Kiberd, Declan, *Inventing Ireland*, London: Jonathan Cape, 1995, p. 263.
96 O'Callaghan, *Rugby in Munster*, p. 177.

CHAPTER FIVE

1 O'Mahony, Bertie, *Munster Football Association: 75 Years of Service to the Beautiful Game*, Cork: Munster Football Association, 1998, p. 27.
2 Taylor, *The Association Game*, pp. 123–131.

3 Hunt, Tom, 'The GAA: Social Structure and Associated Clubs', in Cronin, Murphy, Rouse (eds), *The Gaelic Athletic Association, 1884–2009*, p. 193.

4 http://nifootball.blogspot.ie/2006/08/harry-buckle.html, accessed 1/7/2013.

5 Bromhead, John, 'George Cadbury's Contribution to Sport', *The Sports Historian*, Vol. 20, No. 1, May 2000, pp. 97–117.

6 Baseball was popular with many of Britain's working class in this period though. See for example Johnes, Martin, '"Poor Man's Cricket": Baseball, Class and Community in South Wales c.1880–1950', *International Journal of the History of Sport*, Vol. 17, No. 4, December 2000, and there had been a large number of exhibition games played in Ireland since the middle of the 1870s: *Freeman's Journal*, 27 August 1874; *The Irish Times*, 26 March 1889; *The Irish Times*, 28 March 1889.

7 For examples of this see *Evening Echo*, 18 January 1926; 9 February 1926.

8 Garnham, Neal, *Association Football and Society in Pre-partition Ireland*, p. 48.

9 Pincombe, Ian, 'Out Of Rexville: G.F. Lovell and the South Wales Confectionery Industry, c.1830–c.1940', University College of North Wales, Bangor, unpublished PhD thesis, 2000.

10 Pincombe, *Out of Rexville*, p. 244. In the same era in Ontario, Canada, Westclox placed sport at the heart of its industrial welfare, with the factory particularly famous for its women's softball team; see Sangster, Joan, 'The Softball Solution: Female Workers, Male Managers and the Operation of Paternalism at Westclox, 1923–60', *Labour/Le Travail*, No. 32, Fall 1993, pp. 167–199. See also Gilchrist, Paul, 'Sport under the Shadow of Industry: Paternalism at Alfred Herbert Ltd.', Tomlinson, Alan and Woodham, Jonathan (eds), *Image, Power and Space: Studies in Consumption and Identity*, Maidenhead: Meyer and Meyer Sport, 2007, pp. 3–27.

11 Ryan, Frederick W., 'What the Worker Should Know', Dublin: *Journal of Social and Statistical Inquiry Society of Ireland*, Vol. XIV, Part 2, 1920–1923, pp. 133–143.

12 *Cork Examiner*, 21 April 1924.

13 *The Irish Times*, 19 February 1923.

14 *The Irish Times*, 18 March 1924.

15 *Cork Examiner*, 18 March 1924.

16 Ibid.

17 *Cork Examiner*, 17 March 1926.

18 *Evening Echo*, 12 March 1926.

19 *Cork Examiner*, 18 March 1926.

20 *Cork Examiner*, 17 March 1926.

21 *Cork Examiner*, 21 March 1926.

22 Ibid.

23 Ibid.

24 *FSW*, 27 March 1926.

25 Although there is the qualifier of the heavy snow that day, it was still the biggest crowd mustered for the All-Ireland Championship hurling final in that decade. Attendances veered between that figure of 26, 829 to as low as 7,000 in 1923. Source: Corry, Eoghan, *The GAA Book of Lists*, Dublin: Hodder Headline Ireland, 2005.

26 *Evening Echo*, 20 March 1926.

27 *FSW*, 27 March 1926.

28 For all of these figures see UCD Archives (UCDA): P137/11: FAI Archives, *FAIFS Finance Committee Minute Books*, 12 May 1924.

29 For these figures see UCDA: P137/11: FAI Archives, *FAIFS Finance Committee Minute Books*, 22 April 1926.

30 For these figures see UCCA: UC/ATH/MB/08, *Cork Athletic Grounds Committee Minute Books*.

31 UCCA: UC/ATH/MB/1, *Cork Athletic Grounds Committee Minute Books*, 12 December 1930.

32 From the Athletic Ground Committee's Minute Books however, it appears Cork FC stayed on in the Mardyke for some time.

33 *FSW*, 27 February 1926.

34 The request was rejected in a reply dated 9 March 1926. See UCDA: FAI Archives, P137/2.

35 Cullen, Donal, *Freestaters: The Republic of Ireland Soccer Team 1921–1939*, Essex: Desert Island Books, 2007, pp. 67–76. As well as selection for the international squad a good number of Fordsons players also represented the Free State League in various matches against other leagues, like the Welsh League: Brady, 'Sally' Connolly, Heinemann and Roberts, *Irish Independent*, 3 April 1927; Heinemann also represented the Free State League in the return game in Wales, *Irish Independent*, 22 October 1927, while Charlie Dowdall got selected for the game against the Irish League in March of 1928, *Irish Independent*, 29 February 1928.

36 See letters dated 2 March 1926; 6 March 1926 in UCDA: P137/2, FAI Archives, *International Recognition of FAIFS*.

37 *FSW*, 7 May 1927.

38 *FSW*, 18 February 1928.

39 See Note 72, Introduction.

40 Nyhan, Miriam, 'Narration and Memory: The Experiences of the Workforce of a Ford Plant', *Irish Economic and Social History*, Vol. XXXII, 2006, pp. 18–35.

41 Some examples of cinema prices: Ormond Cinema, Nenagh for Charlie Chaplin's *The Circus*: 2/– or 1/– (*Nenagh Guardian*, 2 November 1929); at the Stella Cinema in Bantry for *Ben Hur* prices in the evening ranged from 3/– to 1/6. Matinees of the show were as low as 9d and 6d for children to see it: *Southern Star*, 18 February 1928.

42 *Cork City FC Gate Receipt Book*, 4 December 1938.

43 *FSW*, 28 August 1926.

44 *FSW*, 30 April 1927.

45 *Evening Echo*, 4 June 1926.

46 *Waterford News*, 8 February 1929.

47 UCDA: P137/26, FAI Archives, *Junior Committee Minutes*, 14 December 1928.

48 *Irish Independent*, 19 August 1930.

49 *Cork Examiner*, 23 July 1932; 27 July 1932.

50 *Evening Echo*, 13 August 1932; 29 August 1932; 2 September 1932.

51 *Evening Echo*, 23 September 1932.

52 *Evening Echo*, 16 September 1932.

53 *Evening Echo*, 17 October 1932.

54 Ibid.

55 *Evening Echo*, 21 October 1932.

56 Ibid.

57 *Evening Echo*, 4 November 1932.

58 *Evening Echo*, 11 November 1932.

59 *Evening Echo*, 25 November 1932.

60 *Evening Echo*, 20 January 1933; CCCA: U600/3 *Cork Sick Poor Society (North Parish) Minute Books*, 15 November 1932.

61 UCCA: UC/FC/MB/08, *UCC Finance Committee Minute Books*, 19 December 1932.

62 UCCA: UC/FC/MB/08, *UCC Finance Committee Minute Books*, 27 March 1933.

63 UCCA: UC/FC/MB/09, *UCC Finance Committee Minute Books*, 19 November 1934.

64 Cork Town Planning Association, *Cork City, A Civic Survey*, Liverpool and London: University of Liverpool and Hodder & Stoughton, 1926, p. 15.

65 Saunders, J.C., *County Borough of Cork Annual Report of the Medical Officer of Health for the Year 1935*, Cork: Eagle Printing Works, 1936, p. 101.

66 Cork Town Planning Association, *Cork City*, p. 26.

67 O'Connor, Emmet, *A Labour History of Ireland, 1824–1960*, Dublin: Gill & Macmillan, 1993, p. 130.

68 CCCA: U216/1/4 *Cork Trades Council Minute Books*, 5 May–11 November 1932; CCCA: U600/3, *Cork Sick Poor Society (North Parish) Minute Books*, 8 November 1932.

69 *Irish Press*, 23 August 1933.

70 O'Connor, *A Labour History of Ireland*, p. 130.

71 *Evening Echo*, 4 November 1932.

72 *Evening Echo*, 11 November 1932.

73 *Evening Echo*, 25 November 1932.

74 UCCA: *UCC Athletic Grounds Committee Minute Books*, 29 November 1933; letter dated 13 November 1933.

75 UCCA: *UCC Athletic Grounds Committee Minute Books*, 29 November 1933; letter dated 13 November 1933; see also entry for 1 February 1934.

76 UCCA: *UCC Athletic Grounds Committee Minute Books*, 24 May 1937.

77 Dáil Debates, Vol. 43, Col. 1419, 3 August 1932, http://historical-debates.oireachtas.ie/D/0043/D.0043.193208030005.html, accessed 27/11/2013.

78 *Evening Echo*, 25 November 1932.

79 Ibid.

80 *Evening Echo*, 2 December 1932.

81 *Evening Echo*, 16 December 1932.

82 Hunt, Tom, 'The GAA: Social Structure and Associated Clubs', in Cronin, Murphy, Rouse (eds), *The Gaelic Athletic Association, 1884–2009*, p. 197

83 *Evening Echo*, 20 April 1934.

84 *The Irish Times*, 23 May 1927.

85 *Evening Echo*, 16 September 1932.

86 *Sport*, 11 April 1925.

87 *Evening Echo*, 7 October 1932.

88 For more on Nattrass, see Jackson, Alex and Toms, David, 'The First Modern Ref', *The Blizzard: The Football Quarterly*, No. 11, December 2014.

89 *Evening Echo*, 14 October 1932.

90 *Evening Echo*, 2 November 1932.

91 *Evening Echo*, 25 November 1932.

92 *Evening Echo*, 3 February 1933.

93 UCCA: UC/FC/MB/08, *UCC Finance Committee Minute Books*, 28 November 1933.

94 *Evening Echo*, 10 February 1933.
95 *Evening Echo*, 24 February 1933.
96 *Evening Echo*, 10 March 1933.
97 *Evening Echo*, 17 March 1933.
98 *Evening Echo*, 9 December 1933; 11 December 1933; 15 December 1933; 18 December 1933; 22 December 1933.
99 *Evening Echo*, 16 January 1934.
100 *Evening Echo*, 16 March 1934.
101 *Evening Echo*, 20 March 1934.
102 Ibid.
103 *Evening Echo*, 4 May 1934.
104 *Evening Echo*, 18 May 1934.
105 *Evening Echo*, 5 January 1934.
106 *Evening Echo*, 6 January 1934.
107 *Cork Examiner*, 4 September 1936.
108 *Cork Examiner*, 31 August 1937.
109 *Evening Echo*, 15 April 1937.

CHAPTER SIX

1 *Munster Express*, 20 November 1920.
2 *Munster Express*, 18 November 1922.
3 See Dyer, Geoff, *The Missing of the Somme*, Edinburgh: Canongate, 2012 edn.
4 *Munster Express*, 18 November 1922.
5 *Munster Express*, 17 November 1923.
6 *Munster Express*, 16 November 1924.
7 *Munster Express*, 19 November 1926.
8 *Munster Express*, 25 November 1927.
9 *Munster Express*, 16 November 1928.
10 *Munster Express*, 14 November 1930.
11 *Munster Express*, 9 February 1924; 1 March 1924; 5 April 1924; 22 November 1924; 29 November 1924.
12 *Munster Express*, 27 December 1924.
13 For a recollection of this brigade see Hanna, Henry, *The Pals at Suvla Bay*, Uckfield: Naval & Military Press, 2009, p. 224.
14 *Munster Express*, 23 June 1923; 12 February 1926; 10 September 1926.
15 His photography studio, Phillips & Whitney, had their photographs of various teams in a wide range of sports used regularly in national newspapers in the 1920s, especially the *Weekly Irish Times*. See for instance issues dated 7 June 1924; 12 March 1927. An obituary of Phillips remembered him as 'the friend to all sportsmen' who was always happy 'to give expert advice on any game', *Munster Express*, 24 March 1944.
16 *Waterford News and Star*, 26 August 1977, for all names and positions held in the Waterford Junior League.
17 George French (1876–1938), music hall entertainer, was born in Edinburgh and raised in Dundee. For some notices of French's Irish shows see *The Irish Times*, 7 September 1912; 12 December 1922; *Freeman's Journal*, 7 May 1901; *Irish Independent*, 5 September 1912. A brief outline of his career can be found in Maloney, Paul, *Scotland and the Music Hall, 1850–1914*, Manchester: Manchester University Press, 2003, p. 104.

18 *Munster Express*, 29 July 1927; 26 September 1930.

19 *Munster Express*, 26 April 1929. The game was also reported on in the *Irish Independent*, 22 April 1929.

20 *Munster Express*, 13 June 1930.

21 *Waterford News*, 29 January 1915; as well as that he apparently lined out for Hampshire Cricket Club at opening bat, though a credible source for this has proved elusive.

22 Keane, Matt, *St Joseph's AFC 70th Anniversary Publication*, Waterford: 1994.

23 *Munster Express*, 15 May 1931, notice reads: 'There were 24 delegates representing 12 Waterford City firms, who intend competing in the new Employers' Football League present at the meeting of the Waterford and District Football League held on Monday night.'

24 Rivlin, Ray, *Shalom Ireland: A Social History of Jews in Modern Ireland*, Dublin: Gill & Macmillan, 2003, pp. 211–236.

25 Ibid.

26 Ibid. Ó Gráda, Cormac, *Jewish Ireland in the Age of Joyce: A Socioeconomic History*, Princeton: Princeton University Press, 2006, p. 187.

27 *FSW*, 5 March 1927.

28 *Waterford News*, 5 December 1884.

29 *Waterford News*, 9 November 1888.

30 *Cork Examiner*, 9 November 1910.

31 *Munster Express*, 18 November 1922.

32 *Munster Express*, 2 December 1922; 30 December 1922.

33 *Munster Express*, 5 March 1926.

34 *Munster Express*, 7 January 1927. For Bishop Foy's School see *Limerick Leader*, 24 February 1926; 5 February 1927. Foy's High School was perhaps best known for its hockey playing, although some idea of the games and, in his words, 'ungentle sports' of the school come from W.B. Stanford's memoirs where he describes break-time games like Tom Tiddler's Ground, Spanish Fly, and other similar leap-frogging games as 'just organised fights': Hinds (ed.) *Stanford: Memoirs*, pp. 30–31.

35 *Munster Express*, 18 March 1927.

36 *Munster Express*, 4 October 1929.

37 *Munster Express*, 1929.

38 *Munster Express*, 17 December 1926; 13 December 1929; 19 September 1930.

39 *Munster Express*, 26 September 1930.

40 *Munster Express*, 9 April 1926; 15 April 1927; 17 August 1928.

41 *Limerick Leader*, 22 February 1920.

42 *The Irish Times*, 30 April 1928.

43 *Munster Express*, 17 August 1928.

44 *Munster Express*, 19 September 1930.

45 *Munster Express*, 12 October 1928.

46 O'Callaghan, *Rugby in Munster*, p. 57.

47 *The Irish Times*, 11 October 1929.

48 *Munster Express*, 20 April 1928; 16 May 1930.

49 *Munster Express*, 18 July 1930. Breen's family's connections with soccer in Waterford would continue, with a relative of his, Patrick Breen, being one of the club's directors in the late 1960s when Waterford FC were so successful.

50 *Munster Express*, 9 February 1924.

51 *Munster Express*, 25 October 1924.

52 *Munster Express*, 30 July 1926; 19 November 1926; 26 November 1926.

53 *FSW*, 22 May 1926.

54 *FSW*, 26 February 1927.

55 In English this means either judge or umpire.

56 *Munster Express*, 21 December 1929.

57 Ibid.

58 *Western Daily Press*, 31 December 1929; *Munster Express*, 21 December 1928.

59 Costello, Murray and Beaumont, *An Introduction to The Royal Hospital Kilmainham: Its Architecture, History and Restoration*, Criterion: Dublin, 1987, p. 16.

60 *Munster Express*, 17 September 1926.

61 *Munster Express*, 13 April 1928.

62 *Munster Express*, 6 August 1937.

63 *Munster Express*, 24 October 1952.

64 *Munster Express*, 16 November 1956 and 23 November 1956.

65 *Munster Express*, 21 August 1928.

66 *Munster Express*, 22 February 1985.

67 *Munster Express*, 2 May 1930.

68 Byrne, Peter, *Football Association of Ireland: 75 Years*, Dublin: Sportsworld Publications, 1996, p. 212. This Alfie Hale is the father of Alfie Hale, who was capped fourteen times for Ireland in the period 1962–73: Byrne, *FAI: 75 Years*, p. 236. On the moves of these men to Bristol Rovers and Bristol City respectively see *Munster Express*, 31 August 1928; see also *Western Daily Press*, 23 August 1928; 28 August 1928.

69 *Munster Express*, 4 February 1927.

70 *Munster Express*, 12 August 1927.

71 *Munster Express*, 27 December 1929.

72 *Munster Express*, 31 July 1931.

73 Hearne, J.M., 'Industry in Waterford City, 1932–1962', in Nolan, William, Power, Thomas and Cowman, Des (eds), *Waterford: History and Society*, Dublin: Geography Publications, 1992, pp. 685–706; See also O'Connor, *A Labour History of Waterford*, p. 223; *Munster Express*, 27 November 1936; Daly, Mary E., 'The Employment Gains From Industrial Protection in the Irish Free State During the 1930s: A Note', *Irish Economic and Social History*, Vol. XV, 1988, pp. 71–75 which notes an overall increase of twenty-five per cent in industrial employment 1932–36.

74 *FSW*, 19 March 1927.

75 *FSW*, 25 February 1928.

76 *The Irish Times*, 12 May 1928.

77 *The Irish Times*, 23 May 1929.

78 *Munster Express*, 26 July 1929.

79 *FSW*, 17 March 1928.

80 Ibid.

81 Ibid.

82 *Munster Express*, 12 July 1929.

83 *Waterford News*, 16 August 1929.

84 Ibid.

85 *Waterford News*, 2 May 1929.

86 *The Irish Times*, 6 March 1930.

87 *The Irish Times*, 15 March 1930.
88 *Munster Express*, 20 December 1929.
89 *Munster Express*, 4 October 1929; 8 August 1930; 8 November 1929.
90 *Munster Express*, 18 July 1930.
91 *Munster Express*, 8 August 1930.
92 *Munster Express*, 4 April 1930.
93 *Munster Express*, 1 August 1930.
94 The spin-off trade associated with the game was even used in the 1940s when a licensed grocer's shop was being auctioned in Waterford city; its proximity to Kilcohan Park and thus the passing trade for both greyhound racing and soccer matches was used as a major selling point by the auctioneer: *Munster Express*, 6 June 1947.
95 *Munster Express*, 1 August 1930.
96 *Munster Express*, 11 May 1928.
97 *Munster Express*, 15 August 1930.
98 Ibid. Reports of Doran playing for Mid-Rhondda include a game against Torquay United, *Western Morning News*, 27 September 1924; Forshaw, when he was with Liverpool, had been selected to be part of a touring side to Australia in 1925, *Derby Daily Telegraph*, 12 March 1925; Lindsay while at Tottenham Hotspur was selected to play in a representative side of Anglo-Scots against Home Scots, *Evening Telegraph*, 7 March 1923; *Dundee Courier*, 21 March 1923; George Wilson went to Bournemouth on a free from Leyton Orient in 1924, *Derby Daily Telegraph*, 14 June 1924.
99 For information on the Welsh sides see Johnes, *Soccer and Society*, pp. 54–58 for Mid Rhondda and pp. 52–58 for more on Llanelli/Llanelly and on Pontypridd see pp. 38–45 in particular.
100 Taylor, *The Leaguers*, pp. 202–207.
101 IFS 20/1932 Finance Act Section 25.
102 *Munster Express*, 21 October 1932.
103 *Munster Express*, 18 November 1932; *The Irish Times*, 15 November 1932.
104 Ó Catháin, Mairtín, '"Struggle or Starve": Derry Unemployed Workers' Movements, 1926–1935', *Saothar*, No. 28 (2003), pp. 49–60.
105 *The Irish Times*, 17 November 1932.
106 *Irish Press*, 29 November 1932.
107 Johnes, *Soccer and Society: South Wales, 1900–1939*, p. 70.
108 Taylor, *The Leaguers*, pp. 248–250.
109 *Cork Examiner*, 25 July 1932.
110 *Cork Examiner*, 27 July 1932.
111 *Munster Express*, 26 August 1932.
112 *Munster Express*, 16 February 1934.
113 *Munster Express*, 29 June 1935.
114 *Munster Express*, 18 September 1936.
115 *Evening Echo*, 11 December 1933.
116 *Munster Express*, 1 December 1933.
117 *Munster Express*, 5 January 1934.
118 *Irish Press*, 29 June 1934.
119 *Munster Express*, 23 April 1937.
120 *The Irish Times*, September 1943; see also http://www.waterford-united.ie/cork-sep-2011-our-finest-forgotten-player/, accessed 11/11/2013.
121 *Irish Press*, 19 April 1937; *Irish Independent*, 19 April 1937.

CHAPTER SEVEN

1 O'Connor Lysaght, D.R., *The Story of the Limerick Soviety: The 1919 General Strike against British Militarism* (3rd Edition), Limerick: Limerick Soviet Commemoration Committee, 2003; Kemmy, Jim (ed.), *The Limerick Anthology*, Dublin: Gill & Macmillan, 1996, pp. 76–80.

2 Kemmy, Jim, 'James Casey, Soviet Treasurer', in Lee, David (ed.), *Remembering Limerick*, Limerick: Limerick Civic Trust, 1997, pp. 264–266.

3 *Limerick Leader*, 15 September 1924.

4 *Limerick Leader*, 12 November 1924.

5 *Limerick Leader*, 7 April 1924; 28 March 1925; 27 April 1925; 25 October 1926.

6 Kemmy, Jim, 'A changing City – A Personal View', in Lee, James (ed.), *Remembering Limerick: Historical Essays Celebrating the 800th Anniversary of Limerick's First Charter Granted in 1197*, Limerick: Limerick Civic Trust, 1997, p. 373.

7 O'Callaghan, *Rugby in Munster*, pp. 76–85.

8 *Irish Independent*, 26 February 1937.

9 *Limerick Leader*, 28 March 1925 for one of the early mentions of the club.

10 *Limerick Leader*, 9 March 1929.

11 McElligott, *Forging a Kingdom*, p.374.

12 *Sport*, 26 March 1927.

13 *Sport*, 23 April 1927; *FSW*, 23 April 1927.

14 *Irish Independent*, 16 April 1928.

15 *Irish Independent*, 6 January 1930.

16 There are only scattered references to the club to be found in the newspapers, including *Freeman's Journal*, 3 December 1921; *Freeman's Journal*, 10 December 1921; *Freeman's Journal* and *Irish Independent*, 12 February 1924; *Nenagh Guardian*, 20 October 1923; *Limerick Leader*, 27 November 1926 for instance.

17 *Freeman's Journal*, 17 December 1923; 24 December 1923; 31 December 1923; 14 January 1924; 21 January 1924; 28 January 1924; *Irish Independent*, 8 January 1924.

18 Certainly mentions of them in the newspapers rarely saw them victorious, as when they beat Cahir Park 3–0 in the Free State Cup, *Freeman's Journal*, 18 March 1924.

19 *Freeman's Journal*, 27 July 1923. It would be a long time before the game in Tipperary was in a sufficiently healthy state to have leagues of its own, with a South Tipperary and District Football League not established until the final quarter of the twentieth century in 1977, in which Cahir is now a member club.

20 *Limerick Leader*, 23 February 1929.

21 *Limerick Leader*, 4 March 1929; 9 March 1929.

22 Ibid., 9 March 1929.

23 McCarthy, Michael, 'The Shannon Scheme Strike', *Old Limerick Journal*, Vol. 4, 1980, pp. 21–6.

24 *Limerick Leader*, 16 August 1930.

25 *Limerick Leader*, 25 August 1930.

26 *Limerick Leader*, 10 January 1931.

27 *Limerick Leader*, 5 December 1931.

28 *Limerick Leader*, 12 December 1931.

29 *Limerick Leader*, 19 March 1932.
30 *Limerick Leader*, 30 January 1932; 20 February 1932.
31 *Limerick Leader*, 30 January 1932.
32 For more on the particular controversy see O'Callaghan, *Rugby in Munster*, pp. 171–173.
33 *Limerick Leader*, 16 April 1932.
34 *Limerick Leader*, 16 August 1930.
35 *Limerick Leader*, 9 April 1932; 23 April 1932; 18 June 1932.
36 *Limerick Leader*, 2 April 1932; 25 June 1932; 13 August 1932; 3 September 1932.
37 *Limerick Leader*, 3 September 1932.
38 *Limerick Leader*, 12 November 1932; 31 December 1932.
39 *Irish Press*, 30 November 1932.
40 *Limerick Leader*, 13 April 1935.
41 *Limerick Leader*, 3 September 1932; 7 September 1935.
42 *Limerick Leader*, 14 April 1934.
43 *Limerick Leader*, 14 May 1934.
44 *Limerick Leader*, 2 June 1934.
45 *Limerick Leader*, 4 June 1930.
46 *Limerick Leader*, 5 January 1935.
47 *Limerick Leader*, 2 November 1935; 9 November 1935.
48 *Limerick Leader*, 18 November 1935.
49 *Limerick Leader*, 7 December 1935.
50 *Limerick Leader*, 28 March 1936.
51 *Limerick Leader*, 26 October 1935; 8 February 1936; 22 February 1936.
52 *Limerick Leader*, 12 May 1934.
53 *Irish Independent*, 16 June 1937.
54 *Limerick Leader*, 12 March 1932.
55 Kemmy, Jim, 'Housing and Social Conditions, 1830–1940', *Old Limerick Journal*, No. 24 (Winter 1988), pp. 69–74.
56 *Limerick Leader*, 19 May 1934.
57 *Limerick Leader*, 5 May 1934.
58 *Limerick Leader*, 9 June 1934; Mr Gilligan most likely meant Primo Carnera, then world heavyweight boxing champion.
59 *Limerick Leader*, 10 March 1934.
60 *Irish Independent*, 26 February 1937; 16 June 1937.
61 *Irish Independent*, 12 April 1937.
62 *Irish Independent*, 20 May 1937.
63 *Irish Independent*, 24 September 1937.
64 *Irish Independent*, 30 December 1937.

CHAPTER EIGHT

1 Garnham, *Association Football*, p. 198; Byrne, Peter, *Green is the Colour*. See also Episode 1 '1863–1929', of Hoban, Gerry and Walpole, Robert (dirs.), *Green is the Colour: The History of Irish Soccer* (DVD), Treasure Entertainment, 2012; Carey, Tadhg, 'Ireland's Footballers at the Paris Olympics, 1924', *History Ireland*, Vol. 20, No. 4, July/August 2012.
2 Collins, Tony, *Rugby's Great Split: Class, Culture and Origins of Rugby League*, London: Routledge, 2006, p. 231.

A NOTE ON SOURCES

1 Cronin, Mike, 'What Went Wrong with Counting? Thinking about Sport and Class in Britain and Ireland', *Sport in History*, Vol. 29, No. 3, 2009, pp. 392–404.
2 O'Callaghan, *Munster in Rugby*, p. 244.

INDEX

Note: illustrations are indicated by page
    numbers in bold.

257

BAS
706.33
Tom
940191